Este
P9-CMS-692

12-27-85

The
Peasant
Kitchen

Also by Perla Meyers

The Seasonal Kitchen

The Peasant Kitchen

a return to simple, good food

Perla Meyers

Vintage Books
A Division of Random House
New York

First Vintage Books Edition,
September 1978

Copyright © 1975 by Perla Meyers

All rights reserved under International and
Pan-American Copyright Conventions.
Published in the United States by Random
House, Inc., New York, and simultaneously
in Canada by Random House of Canada
Limited, Toronto. Originally published by
Harper & Row, Publishers, Inc., in 1975.

Library of Congress Cataloging in
Publication Data

Meyers, Perla
   The peasant kitchen.
   Reprint of the 1st ed. published in 1975
by Harper & Row, New York.
   Includes index.
   1. Cookery, International. I. Title.
[TX725.A1M483 1978]   641.5'94
78-55727   ISBN 0-394-72651-0

Designed by Al Corchia

Manufactured in the United States of America

contents

v

introduction

What is the peasant kitchen?

While working on this book of peasant dishes, I have often been asked "What is the peasant kitchen?" First and most important, the emphasis in the peasant kitchen is on the freshness of the ingredients used. The approach to these seasonal foods is basic and direct, based on the tradition of eating simply, well and inexpensively which has flourished in the kitchens of many nations. In this book, rather than just compiling recipes, I have tried to capture this philosophy on food. This kind of simple, honest treatment of the freshest and best foods available has been developed through the centuries by people who relied on nature's produce and the local offerings of the soil, the seas and the lakes. It is the kind of cooking I grew up with.

I never thought of our kitchen at home as anything but a country, "peasant" kitchen. Although it was large and airy, it was unglamorous and too big to be really efficient, yet it had the charm and appeal that only a working kitchen can have. Since there were no cabinets, everything was open to the eye. Large bottles of home-made vinegars and fruity olive oils crowded next to jars filled with dry herbs, teas, legumes and spices set on the well-scrubbed marble-topped counters. A great variety of well-seasoned earthenware casseroles and other country cookware was piled up underneath the long kitchen table, and big, black wrought-iron skillets hung from large hooks on the wall above the stove. The kitchen opened into a small garden where flowers and herbs grew in terra cotta pots. Though I remember the Mediterranean winters as being damp and chilly, the door to the garden was always open, giving the feeling that it was an extension of the kitchen, bringing the living presence of nature right into the kitchen itself.

Fresh fruits and vegetables were kept in a cool place under the counters. They were never refrigerated because my mother and the cook went to the market two or three times a week to buy just enough for one or two days' meals. Since the family ate both lunch and dinner at home, the kitchen was always bustling with activity. The preparation of food was not a simple matter in those days. We had none of the conveniences that make the life of today's cook easy. Almost everything was made at home; bread was baked daily, cream was whipped by hand, the making of mayonnaise involved a long, careful process. Our cook spent hours making hearty soups and herb vinegars, preserving fruits, baking meats and improvising with leftovers. The preparation of food was a central part of daily life and the kitchen a place to gather in. I often did my homework in the kitchen, at a long marble-topped table where our cook rolled out pastry, kneaded bread and peeled vegetables while telling me endless stories about life in her native Basque village in the northern part of Spain.

Although in those days I considered cooking a chore, my fascination with food continually grew. For many years it was the haute cuisine of France that I mainly wanted to explore. I thought that was where all the excitement and creativity of cooking was found. To me the refined cuisine of Escoffier, Dumaine and Fernand Point represented food at its greatest. I looked for the elegant and the unusual and found it in the cooking of many of the three-star chefs with whom I worked, as student and apprentice, in France, Austria and Switzerland.

In recent years, however, I felt myself more and more an outsider, looking in on this fascinating but unrealistic world of haute cuisine. It is a little like the feeling one has when admiring a beautiful piece of art without wanting to own it. My life-style had begun to change, and with it came a yearning for the days when preparing food was looked on as something natural, inventive and spontaneous, not bound by the rigid rules of *grande cuisine.* I was more and more drawn to the cooking of provincial France, Spain and Italy, to the marvelous cuisines that have remained peasant in nature, where excitement and variety grow out of regional differences and local products. I soon found that I was not alone in this urge to return to simplicity; many of the great three-star chefs were also caught up in the wave of nostalgia. Perhaps more than that, they had come to the realization that fresh produce and quality ingredients cannot be taken for granted any more. The local sausage maker, the small farm that still makes its own cheese and olive oil have become rarities today. So much of the fresh produce has begun to lose its flavor even in regions that have long been famous

in Europe for their fruit, vegetables, cheeses, fish or pork products. Many of the great chefs began to think that we should capture the taste and essence of good things while they are still available. This awareness has brought forth a rebirth of wonderful peasant dishes in many of the best European restaurants. I too was overcome by a desire to let things be and decided to try to re-create the earthy, gutsy taste of dishes that have enriched the cuisines of the countries I care so much about. I soon realized that I had come round full circle to the peasant kitchen I grew up in.

Traditionally, the peasant kitchen was the centerpiece of the home where the pulse of family life was nourished by the preparation and enjoyment of food. Nature's calendar was faithfully reflected here. As the seasons came and went with their always varying produce, the kitchen remained a constant symbol of family unity. Few people these days, unfortunately, have had the pleasure of experiencing such an atmosphere. For too many of us, the kitchen is merely a functional space, a cramped necessity rather than a place where food and the family come together. It's true that modern living does not usually provide us with a kitchen large enough for a family to eat, work and live in. Nevertheless, the philosophy of the peasant kitchen, a philosophy of "good-natured" food prepared with ease and pleasure, is both timeless and timely. It is an attitude that I feel very strongly is best suited for our way of life today. Simple, yet astute and often sophisticated cooking is the mark of the peasant kitchen.

Although the term "peasant" may bring to mind simple, uncomplicated, hearty food, it is not without refinement. It is a cuisine with few rules, a cuisine that does not require precision in measuring ingredients and allows great freedom in the composition of a meal. There are no musts except that of using fresh ingredients at their seasonal best. It is cooking that demands creativity at all times, however, for the peasant cook, whether Spanish, Italian, Hungarian or Scandinavian, often has little to work with. Potatoes, onions, carrots and dry legumes constitute an important part of the everyday diet. Depending on the locality, fish or inexpensive cuts of meat such as pigs' knuckles, lamb shank and oxtails are used in combination with whatever is available to produce inexpensive hearty dishes to satisfy a hungry family. In peasant cooking, nothing is wasted, every scrap of food being used in one way or another. Even vegetable peelings, fish trimmings and old bread are not discarded in the peasant kitchen. With today's high food prices, more and more people are rediscovering these old habits. More and more of us are finding pleasure in growing our own vegetables, in canning and preserving them and in baking our own bread. Like many others, I too want to recapture the good taste of fresh, home-grown food and cook it simply, borrowing from the creativity of the peasant cook. For the city dweller, this may seem hard to do, yet with the right attitude it is still possible to find both quality and flavor in the markets. Don't run into a supermarket expecting to find everything you want on the shelves. Look for a small street market

that takes pride in the freshness of its produce. Find a fish store and a butcher shop that understand both quality and freshness. You'll find that this extra effort will be amply rewarded by the inexpensive yet delicious meals you can achieve.

In spite of our conveniences, in many ways life is simpler for the peasant cook in Europe. Recently I spent a wonderful morning in an outdoor market in Portugal. It was a chilly winter day, and I watched while the peasants brought in their produce. Within an hour the market was covered with mountains of cabbage, carrots, turnips, potatoes and onions. The winter season had real meaning here. Although the choice was limited, you could look at the vegetables and touch them, comparing quality and price. Here is where the inspiration for the day's meal would come from. You couldn't help but feel the life and vibrancy of the market, with its fruits and vegetables, the great heaps of shiny fish, the live chickens and rabbits, fresh cheeses, nuts, and baskets filled with fresh eggs. It was hard not to compare the market's vitality and range of quality with the sterility of the modern supermarket where the seasons scarcely seem to change.

I have to admit that this kind of shopping and cooking does require time. I have not discovered the secret of turning out first class-food in a few minutes with no trouble. Good food, whether it is *grande cuisine* or peasant, demands care. But while fine French food generally requires money and talent as well as time, peasant food is both cheaper and less difficult to prepare. It is unpretentious food and can be cooked successfully by anybody with a love and understanding of good food. Peasant cooking is not a new, "chic" or gimmicky type of cooking, as some new French restaurants would have us believe. It is more like a knowledgeable old friend who is ready and willing to help out in the kitchen.

The hors d'oeuvres table

The hors d'oeuvres table has always played a major role in the peasant kitchens of many countries. Climate and soil have both put their stamp on the hors d'oeuvres of different countries, and hors d'oeuvres are just as important in Northern European cooking as in Mediterranean cooking.

More than a beginning to the meal, the hors d'oeuvres table was, and still remains, a lifestyle in itself. In Mediterranean Europe, hors d'oeuvres are synonymous with the sunswept sidewalk cafés of the South of France, the bars on the wharfs of Greece, the Italian trattorias and the tavernas of Spain. These are all places where people get together for a glass of wine or an apéritif before lunch or dinner, to discuss the events of the day while nibbling on tidbits of shellfish, olives, raw vegetables, cheeses and local specialties.

Over the years innumerable hors d'oeuvres salads have been created by peasant cooks in every country in Europe. What began as a necessity for using leftovers imaginatively became, by virtue of the cook's

ingenuity, an infinite array of appetizers both hot and cold, using fish, meat, vegetables, eggs and dry legumes in delicious and unusual variations.

One of the best examples of this kind of creativity is the Italian antipasto table. It exudes the brilliance, freshness and sense of drama of the Italian cook. Here is a profusion of color. Bright red tomatoes, deep purple eggplants, pale green artichokes, fennel, celery, olives, radishes, etc., create a wonderful backdrop for marvelous salads combining rice, white beans and chick peas with meats, seafood and cooked vegetables. Thinly sliced sausages and hams are arranged in artful patterns and garnished with red peppers, olives, hard-boiled eggs and gherkins. The Scandinavian smorgasbord is a Northern European example of the creative imagination displayed by peasant cooks. Here again there is an innumerable variety of beautifully prepared dishes both hot and cold that make marvelous use of the catch of the sea: herrings, eels, crayfish and salmon, to name a few.

The equivalent of the Italian antipasto in Spain is the *tapas*. You see them displayed in earthenware bowls on the long counters of Spanish taverns with the specialties of the day scribbled on the mirrors behind the counter. These appetizers are just as varied and exciting as the Italian ones. They may include pickled sardines, country omelets made with spinach, cold potato and onion pie cut into wedges, as well as spicy sausages or shrimp cooked in hot garlic-flavored olive oil.

introduction

The hors d'oeuvres table in France varies dramatically with each region. In Alsace there is a profusion of sausage terrines and pâtés. On the Atlantic coast there are innumerable varieties of shellfish. But nowhere is the hors d'oeuvres table as exciting as in the South of France. Here we sense the freedom of spirit of the Mediterranean cooks with their instinctive flair for good food. Baskets of beautiful vegetables, picked at just the right degree of ripeness, are accompanied by a piquant Provençale dip or a garlicky mayonnaise. Tiny mushrooms, artichokes and onions are marinated in a marinade of fruity olive oil, wine and aromatic herbs. Country sausages, hams, olives, anchovies, grilled peppers and mountain cheeses all work together to create the essence of the hors d'oeuvres table.

In the peasant kitchens of most of these countries a small selection of appetizers traditionally was served at every meal. They might include a few sardines, a dish of mixed olives, a plate of small ripe tomatoes, a few radishes and some hard-boiled eggs, along with a loaf of crusty bread and a bowl of sweet butter. Originally, such hors d'oeuvres made a simple yet piquant introduction to the meal. In recent years, however, with eating habits changing and food becoming increasingly expensive, the average European housewife has begun to serve her family this kind of simple assortment for the midday meal or family supper, perhaps accompanied by a hearty soup or an omelet. It can be a satisfying and economical kind of meal since it allows the cook total freedom in the kitchen and can be made as simple or as elaborate as the budget allows. This illustrates the beauty of the peasant kitchen, where everything is made use of, either in the soup pot or in the salad bowl. Until now, the hors d'oeuvres table has not been incorporated into our way of life. Hors d'oeuvres have been predictably limited to finger foods, with dips and cheeses served for pre-dinner entertaining, while the buffet table has invariably been composed of a glazed ham, turkey or roast beef, all of which are expensive and unimaginative.

I feel very strongly that it is time for us to change this stereotyped way of eating and entertaining. An interesting and varied hors d'oeuvres table can be prepared with ingenuity and a minimum of effort. Most important to remember is that it must be fresh and appealing to the eye and varied enough to arouse the appetite for things to come or to satisfy the appetite as a light supper or lunch. It is simply a matter of taste, care and the willingness to experiment.

PERLA MEYERS
June 1975

The
Peasant
Kitchen

Symbols

● **Inexpensive**   ◉ **Moderate**   ✿ **Expensive**

■ **Easy**   ▪ **Intermediate**   ⊞ **Difficult**

Many French gastronomic terms have been absorbed into our language over the years, but some seem to have lost something in translation. This is particularly true of hors d'oeuvres. Whereas hors d'oeuvres in France can be anything from an elegant *pâté de fois gras* to a peasant country terrine, from an elaborately prepared eggs *en gelée* to a simple potato omelet, in this country hors d'oeuvres have become synonymous with finger foods, or in many cases with cheese. An undistinguished dip, or tiny crackers topped with a commercial spread or a variety of cheeses, dominate the pre-dinner scene. This is particularly sad, since the world of hors d'oeuvres is so rich and exciting, and when properly understood, so right for our way of life.

Hors d'oeuvres play a major role in several cuisines. The Italian antipasto is a marvelous combination of all that is fresh and good. Spanish *tapas* are marvelous teasers, usually composed of different shellfish prepared in many ways, simple as well as elaborate; and Scandinavian smorgasbords —herrings, meats, and vegetables beautifully prepared and carefully served—are indeed masterpieces.

In Mediterranean countries hors d'oeuvres are a way of life. They go hand in hand with the apéritif, a glass of wine or dry sherry sipped before lunch or dinner at a sidewalk café, the neighborhood bistro or *tasca* bar. Here is where one can enjoy a few good olives, some freshly cooked shrimp, a few oysters, or some good country sausage before heading home for the noon or evening meal. Even in poor homes some kind of simple hors d'oeuvre is served. It may be just a few spring radishes accompanied by coarse salt and fresh country bread or a few sardines and a bowl of hard-boiled eggs.

In arranging an hors d'oeuvre table, the right balance and composition of foods is important; for example, a selection of country sausages or good country ham, sardines, stewed mushrooms, marinated olives or onions, and some shellfish, such as shrimp or mussels, makes for variety and contrast of tastes.

Hors d'oeuvre salads, evolved over the years from the peasant cuisine of each nation, make a natural way of using leftovers, such as cooked vegetables, roasts and fish, creatively. Most of these salads depend on fresh local produce. Thus, in the Middle East marvelous salads are made from chick-peas and eggplants. In Scandinavia, where herrings abound, innumerable salads have been created combining the fish with beets, potatoes, and apples. In Italy seafood and vegetable salads are the focal point of the antipasto table, since none of Italy is far from the sea.

In France the hors d'oeuvre salads vary greatly from place to place, depending on the region's specialties. In Lyons and Alsace, pâtés, sausages and other pork products are the main attraction on the hors d'oeuvre table, and salads will usually include bits of ham, sausage, or head cheese in combination with a seasonal vegetable. The south of France, which is poorer in these products, makes excellent use of the local olives, tomatoes, and shellfish, with a lavish use of herbs and olive oil. *Ratatouille*, a Provençal ragoût of stewed tomatoes, zucchini, eggplants and onions, is a classic salad of the region and so is *salade Niçoise*, a combination of tuna, olives, anchovies, and greens that has become increasingly popular in this country. From the Basque province of France come hearty salads made with red peppers and the local smoked ham.

Although the versatility of salads is endless, it is important to understand that freshness is essential, that the ingredients used must have an affinity to one another and that a good balance must be kept between the main components of the salad and its dressing. Most hors d'oeuvre salads are bound with either a vinaigrette (an oil- and vinegar-based dressing) or a mayonnaise. Both can be varied endlessly with herbs and spices, but must never dominate the salad itself. And "stretching" a salad by adding too much minced celery, potatoes, or rice dilutes the taste and quality of the main ingredients. The salad bowl is not a wastebasket; each salad requires careful preparation and seasoning.

With the popularity of salads in this country, it is surprising that they have been limited for so long to the lunch table. In areas such as Florida, Arizona, and California, where the climate naturally calls for fresh, cool meals, several hors d'oeuvre salads accompanied by French bread and a glass of wine can make the perfect supper. And in the eastern part of the United States, hors d'oeuvre salads are equally suitable for simple meals and pre-dinner entertaining, possibly with the addition of two or three good sausages or country ham. Their fantastic versatility should provide any cook with a whole new and exciting world of food.

Butter and anchovy dip

Makes: about 1½ cups
Preparation time: 10 minutes

Ingredients

2   cans flat anchovy fillets, well drained
2   cloves garlic, mashed
Juice of ½ lemon, more if necessary
½   cup fruity olive oil
½   pound butter, softened
Cayenne pepper
¼   teaspoon dry mustard
Salt, if necessary

Preparation

1. In the container of a blender combine the anchovies, garlic, lemon juice, and olive oil. Blend the mixture at high speed until smooth, then pour it into an earthenware serving bowl. Add the butter, mustard, and a large dash of cayenne pepper and mash the mixture with a fork until smooth and well blended. Taste and correct the seasoning, adding salt if necessary.

2. The dip must be quite spicy. Let it stand for 2 hours to develop flavor. Just before serving, taste again and add more lemon juice or cayenne if necessary. Serve as an accompaniment to a raw vegetable basket and hard-boiled eggs.

Remarks

The dip can be made several days ahead of time and either refrigerated or frozen. Bring it back to room temperature and whisk until thoroughly smooth and well blended.

Salsa anchoiada

Makes: about 1½ cups
Preparation time: 10 minutes

Much like the southern French *tapenade*, this piquant anchovy and black olive dip is typical of the creative simplicity of Mediterranean cooking. Serve it with a basket of raw vegetables, crusty French bread, and a bowl of hard-boiled eggs.

Ingredients

1   cup pitted, coarsely chopped black
    Greek olives
1   can flat anchovy fillets, drained
3   tablespoons well-drained Italian capers
1   teaspoon dry mustard
Juice of 1 large lemon
1   tablespoon Basil paste (see page 210)
    or ½ cup chopped fresh basil
1   tablespoon minced fresh oregano or
    ½ teaspoon dried
2   cloves garlic, minced
Heavy grinding of black pepper
¾   cup fruity olive oil

Preparation

1. In the container of a blender combine all the ingredients except the oil and blend at high speed for 30 seconds. Then, blending all the while, add the oil in a slow stream until the sauce is thick and smooth. Pour into an earthenware bowl and taste and correct the seasoning.

2. If used the same day do not refrigerate. Otherwise, bring the dip back to room temperature at least 45 minutes before serving. Whisk the blend well and serve.

(continued)

hors d'oeuvres and salads

Caviar dip

Makes: 2 cups
Preparation time: 10 minutes

Remarks

Canned olives are not acceptable for this dip, as they totally lack flavor. And while good fruity olive oils are usually not available in the supermarket, it is well worth the effort to look for them in specialty stores.

Notes

Ingredients

2 cups Mayonnaise (page 208)
2 tablespoons minced scallion
Juice of 1 lemon
2 tablespoons chili sauce
Dash of Worcestershire sauce
2 to 3 ounces imported Danish lumpfish
    caviar
Salt and freshly ground white pepper
2 tablespoons minced fresh dill (optional)

Preparation

1. In the container of a blender combine the mayonnaise, scallion, lemon juice, chili sauce, and Worcestershire and blend at high speed for 30 seconds. Pour the mixture into a serving bowl; add the caviar, salt, and pepper and chill for 2 to 4 hours before serving.

2. Thirty minutes before serving, bring the mayonnaise back to room temperature, taste, correct the seasoning, and add the optional dill. Serve with a raw vegetable basket.

Remarks

For a variation, substitute ½ cup tightly packed, finely minced smoked salmon for the caviar.

Cervelle des canuts

Serves: 4 to 6
Preparation time: 10 minutes

One of the most delicious cheese desserts of the Lyons area is this mixture of *crème fraîche*, fresh herbs, and cream cheese. The unusual name comes from the "canuts," the old-time silk weavers of Lyons. Serve the dish as a dessert on individual plates accompanied by crusty French bread, or as a dip accompanied by cherry tomatoes, black olives, and peeled cucumber sticks.

Ingredients

3   tablespoons white wine vinegar
2   tablespoons olive oil
½   cup finely minced fresh herbs (parsley, chives, chervil, and tarragon)
1   cup whipped cream cheese
1½ cups Crème Fraîche (page 206)
2   cloves garlic, mashed
Salt and freshly ground black pepper

Preparation

1. In a bowl combine the vinegar, olive oil, and herbs. Let the mixture stand for an hour or two to develop flavor.

2. Add the cream cheese, *crème fraîche*, and garlic. Whisk the mixture until it is smooth and well blended, then season with salt and pepper and chill for 4 to 6 hours, or overnight.

3. An hour before serving, bring back to room temperature, then taste and correct the seasoning. Pour into a glass bowl or spoon into individual dishes.

Spicy curry dip

Makes: 2 cups
Preparation time: 10 minutes

Ingredients

2   cups Mayonnaise (page 208)
1   tablespoon curry powder
Large pinch of ground cumin
Pinch of ground turmeric
2   hot green chili peppers, finely minced
Salt and freshly ground white pepper
Lemon juice

Preparation

In an earthenware bowl combine the mayonnaise, curry powder, cumin, turmeric, and chili pepper. Stir the mixture until it is well blended, then add salt, pepper, and lemon juice to taste. Chill for at least 1 to 2 hours to develop flavor, then serve.

Remarks

Green chili peppers are sold in cans in good supermarkets or Spanish or Mexican specialty stores. The dip will keep, refrigerated, for 2 weeks in a covered jar.

Notes

hors d'oeuvres and salads

Provençal herb sauce

Makes: about 1½ cups
Preparation time: 10 minutes

Here is a sauce that can be used as a dip
as well as a sauce for grilled fish or
cold roast meats. It must be made with
fresh herbs, but can be frozen successfully.
To achieve the real Provençal flavor of
the sauce, you must use a fruity olive oil
such as Plagniol, a marvelous oil from
Nice; the Italian Sasso; or Aiana, an
excellent Greek brand.

Ingredients

½ cup tightly packed fresh parsley
1   cup tightly packed fresh basil leaves
2   large cloves garlic
2   tablespoons fresh thyme leaves
2   tablespoons sweet marjoram or
    summer savory
¾ to 1 cup fruity olive oil
2   tablespoons finely minced chives
3   tablespoons finely diced zucchini,
    skin only
Salt and freshly ground black pepper
Juice of 1 lemon

Preparation

In the container of a blender combine the
parsley, basil, garlic, thyme, and marjoram
or savory. Add the oil in a slow steady
stream and blend the mixture at high speed
until smooth. Pour into a serving bowl
and add the chives, zucchini, salt, pepper,
and lemon juice. Whisk the mixture until
well blended, then taste and correct the
seasoning. Serve at room temperature.

Remarks

If refrigerated, bring the sauce back to
room temperature before serving.

Tuna dip veneziana

Makes: about 2½ cups
Preparation time: 10 minutes

Though "dips" play a major role in American pre-dinner entertaining, they have
not been ignored in other cuisines. Indeed,
countries such as Italy and France have
created classics, such as the Italian *bagna
cauda* or the *tapenade* from the south of
France. Here is one from Venice that can
be served with hard-boiled eggs and raw
vegetables, and also as a sauce for
poached or grilled fish.

Ingredients

2   cups Mayonnaise (page 208)
1   can (7½ ounces) tuna in oil, drained
Juice of 1 large lemon
1   large clove of garlic, mashed
½ small white onion, chopped
Salt and freshly ground white pepper

Garnish:
Black Greek olives
Green pepper rings

Preparation

1. In the container of a blender combine
the mayonnaise, tuna, lemon juice, garlic,
and onion. Blend the mixture at high speed
until smooth and well blended, then pour
into a serving bowl and chill.

2. Just before serving, bring the dip back
to room temperature, taste and correct the
seasoning, and garnish with black olives
and green pepper rings.

Remarks

The dip will keep for several days. When
making it well in advance, it is best to
add the onion and garlic 2 to 3 hours
before serving.

Spring salad bowl

Serves: 4
Preparation time: 15 to 20 minutes
Cooking time: 10 to 12 minutes

The customs of serving salads vary astonishingly around the world. The Spanish serve their salad before the meal, the Americans during, and the French after. I personally find a crisp spring salad an interesting beginning to an informal dinner. This one, offering the best selections from the spring vegetable garden, is a welcome and colorful addition to the season's table.

Ingredients

1   head Boston lettuce
4 to 6 mushrooms, finely sliced
Juice of ½ lemon
7   tablespoons olive oil
Salt and freshly ground pepper
12 stalks asparagus
1½ teaspoons Dijon mustard
2   tablespoons tarragon vinegar
1   teaspoon granulated sugar
2   tablespoons finely minced chives
1 to 2 tablespoons finely minced chervil
    or dill (optional)
2   endives, cut into fine strips lengthwise
2   medium-sized beets, cooked and finely
    cubed
1   hardboiled egg, minced

Garnish:
Pimiento strips

Preparation

1. Wash the lettuce thoroughly under cold running water, then place in a plastic bag. Pierce the bag in several places with the tip of a knife, shake several times, and refrigerate until serving time.

2. Place the mushrooms in a bowl, sprinkle them with lemon juice and a little of the olive oil, season with salt and a grinding of black pepper, and chill until serving time.

3. Clean the asparagus stalks with a vegetable peeler and remove the tough ends, leaving the stalks 5 to 6 inches long. In a large, flameproof casserole bring salted water to a boil. Tie the asparagus into even bundles, drop them into the boiling water, and cook, uncovered, over high heat for 10 to 12 minutes, or until barely tender. Drain the asparagus and run them under cold water to stop further cooking, then untie them and spread on paper towels. Set aside but do not refrigerate.

4. In a wooden salad bowl combine the mustard, vinegar, remaining olive oil, sugar, salt, and pepper. Whisk the mixture until it is creamy and well blended, then add the chives and optional chervil or dill and let the dressing stand for 30 minutes. Dip each asparagus stalk in the dressing and set aside again.

5. Just before serving, whisk the dressing again, top with lettuce leaves, endives, and mushrooms, and toss lightly. Put the beets in the center of the bowl. Divide the asparagus into 4 parts and place them at the edge, arranging a strip of pimiento around each portion. Sprinkle with minced egg and serve immediately, with buttered pumpernickel or French bread.

hors d'oeuvres and salads

Summer salad bowl

Serves: 4 to 6
Preparation time: 15 minutes
Cooking time: 1 to 1½ hours

The summer salad bowl should include the best and freshest of the season's vegetables—although you should use only those that have a good affinity for one another. Try, too, to give the salad your own creative touch.

Ingredients

4   medium-sized beets
1   small head cauliflower
½   pound very young string beans
4   medium-sized new potatoes
3   tablespoons tarragon vinegar
8   tablespoons olive oil
1   teaspoon French herb or Dijon mustard
1   clove garlic, mashed
2   tablespoons minced fresh chervil or
    1 teaspoon dried
Salt and freshly ground black pepper

Garnish:
Boston lettuce leaves
1   small red onion, finely sliced
2 to 3 hard-boiled eggs, cut in half
Black Greek olives

Optional:
1   cup of cooked chicken or smoked ham
    cut into julienne

Preparation

1. Clean the beets, but do not peel them. Drop them into plenty of boiling salted water, and cook them, partially covered, until they are tender when pierced with the tip of a sharp knife. You may have to add water to the pot to keep them completely covered with water during cooking. As soon as the beets are done, run them under cold water and slip off their skin. Cube and chill until serving time.

2. Break the cauliflower into florets, wash thoroughly under cold running water, and set aside.

3. Clean the beans, snapping off the tips at both ends.

4. In a large saucepan bring salted water to a boil. Add the beans and cook them until they are tender but still slightly crisp, then remove them from the water with a slotted spoon and run under cold water to stop further cooking. Chill the beans until serving time.

5. Drop the cauliflower florets into the bean water and cook for 8 minutes, or until they are tender but not falling apart. Drain and chill.

6. In another saucepan bring salted water to a boil. Add the potatoes and cook them until they are tender, then drain and cool. When they are cool enough to handle, peel and slice thin.

7. In a small jar combine the vinegar, oil, mustard, garlic, and chervil, a pinch of salt and a grinding of black pepper, and shake the jar to blend the dressing thoroughly. Set aside.

8. Line a round, shallow salad bowl with lettuce leaves. Arrange the cauliflower, beans, potatoes, and beets in 4 separate mounds on the leaves, then garnish the dish with sliced onion, hard-boiled eggs, black olives, and the optional chicken or ham. Pour the dressing over the salad but do not toss.

Salade lyonnaise

Serves: 4 to 6
Preparation time: 20 minutes
Cooking time: 10 minutes

Toss the salad at the table. Serve accompanied by finely sliced, buttered pumpernickel bread and a chilled rosé wine.

Remarks

This kind of salad is usually a "leftover" salad. Cook each vegetable sometime during the week, making sure you have some leftovers. The salad will then happen naturally, and can be assembled in 5 minutes. I often serve it with a side dish of matjes herring garnished with finely sliced red onion.

Notes

Ingredients

1   Greening apple, peeled, cored, and diced
Juice of 1 lemon
1   small celery root (celeriac), peeled and cubed
2   tablespoons wine vinegar
1   teaspoon Dijon mustard
¼   teaspoon dry mustard
3   tablespoons finely minced scallion
1   large clove garlic, mashed
6   tablespoons olive oil
Salt and freshly ground black pepper
2   tablespoons Crème Fraîche (page 206) or sour cream
1   romaine lettuce heart
3   cups tightly packed fresh spinach leaves
¾   cup finely diced Gruyère or Swiss cheese
¾   cup finely diced smoked ham
8 to 10 slices of garlic sausage, peperoni, or Polish sausage
3   hard-boiled eggs, peeled and cut in half lengthwise (optional)

Preparation

1. Combine the diced apple and lemon juice in a small bowl and chill until serving time.

2. In a small saucepan bring salted water to a boil. Add the celery root and cook for 10 minutes, or until tender. Drain and set aside.

3. In a large salad bowl combine the vinegar, mustards, scallion, and garlic. Whisk the mixture until it is thick and smooth, then add the olive oil, salt, and pepper and whisk the sauce until the oil is

well blended. Add the crème fraîche and whisk again until the sauce is smooth.

4. Tear the romaine lettuce into 2-inch pieces and add it to the bowl together with the spinach, apple, celery root, cheese, and ham. Garnish with finely sliced sausage and optional hard-boiled eggs, then sprinkle with freshly ground black pepper and chill.

5. Twenty minutes before serving time, bring the salad back to room temperature and toss it at the table. Serve accompanied by black bread and a bowl of sweet butter.

Notes

Asparagus and ham rolls primavera

Serves: 4 to 6
Preparation time: 40 minutes
Cooking time: 12 minutes

Ingredients

21 to 27 large stalks asparagus
2   whole eggs
1   teaspoon Dijon mustard
1   tablespoon white wine vinegar
Salt and freshly ground white pepper
1   cup vegetable oil
2   tablespoons minced fresh parsley
1   tablespoon minced scallion
2   tablespoons finely minced chives or fresh dill
6   slices excellent-quality cooked ham

Preparation

1. Peel the asparagus with a vegetable peeler. Remove the tough ends, leaving the stalks 5 to 6 inches long. Tie the stalks into even bundles, leaving one or two stalks loose for testing.

2. Bring 6 to 7 quarts of salted water to a boil in a large, heavy, flameproof casserole, add the asparagus, and cook over high heat for 10 to 12 minutes, starting to test for doneness with the sharp tip of a knife after 8 minutes. (The asparagus should still be slightly crisp when done.) As soon as the asparagus are ready, drain them and run them under cold water to stop further cooking. Untie the bundles and spread the stalks on a double layer of paper towels. Cool.

3. In the container of a blender combine the eggs, mustard, vinegar, salt, and pepper and blend at high speed for 1 minute. Continuing to beat, start adding the oil in a slow stream. As soon as the mixture thickens, add the oil more quickly, until the mixture is thick and smooth. Add the parsley and scallion and blend.

4. Mince 3 stalks of the asparagus fine and add them to the sauce. Blend the mixture again at high speed until it is smooth, then taste for seasoning, adding a large grinding of pepper. Pour the sauce into a bowl, add the chives or dill, and chill for 2 to 3 hours.

5. One or two hours before serving, roll 3 to 4 asparagus into a slice of ham. Place the roll on a rectangular platter and continue until all the asparagus and ham are used up. Cover the rolls completely with the sauce and serve chilled but not cold.

Remarks

Leftover asparagus sauce can be served with grilled or poached salmon or poached shrimp.

Notes

Stuffed avocados à la danoise

Serves: 4
Preparation time: 35 minutes

The happy marriage of salmon and dill has always been recognized in Scandinavian cooking. The avocado, with its subtle flavor, adds a delicious finishing touch to this light appetizer.

Ingredients

1   cup watercress leaves
1   whole egg
Juice of 1 lemon
1   teaspoon Dijon mustard
Salt and freshly ground white pepper
⅔ to ¾ cup vegetable oil
2   tablespoons minced fresh dill
1   tablespoon minced scallion, green
     part only
2   ripe avocados
1½ cups flaked, freshly poached salmon
     (see page 141)

Garnish:
Boston lettuce leaves
Sprigs of fresh dill

Preparation

1. Bring salted water to a boil in a small saucepan, add the watercress leaves, and poach them over medium heat for 1 minute. Drain the leaves, run them under cold water, and dry on paper towels. Set aside.

2. In the container of a blender place the egg, juice of ½ lemon, Dijon mustard, salt, and pepper. Turn the blender on to high speed and, slowly adding the oil, blend until the mixture becomes thick. Add the watercress leaves, dill, and scallion and blend again until the mixture is smooth. Taste the sauce for seasoning, adding salt

and pepper to taste (you may find you like a stronger dill flavor). Chill the sauce for 2 to 4 hours.

3. An hour before serving, cut the avocados in half lengthwise, remove the pits, and sprinkle the cavities with lemon juice, salt, and pepper.

4. Mix the salmon with the dill sauce and spoon into the avocado cavities. Top each avocado with a sprig of dill and place on a bed of lettuce leaves. Serve chilled but not cold, accompanied by thinly sliced black bread and a bowl of sweet butter.

Notes

Cold green bean salad julienne

Serves: 6
Preparation time: 10 minutes
Cooking time: 8 to 10 minutes

Ingredients

1½ pounds young string beans
½ pound fresh mushrooms
½ cup olive oil
2 tablespoons red wine vinegar
2 teaspoons Dijon mustard
1 large shallot, finely minced
1 small clove garlic, mashed
Salt and freshly ground black pepper
¾ cup finely diced Westphalian ham or prosciutto
2 tomatoes, quartered
1 hard-boiled egg, finely minced (optional)

Preparation

1. Snap tips off beans, wash them thoroughly under cold running water, and set aside.

2. Wipe the mushrooms with a damp paper towel; remove the stems and reserve for stocks and soups. Slice the mushrooms into ¼-inch slices, then cut the slices into thin julienne. Set aside.

3. Bring salted water to a boil in a large saucepan, add the beans and cook for 8 to 9 minutes, or until barely tender, then drain and run under cold water to stop further cooking. Cool. If the beans are large, cut them into 2- to 3-inch pieces.

4. In a large glass serving bowl, combine the oil, vinegar, mustard, shallot, and garlic. Whisk the dressing until it is well blended, then season with salt and pepper. Add the mushrooms to the bowl and let them marinate for 30 minutes. Add the beans and prosciutto or ham and toss the

salad lightly. Taste and correct the seasoning.

5. Garnish with quartered tomatoes and optional minced egg, then serve at room temperature, accompanied by French bread and a bowl of sweet butter.

Notes

Green bean and radish salad à la danoise

Serves: 4 to 6
Preparation time: 20 minutes
Cooking time: 10 to 12 minutes

Ingredients

1   pound fresh string beans
2   cups thinly sliced radishes
1½ tablespoons lemon juice
1   teaspoon Dijon mustard
6   tablespoons olive oil
1   teaspoon granulated sugar
2   tablespoons finely minced fresh dill
Salt and freshly ground black pepper
1 to 2 tablespoons finely chopped walnuts

Preparation

1. If possible, use very young, small string beans for this salad. Snap off their tips and leave them whole, then rinse them under cold running water and set aside.

2. Bring salted water to a boil in a large, flameproof casserole. Drop the beans, a few at a time, into the boiling water and cook for 10 to 12 minutes, or until tender but still slightly crisp. Drain the beans and immediately run them under cold water to stop further cooking. Cool, then combine them with the radishes in a serving bowl.

3. In a small mixing bowl combine the lemon juice, mustard, olive oil, and sugar. Whisk the mixture until it is well blended, then add the minced dill, a pinch of salt and pepper. Pour the dressing over the beans, toss, and chill for 2 to 4 hours before serving. Just before serving, sprinkle with walnuts.

Remarks

If the beans are large or of the flat Kentucky variety, cook them whole, and as soon as they are cool, cut them into 2-inch pieces. To vary it, you may garnish the salad with minced hard-boiled egg and tiny smoked sardines.

Notes

Hot bean and sausage salad
Serves: 4
Preparation time: 20 minutes
Cooking time: 1¾ hours

Ingredients
1 cup dried white beans
Salt and freshly ground black pepper
1 bay leaf
1 onion stuck with 1 whole clove
2 garlic sausages or 4 fried pork sausages
1 cup cubed slab bacon
2 tablespoons butter
6 tablespoons olive oil
2 tablespoons minced shallots
2 large cloves garlic, minced
2 tablespoons minced fresh parsley
2 tablespoons white wine vinegar

Preparation
1. Combine the beans with water to cover in a large, flameproof casserole. Bring to a boil, then remove from the heat and let the beans stand, covered, for 1 hour.

2. Salt the water in which the beans are soaking, add the bay leaf and onion, and bring to a boil. Reduce the heat and simmer the beans, at the lowest possible heat, for 1½ hours, or until very tender. (They must cook at the lowest possible heat or they will remain tough.) If you are using garlic sausages, add them 10 minutes before the beans are done.

3. While the beans are cooking, drop the bacon cubes into boiling water and cook for 3 minutes. Drain and dry thoroughly with paper towels, then fry, in the butter in a small, heavy skillet, until almost crisp. Remove to a double layer of paper towels and set aside.

Bean and caviar salad

Serves: 4 to 6
Preparation time: 10 minutes
Cooking time: 1 to 1½ hours

4. When the beans are done, remove the sausages to a side dish, slice, and reserve. Drain the beans, discard the onion and bay leaf, and set aside.

5. In a large, heavy skillet heat the oil, add the minced shallots, garlic, and parsley and cook until soft but not browned. Add the vinegar, beans, and bacon, then toss lightly and season with salt and pepper. Add the sliced sausages.

6. Serve warm, with crusty bread and a well-seasoned salad.

Notes

Teaming white beans with caviar brings new life to the antipasto table. These beans, a staple of Tuscan cooking, are often used for both hot and cold dishes in that region. A favorite is the tuna and white bean salad, but I find caviar provides an interesting yet inexpensive change.

Ingredients

2 tablespoons red wine vinegar
¼ teaspoons dry mustard
6 tablespoons fruity olive oil
Salt and freshly ground black pepper
1 clove garlic, mashed
3 to 4 cups Cooked White Beans (page 210)
1 small red onion, thinly sliced
3 tablespoons lumpfish caviar (preferably Danish)
Juice of ½ lemon

Garnish:
Finely minced fresh parsley

Preparation

1. In a serving bowl combine the vinegar, mustard, olive oil, salt, pepper, and garlic, whisking the mixture until it is well blended. Add the cooked beans and toss, then add the onion. Chill.

2. Thirty minutes before serving, bring the salad back to room temperature. Add the caviar and lemon juice, sprinkle with finely minced parsley, and toss the salad lightly. Taste for seasoning and serve.

hors d'oeuvres and salads

Cold beet salad aux fines herbes

Serves: 6 to 8
Preparation time: 15 minutes

Remarks

When cooking white beans for a salad,
sprinkle the drained hot beans with olive oil
and a little lemon juice to keep them
from sticking. For a stronger flavor, mash
two anchovy fillets into the dressing before
adding the beans.

Notes

I am always looking for new ways to
prepare beets. I find them an intriguing
vegetable that should not be limited to the
usual two or three preparations. This
summer salad combines three of my
favorites: fresh herbs, *crème fraîche* and,
of course, beets.

Ingredients

1   cup Crème Fraîche (page 206)
2 · tablespoons olive oil
1½ tablespoons red wine vinegar
2   tablespoons finely minced fresh
    tarragon or 1 teaspoon dried
2   tabléspoons finely minced fresh herbs
    (parsley, chervil, and chives)
4   cups freshly cooked, cubed beets
Salt and freshly ground white pepper

Garnish:
2   tablespoons finely minced fresh parsley

Preparation

1. In a serving bowl combine the *crème
fraîche*, olive oil, vinegar, and herbs. Stir
the mixture until well blended, then add the
beets and fold them into the dressing.
Season with salt and pepper and chill for
2 to 4 hours before serving.

2. Forty-five minutes before serving, bring
the salad back to room temperature.
Taste and correct the seasoning, then
sprinkle with parsley and serve as part of
an hors d'oeuvre table or as a garnish
to roast chicken, poached fish, or cold
roast beef.

Demels beet and herring salad

Serves: 4 to 6
Preparation time: 15 minutes

Even though the French have always
earned the greatest credit for their hors
d'oeuvre tables, in my opinion the Viennese
have created some of the most flavorful
hors d'oeuvre salads. This one is from
Demels Café in Vienna.

Ingredients

1   cup Swedish-style herring, cut into
    ½-inch cubes
3   hard-boiled eggs, coarsely chopped
3   small beets, cooked, peeled and cubed
½   green bell pepper, finely cubed
1   small dill gherkin, finely diced
2   tablespoons finely minced scallion,
    green part and all
3 to 4 tablespoons Mayonnaise (page 208)
Heavy grinding of white pepper
Pinch of salt

Garnish:
2   sieved hard-boiled egg yolks
Sprigs of fresh dill or parsley

Preparation

1. In a mixing bowl combine the herring
pieces, eggs, beets, green pepper, gherkin,
and scallion. Add the mayonnaise and
white pepper and taste the mixture before
adding salt. Blend the mixture carefully
with a wooden spoon and chill for 2 to 4
hours.

2. When ready to serve, pour the salad
into a rectangular hors d'oeuvre dish or
glass serving bowl and garnish with the
sieved egg yolks and sprigs of dill or
parsley. Serve with thinly sliced pumpernickel and a bowl of sweet butter.

Boreks variés

Serves: 14 to 16
Preparation time: 1 hour
Cooking time: 45 minutes

Greek *boreks* are small pastry triangles
usually filled with a mixture of cheese and
spinach and served as hors d'oeuvres.
The dough used for *boreks* is called phyllo
dough; somewhat similar to strudel dough,
it is used in both Greek and Turkish
cooking. Though the traditional filling
can be excellent when well prepared, I
find that you can be extremely inventive
with this fine dough, and have created
some fillings that are both delicious and
easy to prepare.

Ingredients

1   package phyllo pastry dough
1   cup melted butter
Filling of your choice (see below)

Preparation

1. Preheat the oven to 350 degrees.

2. For making the triangles you will need a
large smooth working area, several cookie
sheets, and a slightly damp towel for
covering. Place one sheet of phyllo dough
on a wooden board or table. Quickly brush
the entire sheet with melted butter and
top carefully with another sheet. Brush
again with melted butter. (Make sure you
cover the remaining dough with the damp
towel or the dough will dry out before you
can use it.) Continue until all the dough
is used up. With a sharp knife cut the stack
of buttered sheets into 6 even strips about
3 inches wide. Place 1 teaspoon of the
filling on the bottom of a strip of dough
and fold the strip into a triangle; continue
to fold it over and over on itself as if you
were folding a flag. Brush the triangle

Chicken liver and herb filling

again with melted butter and place it on a cookie sheet. Continue making triangles with the next batch until all the phyllo pastry and filling are used up. Bake the triangles for 25 to 30 minutes, or until nicely browned. Serve immediately.

Remarks

The *boreks* can be made days and even weeks in advance and frozen on the cookie sheets. When the *boreks* are to be served as an appetizer at the table, you can make them slightly larger and serve only one or two fillings at a time.

Notes

Ingredients

½ pound fresh chicken livers
3 tablespoons butter
2 tablespoons finely minced shallots
Salt and freshly ground black pepper
8 ounces cream cheese, at room temperature
1 teaspoon finely minced garlic
1 tablespoon finely minced fresh parsley
1 tablespoon finely minced fresh tarragon or ¼ teaspoon dried

Preparation

1. Carefully clean the chicken livers, removing any dark or green spots, then dry well with paper towels and cut into small cubes. Set aside.

2. In a heavy, 10-inch skillet heat the butter. When it is very hot, add the shallots and chicken livers and cook over high heat until nicely browned on both sides. Season with salt and pepper and scrape the mixture into a mixing bowl.

3. Add the cream cheese, garlic, parsley, and tarragon. Mash the mixture with a fork until it is well blended, then taste for seasoning; it should be quite peppery. Chill the mixture for 30 minutes to an hour before filling the dough.

Mushroom and dill filling

Ingredients

3 tablespoons butter
2 tablespoons finely minced scallion
½ pound fresh mushrooms, finely minced
2 tablespoons heavy cream
8 ounces cream cheese, at room
   temperature
2 tablespoons finely minced fresh dill
2 tablespoons freshly grated Parmesan
   cheese
Salt and freshly ground white pepper

Preparation

In a small, heavy skillet heat the butter.
When it is very hot, add the scallion and
mushrooms and cook the mixture over
high heat until it is lightly browned and all
the mushroom water has evaporated. Add
the cream and continue cooking until
the mixture is thick and all the moisture
has evaporated. Scrape into a mixing bowl
and add the cream cheese, dill, Parmesan,
salt, and pepper. Mash well with a fork,
then taste for seasoning. Chill the filling for
30 minutes before filling the dough.

Notes

Crabmeat and curry filling

Ingredients

1 cup cooked, flaked lump crabmeat
8 ounces cream cheese, at room
   temperature
1 egg yolk
½ teaspoon curry powder
1 tablespoon finely minced fresh chives
1 tablespoon finely minced scallion
2 teaspoons lemon juice
Salt and freshly ground white pepper

Preparation

Carefully pick over the crabmeat, removing
all the pieces of shell. In a bowl combine
the cream cheese, egg yolk, curry powder,
and herbs. Mash the mixture with a fork
to blend well, then add the crabmeat and
lemon juice. Blend the mixture carefully
and season with salt and pepper. Chill for
30 minutes before filling the dough.

Remarks

Finely diced, cooked shrimp or canned
tuna can be substituted for the crabmeat.

Notes

Eggplant and shellfish salad

Serves: 8
Preparation time: 45 minutes (plus 1 to 2
hours draining time)
Cooking time: 25 minutes

Ingredients

3   medium eggplants, peeled and cut into
    1-inch cubes
Salt
1   cup olive oil, approximately
½   cup thinly sliced almonds
2   cups sliced onion
2   cloves garlic, finely minced
2   cups finely diced celery
2   medium tomatoes, peeled, seeded, and
    chopped
⅔   cup tomato puree
2   tablespoons well-drained capers
1   cup small black olives (oil cured)
2   large red peppers, charred, seeded,
    and sliced (see page 31)
Freshly ground black pepper
1   small can (3½ ounces) tuna
1   cup cooked, peeled, diced shrimp

Optional:
12 to 15 mussels, well cleaned, cooked,
    and shelled

Garnish:
Juice of ½ lemon
Finely minced fresh parsley
Finely sliced rounds of red pepper
Rolled anchovy fillets

Preparation

1. Place the eggplant on a double layer
of paper towels, sprinkle with salt, and let
drain for 1 or 2 hours.

2. While the eggplant is draining, heat 2
tablespoons of the oil in a small, heavy
skillet. Add the almonds and cook them
until lightly browned, then remove them to
a double layer of paper towels to drain.

3. Dry the eggplant thoroughly with paper
towels. In a large, heavy skillet, heat ¼ cup
of the oil. Add the eggplant cubes, a few
at a time (do not crowd your pan), and
sauté until they are nicely browned.
Remove to a colander and continue sautéing, adding a little more oil when necessary.

4. When all the eggplant is done, add a
little more oil to the pan, then the onion,
and cook over low heat until soft and
lightly browned. Add the garlic, celery,
tomatoes, and tomato puree, cover the
skillet, and cook the mixture until the celery
is tender, or for about 10 minutes.

5. Return the eggplant to the pan, together
with the capers, olives, and red peppers.
Season with salt and pepper and simmer
the mixture for another 5 minutes, then
add the almonds, tuna, shrimp, and
optional mussels. Heat through, correct
the seasoning, and pour into a serving
bowl. Chill for 6 to 8 hours.

6. Just before serving toss the salad
lightly, sprinkle with lemon juice and
parsley, and garnish with thinly sliced
red pepper rounds and rolled anchovy
fillets.

Notes

Swiss endive and gruyère salad

Serves: 6 to 8
Preparation time: 15 minutes

The endive, with its tangy, slightly bitter taste, is one of the most versatile of greens. It can be served as a vegetable accompanying a roast or as an addition to the salad bowl. As an appetizer the endive combines especially well with beets, shrimp, or radishes. Here is a salad that takes only minutes to prepare and is particularly suitable for simple dinners or lunch.

Ingredients

4 to 6 endives
1 cup thinly sliced radishes
1½ cups Gruyère or imported Swiss cheese cut into 1½-inch matchsticks
Juice of 1 lemon
1 teaspoon granulated sugar
3 tablespoons thinly sliced scallion
½ cup olive oil
1 teaspoon Dijon mustard
Salt and freshly ground white pepper

Preparation

1. Wash the endives quickly under cold running water. Do not soak them, as this increases their bitter flavor. Remove the outer leaves, then cut the endives in half lengthwise and then into ½-inch strips.

2. Place the endives, radishes, and cheese in a salad bowl and set aside.

3. In a small bowl combine the lemon juice, sugar, scallion, olive oil, and mustard. Whisk the mixture until it is completely blended, then add a pinch of salt and pepper. Taste the dressing; it should be quite sweet. Set aside.

4. An hour before serving, pour the dressing over the endive and cheese mixture and toss lightly. Chill.

5. Remove the salad from the refrigerator 15 minutes before serving. Taste for seasoning, adding a heavy grinding of fresh pepper. Serve with French bread and a bowl of sweet butter.

Notes

hors d'oeuvres and salads

Endive and walnut salad

Serves: 4 to 6
Preparation time: 10 minutes

The endive, by far the most interesting of the winter greens, is good in salads as well as braised or otherwise cooked. Unfortunately, it is quite expensive and often not available in some parts of the country. Do try to find it, or urge your local greengrocer to get it for you. A well-flavored endive salad is a perfect beginning to a light winter or spring meal.

Ingredients

4 to 6 endives
¼ teaspoon dry mustard
1 teaspoon Dijon mustard
1 tablespoon wine vinegar
3 tablespoons olive oil
2 tablespoons Crème Fraîche (page 206)
Salt and freshly ground white pepper
1 tablespoon lemon juice
2 tablespoons finely chopped walnuts
2 ounces (¼ cup) Roquefort cheese, finely diced

Preparation

1. Wash the endives thoroughly under cold running water, but do not soak them, as this brings out bitterness. With the tip of a sharp knife, remove the hard, round core of the endive, separate the leaves and drain them on a kitchen towel. Chill.

2. In a serving bowl combine the dry mustard with the Dijon mustard and vinegar. Whisk the mixture until it is well blended and let it stand for 30 minutes to 1 hour. Add the oil and *crème fraîche,* season with salt and pepper, and whisk again to combine well. Set aside.

3. Just before serving, arrange the endives in a bowl. Sprinkle with the lemon juice, walnuts, and Roquefort cheese and toss the salad with the dressing at the table.

Remarks

The cheese must not overpower the endives. If you cannot get good-quality Roquefort, substitute a mild, imported Gorgonzola.

Notes

Lentil and sausage salad

Serves: 4 to 6
Preparation time: 15 minutes
Cooking time: 40 to 50 minutes

A lentil salad is a marvelously robust winter salad, perfect for Sunday suppers and after-ski entertaining. Serve it with black bread and a bowl of sweet butter.

Ingredients

2   cups dried lentils
Salt
1   Bouquet Garni (see page 214)
1   carrot, peeled and cut in half
1   large onion, peeled and stuck with
    1 whole clove
1   stalk celery
2   tablespoons red wine vinegar
1½ teaspoons Dijon mustard
½ cup olive oil
1   large clove garlic, mashed
2   tablespoons finely minced fresh parsley
⅓ cup finely minced scallion
Freshly ground black pepper
2   frankfurters, cooked and thinly sliced

Preparation

1. Wash the lentils in several changes of cold water, then place in a large saucepan and cover with 2 inches of cold water. Add a large pinch of salt, the *bouquet garni*, carrot, onion, and celery. Bring to a boil, then reduce the heat and simmer, partially covered, for 40 minutes, or until just tender. Drain the lentils, discarding the vegetables and *bouquet garni*, and set aside.

2. In a serving bowl combine the vinegar and mustard. Whisk the mixture until it is smooth and well blended, then add the olive oil, garlic, parsley, scallion, salt, and a heavy grinding of black pepper. Whisk the dressing until well blended. Add the warm lentils and sausage slices, toss, and serve at room temperature.

Notes

hors d'oeuvres and salads

Marinated mushrooms

Serves: 6 to 8
Preparation time: 10 minutes
Cooking time: 3 minutes

Ingredients

2   pounds small mushrooms
¾   cup olive oil
3   cloves garlic, peeled and thinly sliced
Juice of 2 lemons
2   tablespoons white wine vinegar
Salt
2   bay leaves
1   sprig of fresh parsley
1   sprig of fresh thyme or ½ teaspoon
    dried
6   peppercorns

Garnish:
2   tablespoons finely minced fresh parsley,
    chervil, or fennel tops

Preparation

1. Wipe the mushrooms with a damp paper
towel (do not wash) and trim the mushroom
stems. Cut the mushrooms in half lengthwise through the stems or quarter the
larger ones.

2. Heat the oil in a large heavy skillet. Add
all the other ingredients except the
garnish and simmer the mixture for 2 to 3
minutes. Remove the skillet from the
heat, cover, and let the mushrooms cool
in the liquid.

3. Pour the mushrooms, together with their
poaching liquid, into an earthenware bowl.
Garnish with the minced parsley, chervil,
or fennel and serve at room temperature,
as part of an hors d'oeuvre table or as
an accompaniment to grilled fish.

Remarks

The mushrooms are even better when
left to marinate for several days. Store
them in the refrigerator in a covered jar
and bring them back to room temperature
30 to 40 minutes before serving.

Notes

Viennese stuffed mushrooms

Serves: 6 to 8
Preparation time: 15 minutes
Cooking time: 10 minutes

Ingredients

12 to 16 large fresh mushrooms (2 to 3
    inches in diameter), plus an additional
    ½ pound mushrooms
3 tablespoons butter
2 large shallots, finely minced
Salt and freshly ground white pepper
6 ounces cream cheese, softened
2 tablespoons minced fresh dill
2 tablespoons finely grated fresh
    Parmesan cheese

Garnish:
Sprigs of fresh parsley

Preparation

1. Carefully remove the stems from the
large mushrooms; mince and set aside.
Wipe the mushroom caps carefully with
damp paper towels. Set aside. Finely mince
the remaining ½ pound of mushrooms.

2. Heat 2 tablespoons of the butter in a
small, heavy skillet. Add the minced mushrooms, mushroom stems, and shallots
and cook the mixture over high heat until
it is lightly browned and all the mushroom
water has evaporated. Season with salt
and pepper.

3. In a mixing bowl combine the cream
cheese, dill, and mushroom mixture. Add
the Parmesan, then mash the mixture
with a fork until it is well blended. Taste
and correct the seasoning and chill for
30 minutes.

4. Preheat the broiler.

5. Butter a baking dish with the remaining
butter. Fill the mushroom caps with the
mushroom and cream cheese mixture,
then place under the broiler and cook for
3 to 5 minutes, or until lightly browned.
Do not overcook. Carefully transfer the
mushrooms to a serving platter, garnish
with sprigs of parsley, and serve immediately.

Remarks

For variety, omit the dill. Instead, sauté 2
tablespoons of pine nuts in 2 tablespoons
of butter until lightly browned. Add to the
cream cheese and mushroom mixture
and fill the mushroom caps.
For a more elegant presentation, cut bread
rounds with a cookie cutter, sauté them
in a mixture of butter and oil, and then
arrange a mushroom cap on each toast
round.

Notes

hors d'oeuvres and salads

Mussel and potato salad rovigo

Serves: 4 to 6
Preparation time: 40 minutes
Cooking time: 25 to 30 minutes

Mussels are used extensively in Mediterranean cooking in both hot and cold dishes. They combine extremely well with cold rice as well as with potatoes and other vegetables. For variety you may add ½ pound of thinly sliced raw mushrooms to the salad bowl.

Ingredients

1½ pounds new potatoes
2 tablespoons dry white wine
2 tablespoons olive oil
Salt and freshly ground black pepper
4 pounds fresh mussels, well scrubbed
2 tablespoons minced shallots
3 tablespoons minced fresh parsley
2 whole eggs
2 teaspoons Dijon mustard
2 teaspoons hot prepared mustard
   (preferably Colman's)
1 tablespoon white wine vinegar
¾ to 1 cup vegetable oil

Garnish:
2 hard-boiled eggs, cut in half
2 tablespoons well-drained capers
4 rolled anchovy fillets

Preparation

1. Scrub the potatoes thoroughly under cold running water.

2. Bring salted water to a boil in a large saucepan. Add the potatoes, and boil, uncovered, until they are just tender when pierced with the tip of a sharp knife. Drain, and when they are cool enough to handle, peel and cut into thin slices. Place in a mixing bowl, sprinkle with the white wine, olive oil, salt, and pepper. Toss lightly and set aside.

3. Preheat the oven to 325 degrees.

4. Put the mussels in a large heatproof casserole. Cover the casserole, place it in the center of the oven, and steam the mussels open. Discard the shell and remove the black "border" around the mussels. Add to the bowl, together with the shallots and 2 tablespoons of the minced parsley. Set aside.

5. In the container of a blender combine the eggs, mustards, vinegar, salt, and pepper. Blend the mixture at top speed for 30 seconds, then, continuing to blend, add the vegetable oil by driblets. As soon as the mixture thickens add the oil in a light stream until the sauce stops absorbing more oil and is very thick. Taste and correct the seasoning. Add enough sauce to bind the salad, toss lightly, and chill for an hour or two.

6. Thirty minutes before serving, bring the salad back to room temperature, pour into a serving bowl and garnish with the remaining parsley, and the eggs, capers, and anchovy fillets.

Notes

Potato and pepper salad galicia

Serves: 4 to 6
Preparation time: 25 minutes (plus 1 to 2 hours marinating time)
Cooking time: 20 to 30 minutes

More of a "buffet" salad than an actual appetizer, this hearty salad from northern Spain is an excellent accompaniment to shish kebab, grilled fish, or cold roast chicken.

Ingredients

2 to 3 red peppers
6 tablespoons olive oil
2 tablespoons red wine vinegar
1 large clove garlic, mashed
Salt and freshly ground black pepper
1 small red onion, thinly sliced
6 medium-sized mushrooms, thinly sliced
8 to 10 medium-sized new potatoes
1½ cups cubed bacon

Garnish:
1 tablespoon well-drained capers
2 tablespoons finely minced fresh parsley

Preparation

1. Preheat the broiler.

2. Place the peppers in a roasting pan and broil them until their skin is well charred on all sides, then remove from the broiler and peel under cold running water. Remove the seeds and slice them. Set aside.

3. In a large serving bowl combine the oil, vinegar, garlic, salt, and a heavy grinding of black pepper. Whisk the mixture until it is well blended, then add the onion and mushrooms and let marinate for 1 to 2 hours.

4. Bring salted water to a boil in a large saucepan. Add the potatoes and cook until they are tender when pierced with the tip of a sharp knife but not falling apart. Peel, slice, and add them to the serving bowl while they are still warm. Toss them lightly to cover well with the dressing, then add the peppers and set aside.

5. Sauté the bacon cubes in a small, heavy skillet until they are almost crisp, then drain on a double layer of paper towels and add to the salad bowl. Toss the salad again and correct the seasoning.

6. Sprinkle the salad with capers and parsley and serve at room temperature.

Notes

Middle eastern chick-pea salad

Serves: 4 to 6
Preparation time: 5 minutes
Cooking time: 2 to 3 hours

Chick-peas are a round, hard corn-colored dry vegetable that plays an important part in Middle Eastern cooking. Other Mediterranean countries such as Spain and Italy make good use of chick-peas in soups, salads, and stews. Though canned chick peas are available in every supermarket, I find that they are usually still somewhat tough and more expensive by far than when cooking them yourself.

Ingredients

1 to 1½ cups dried chick-peas
1   tablespoon red wine vinegar
Juice of 1 or 2 large lemons
6   tablespoons olive oil
¼   teaspoon dry mustard
1   teaspoon Dijon mustard
1   clove garlic, mashed
1   large, ripe tomato, cubed
1   cucumber, peeled, seeded, and diced
1   green pepper, cored, seeded, and diced
6   radishes, diced
3   tablespoons finely minced scallion
2   tablespoons finely minced fresh parsley
Salt and freshly ground black pepper

Preparation

1. Soak the chick-peas in plenty of water to cover. Add ½ teaspoon baking soda and let them stand overnight.

2. The next day drain the chick-peas and place them in a heavy, ovenproof casserole. Cover the chick-peas with water and place the casserole, tightly covered, in a 325-degree oven. Cook for 2 to 3 hours, or until tender. Do not salt until the chick-

peas are almost done. Remove the casserole from the oven and let the chick-peas cool in their cooking liquid.

3. In a large glass serving bowl combine the vinegar, juice of 1 lemon, olive oil, mustards, and garlic. Whisk the mixture until the dressing is well blended, then add the drained chick-peas, tomato, cucumber, green pepper, radishes, scallion, and parsley. Toss the salad, season with salt and pepper, and chill for 2 to 4 hours.

4. Thirty minutes before serving, bring the salad back to room temperature. Taste and correct the seasoning, adding the juice of a second lemon if necessary; the salad should be quite tangy. Serve as an appetizer or as part of an hors d'oeuvre table.

Remarks

When serving the salad as an appetizer, I often serve a side dish of sardines in olive oil, sprinkled with lemon juice and finely minced chives.

Notes

Mediterranean chick-pea salad

Serves: 4 to 6
Preparation time: 15 minutes

Ingredients

3 to 4 cups cooked chick-peas (see
    page 28)
1   can (7½ ounces) tuna in olive oil
½   cup thinly sliced pimiento
1   green pepper, roasted, peeled, seeded
    (see below), and sliced
1   small red onion, peeled and thinly
    sliced
2   tablespoons well-drained capers
2   tablespoons minced fresh parsley
½   cup pitted black olives (preferably
    Greek)
Salt and freshly ground black pepper
2   tablespoons red wine vinegar
½   cup olive oil
1   teaspoon Dijon mustard
1   large clove garlic, mashed
Juice of 1 lemon

Preparation

1. In a large serving bowl combine the
cooked chick-peas, tuna, pimiento, green
pepper, onion, capers, parsley, black
olives, salt and pepper. Set aside.

2. In a small screw-top jar combine the
vinegar, olive oil, mustard, garlic, salt, and
pepper. Cover the jar and shake it until
the dressing is smooth and well blended,
then pour over the salad. Toss lightly
and chill.

3. Just before serving, bring the salad back
to room temperature and sprinkle with
lemon juice. Taste and correct the seasoning. Serve as part of an hors d'oeuvre
table or by itself, accompanied by a bowl
of hard-boiled eggs and French bread.

Remarks

To roast peppers, place them on a baking
sheet, set under the broiler and cook
until the skins are almost charred on all
sides. Remove the peppers from the baking
sheet and peel off the skins under cold
running water. It is useful to prepare
several peppers at one time, place them
in a jar, cover with olive oil, and store in
the refrigerator.

Notes

Greek radish salad

Serves: 6 to 8
Preparation time: 15 minutes

In my first garden I planted several rows of radishes. A few weeks later I had a huge surplus of this delicious early summer vegetable. The result: a light salad that has since become a staple of the spring-summer kitchen.

Ingredients

1 tablespoon lemon juice
6 tablespoons olive oil
½ teaspoon Dijon mustard
4 to 5 cups thinly sliced radishes
8 to 10 black Greek olives, thinly sliced
¾ to 1 cup crumbled feta cheese
2 tablespoons finely minced fresh parsley
1 small red onion, thinly sliced
Freshly ground black pepper
Salt

Preparation

1. In a small jar combine the lemon juice, olive oil, and mustard. Shake the jar to blend the dressing thoroughly, then set aside.

2. In a large serving bowl combine the radishes, olives, feta, parsley, and onion. Add the dressing and a heavy grinding of black pepper. Toss the salad and taste it for seasoning. (Feta cheese can be slightly salty, so the salad may only need a small pinch of salt.) Chill for 2 to 4 hours before serving, then serve with French bread and a bowl of sweet butter.

Remarks

If you want to reduce the saltiness of feta cheese, place it in a bowl and cover with cold water. Place the bowl in the refrigerator and use the cheese a day or two later. The cheese will keep for two weeks in the refrigerator.
As an additional garnish you can serve a plate of sardines dressed in a little lemon juice and olive oil.

Notes

Stuffed tomatoes aïoli

Serves: 4 to 6
Cooking time: 10 minutes

Here is an excellent filling using leftover poached fish such as salmon, cod, whiting, or sole. The tomatoes can be served as part of an hors d'oeuvre table or as an appetizer for a summer or early fall meal. Try not to use tomatoes that are "pretty" but flavorless, like hothouse winter tomatoes. You are not after looks but taste!

Ingredients

4 to 6 medium-sized, ripe tomatoes
Salt and freshly ground black pepper
1   large egg
1   teaspoon wine vinegar
1   clove garlic, mashed
½ to ¾ cup olive oil
1   cup flaked, poached fish or 1 cup tuna
    in oil, well drained
½ cup fresh, cooked peas
1   tablespoon minced fresh parsley
1   tablespoon minced chives
Juice of ½ lemon

Garnish:
Boston lettuce leaves

Preparation

1. Cut the tops off the tomatoes and set aside. Carefully scoop out the pulp without breaking the skins, and reserve the pulp for sauces and stocks. Sprinkle the tomatoes with salt and pepper, turn them upside down on a plate and let drain for 30 minutes to 1 hour.

2. In the container of a blender combine the egg, salt, pepper, vinegar, and garlic.

Blend the mixture at top speed for 30 seconds, then, still blending, add the oil by driblets until the mixture starts to thicken, then add the remaining oil in a light stream. Blend the mayonnaise until it is thick and creamy and does not absorb any more oil. Taste and correct the seasoning, then set aside.

3. In a bowl combine the fish, peas, parsley, chives, and lemon juice. Fold ¼ cup of the mayonnaise into the mixture and chill for 30 minutes. Taste and correct the seasoning, then fill the tomatoes with the fish mixture and top with the tomato "cap." Chill until serving time.

4. Just before serving, line a serving platter with lettuce leaves. Arrange the tomatoes on top, and serve with French bread and a side bowl of Lemon Vinaigrette (see page 221).

Remarks

If your tomatoes are large and you seem to have too little filling you may "stretch" it by adding to it 2 hard-boiled eggs, coarsely chopped.

Notes

hors d'oeuvres and salads

Eggs and tomato salad andalouse

Serves: 6
Preparation time: 15 minutes

Summer is the time for simple, easy-to-prepare appetizers. But that doesn't mean they should be unimaginative.

Ingredients

5   tablespoons olive oil
2   tablespoons wine vinegar
2   tablespoons minced fresh parsley
2   tablespoons minced fresh basil or
     ½ teaspoon dried
1   tablespoon well-drained tiny capers
1   tablespoon minced chives
Salt and freshly ground black pepper
2   large, ripe beefsteak tomatoes
1   teaspoon unflavored gelatin
3   tablespoons water
1   cup Mayonnaise (see page 208)
6   hard-boiled eggs
6   pimiento strips
6   rolled anchovy fillets

Garnish:
Sprigs of fresh basil or parsley
Black Greek olives

Preparation

1. In the container of a blender combine the oil, vinegar, parsley, and basil. Blend the mixture at high speed until it is smooth, then pour into a bowl. Add the capers and chives and season the dressing with salt and pepper.

2. Cut the tomatoes into 6 slices ½ inch thick and place them on a round serving platter. Lightly cover each slice with the dressing and set aside.

3. In a small saucepan combine the gelatin with the water. Heat the gelatin until it is dissolved, then fold it into the mayonnaise.

4. Cut a ¼-inch slice lengthwise off each egg and coat the egg completely with mayonnaise. As soon as the mayonnaise is set, place each egg on a tomato slice. Roll a strip of pimiento around a rolled anchovy fillet and place on top of each egg. Chill the eggs until serving time.

5. Just before serving, garnish the platter with sprigs of basil or parsley and black olives.

Remarks

This appetizer is an excellent way of using such leftovers as cold roast chicken or poached salmon as a garnish.

Notes

Balkan rice salad

Serves: 6 to 8
Preparation time: 30 minutes
Cooking time: 45 minutes

Here is a delicious salad that I often make when I have leftover curried rice. Aside from making an excellent addition to the hors d'oeuvre table, the salad goes particularly well with shish kebab and grilled fish.

Ingredients

2   medium-sized zucchini
⅔   cup olive oil, more if necessary
3   tablespoons wine vinegar, more if necessary
1   cup thinly sliced red onion
1   cup chopped pimiento
1   large clove garlic, mashed
Salt and freshly ground black pepper
2   tablespoons butter
1   small onion, minced
1   tablespoon tomato paste
1   teaspoon curry powder
1   cup raw Italian (Arborio) rice
2   cups Chicken Stock (see page 203) or bouillon
1   large green pepper, roasted, peeled, and chopped (see page 31)
1   can (7½ ounces) tuna in olive oil
2   tablespoons minced fresh parsley
½   cup sliced green olives
½   cup sliced black Greek olives

Preparation

1. Wash the zucchini thoroughly under cold running water and cut off the tips on both ends. Drop the zucchini into fast-boiling salted water and cook them over medium heat for 20 minutes, then drain and run under cold water to stop further cooking. Drain on paper towels, then cut in half lengthwise and then into ½-inch cubes. Place the cubes in a mixing bowl and set aside.

2. In a bowl combine the oil, vinegar, onion, pimiento, and garlic. Season the mixture with salt and pepper, then pour it over the zucchini. Let the zucchini marinate in the dressing for 4 to 6 hours.

3. Heat the butter in a heavy-bottomed saucepan, then add the minced onion and cook it over medium heat until it is soft but not browned. Add the tomato paste and curry and stir the mixture for 1 minute. Add the rice and stir to coat it completely with the onion mixture, then add the stock. Bring it to a boil, reduce the heat, and simmer, covered, for 20 minutes. Remove the rice to a serving bowl and cool.

4. Add the zucchini mixture to the rice, as well as the green pepper, tuna, parsley, and olives. Toss the salad and taste for seasoning; it may need a little more oil and vinegar. Serve the salad slightly chilled or at room temperature.

Remarks

This kind of salad gives you a good opportunity to be creative in the kitchen. You can add to or leave out some of the ingredients and discover a whole new dish.

Notes

Stuffed tomatoes à la danoise

Serves: 6
Preparation time: 10 minutes
Cooking time: 5 minutes

It is a sad fact that in a country where fruits and vegetables are shipped from three thousand miles away, and where tomatoes are available year round, we can rarely buy a vine-ripened tomato. A stuffed tomato can be a delicious and refreshing beginning to a meal, yet unless the tomato itself is flavorful even the most interesting filling will not make it so.

Ingredients

6   medium-sized, ripe tomatoes
Salt
2   tablespoons butter
½   pound fresh mushrooms, finely minced
½   cup finely minced scallion, green
     part and all
Freshly ground white pepper
4   ounces softened cream cheese
3 to 4 tablespoons sour cream
2   tablespoons finely minced fresh dill

Garnish:
Sprigs of fresh dill

Preparation

1. Cut a slice off the top of each tomato. Carefully loosen the interior with the tip of a sharp knife and remove it. Discard the seeds, but reserve the flesh for soups, stocks, and sauces. Sprinkle the tomato shells with salt and place them, upside down, on a double layer of paper towels to drain for 30 minutes to 1 hour.

2. Melt the butter in a heavy, 10-inch skillet. Add the mushrooms and cook over high heat until they are lightly browned, then add the minced scallion and continue cooking until the scallion is soft and all the mushroom juice has evaporated. Season the mixture with salt and pepper and set aside.

3. In a mixing bowl combine the cream cheese, sour cream, and minced dill. Mash the mixture with a fork until it is well blended, then add the mushroom and scallion mixture and blend again. Season with salt and pepper and chill for 30 minutes to 1 hour.

4. Fill the tomatoes with the mushroom mixture, then top each with a sprig of dill and a tomato cap. Place the tomatoes on a round serving platter and serve at room temperature.

Remarks

For a variation you can stuff raw mushrooms with the filling. These should first be marinated for 4 to 6 hours in Vinaigrette Provençale (see page 221), then drained and dried with paper towels before being stuffed.

Notes

Stuffed tomatoes forestière

Serves: 6 to 8
Preparation time: 15 minutes
Cooking time: 5 minutes

Ingredients

6 to 8 medium-sized, ripe tomatoes
Salt
6   ounces cream cheese, softened
⅔ cup sour cream
2   tablespoons minced scallion
2   tablespoons finely minced fresh dill
1   clove garlic, mashed
3   cups fresh spinach, cleaned
Freshly ground white pepper

Garnish:
Sprigs of fresh dill

Preparation

1. Cut the tops off the tomatoes and set
aside.

2. Carefully scoop out the seeds and pulp,
reserving the pulp for another use. Sprinkle
the tomatoes with salt and let them drain,
upside down, on a double layer of paper
towels for 30 minutes to 1 hour.

3. In a mixing bowl combine the cream
cheese, sour cream, scallion, minced dill,
and garlic. Mash the mixture with a fork
until it is smooth and well blended, then
set aside.

4. Bring salted water to a boil in a large,
flameproof casserole. Add the spinach and
cook for 5 minutes, then drain and set
aside to cool.

5. As soon as the spinach is cool enough
to handle, squeeze all the moisture out
of it with your hands until the spinach is the
size of a small ball. Mince the spinach

fine and add to the mixing bowl. Blend the
mixture thoroughly with a fork, season
with salt and pepper, and chill for 30
minutes to 1 hour.

6. Fill the tomatoes with the spinach and
cream cheese mixture, then top each
one with a sprig of dill and a tomato cap.
Arrange on a serving platter and serve
chilled, accompanied by buttered pumpernickel.

Remarks

I often turn this light appetizer into a
simple supper meal by garnishing the
platter with quartered hard-boiled eggs,
thinly sliced radishes and cucumbers, and
some sardines. Serve a side dish of
Lemon Vinaigrette (see page 209) and an
assortment of good cheeses.

Notes

hors d'oeuvres and salads

Zucchini and pepper salad bagutta

Serves: 4 to 6
Preparation time: 35 minutes
Cooking time: 40 to 50 minutes

Milan's Ristorante Bagutta is a friendly Tuscan restaurant where I spent one of my most enjoyable working sessions in recent years. The antipasto table is arranged daily with a centerpiece of raw vegetables and fresh fish. The salads are simple but of the utmost freshness. This zucchini and pepper salad is one of them.

Ingredients

6   medium-sized zucchini
2   large green bell peppers
2   large red bell peppers
⅔ cup fruity olive oil
Salt and freshly ground black pepper
Juice of 1 lemon
1   tablespoon red wine vinegar

Garnish:
2   tablespoons minced fresh parsley
1   large clove garlic, finely minced
1 to 2 tablespoons finely minced fresh basil

Preparation

1. Scrub zucchini and cut off ends but do not peel. Cube the zucchini, then put in a colander over a bowl, sprinkle with salt, and let drain for 30 minutes to 1 hour.

2. Preheat the broiler.

3. Place the green and red peppers on a baking sheet and broil them on all sides until skin is almost charred. Remove to a double layer of wet paper towels and wrap them, and as soon as they are cool enough to handle, peel off the skin under cold running water. Remove the cores and seeds and cut the peppers into thin slices. Set aside.

4. Dry the zucchini cubes thoroughly on paper towels.

5. Heat ¼ cup of the olive oil in a heavy, 10- to 12-inch skillet. Add the zucchini and cook over medium heat until nicely browned on all sides, shaking the pan from time to time to cook evenly. When the zucchini are done, season with salt and pepper, then add the sliced peppers and cook for 2 more minutes. Pour the mixture into a sieve and let drain for 10 minutes.

6. Put the vegetable mixture in a serving bowl. Add the remaining olive oil, the lemon juice, and vinegar and sprinkle with the parsley, garlic, and basil. Toss the salad lightly and chill for an hour or two.

7. Thirty minutes before serving, bring the salad back to room temperature, correct the seasoning, and serve as an appetizer accompanied by finely sliced prosciutto, or as part of an hors d'oeuvre table.

Notes

Zucchini and tomato salad

Serves: 6
Preparation time: 10 minutes
Cooking time: 15 to 20 minutes

As simple as it may be, a zucchini and tomato salad makes a delicious and refreshing summer appetizer, either by itself or together with a platter of prosciutto or Italian salami.

Ingredients

6   small zucchini
Juice of 1 lemon
Salt and freshly ground black pepper
1   small red onion, thinly sliced
Finely minced fresh parsley to taste
½ cup finely diced pimiento
4 to 6 Italian plum tomatoes, quartered

The Dressing:
½ cup olive oil
3   tablespoons red wine vinegar
1   large clove garlic, mashed
2   tablespoons finely minced fresh basil
    or 1 teaspoon dried

Preparation

1. Wash the zucchini thoroughly under cold running water and slice off both tips. Bring 4 quarts of salted water to a boil, add the zucchini and cook over medium heat for 10 or 15 minutes, or until they are easily pierced with the tip of a sharp knife, being careful not to overcook. As soon as the zucchini are done, run them under cold water to stop them from further cooking. Drain and place on a double layer of paper towels to cool.

2. As soon as the zucchini are cool enough to handle, cut them in half lengthwise and sprinkle with lemon juice, salt, and pepper. Set aside.

3. In a small jar combine the olive oil, vinegar, garlic and basil. Shake the jar to blend and chill for 30 minutes.

4. An hour or two before serving, sprinkle the zucchini with the onion rings, parsley, and pimiento. Arrange the quartered tomatoes around them and pour the dressing over both vegetables. Season with salt and freshly ground black pepper. Serve chilled but not cold.

Remarks

This salad can also be garnished with flaked tuna fish, cold leftover poached salmon, rolled anchovy fillets, or cooked shrimp. It goes wonderfully well with roast or grilled meats, too. If you serve it along with a meat course, cut the zucchini into ½-inch cubes and mix together with the quartered tomatoes in a serving bowl.

Notes

Cold beef salad vinaigrette

Serves: 6 to 8
Preparation time: 10 minutes

Ingredients

½ cup olive oil
3   tablespoons red wine vinegar
2   teaspoons Dijon mustard
1   large clove garlic, mashed
Salt and freshly ground black pepper
4 to 5 cups cold, cubed braised or roast beef
1   green pepper, cored, seeded, and finely cubed
½ cup finely minced scallion
½ cup finely minced pimiento
½ cup pitted green olives, cut in half
2   small dill gherkins, finely minced
2   tablespoons well-drained capers
½ cup cooked peas
2   tablespoons finely minced fresh parsley

Garnish:
Quartered tomatoes and green pepper rings

Remarks

This salad will keep for several days. If refrigerated, bring it back to room temperature. Other diced vegetables can be added, such as cooked green beans and potatoes and raw mushrooms.

Notes

Preparation

1. In a small mixing bowl combine the oil, vinegar, mustard, garlic, salt, and pepper to taste. Whisk the dressing until it is smooth and well blended, then set aside.

2. In a large bowl combine the beef, green pepper, scallion, pimiento, olives, gherkins, capers, peas, parsley, salt and pepper. Add the dressing, toss lightly, and let the salad stand in a cool place for 2 to 4 hours.

3. At serving time, taste and correct the seasoning. Pour the salad into a deep rectangular serving dish, garnish with green pepper rings and quartered tomatoes, and serve accompanied by French bread.

Ham cornets à la russe

Serves: 6 to 8
Preparation time: 30 to 40 minutes
Cooking time: 6 minutes

Ingredients

1   cup finely diced celery
1   cup diced carrot
1   cup diced green beans
1   cup finely diced potatoes
1   cup fresh, cooked peas
¾ to 1 cup Mayonnaise (see page 208)
Salt and freshly ground white pepper
12 to 16 stalks asparagus, cooked
6 to 8 slices of Westphalian or smoked
    ham

Garnish:
Sprigs of fresh parsley
Pimiento strips

Preparation

1. In a large casserole bring salted water
to a boil. Add the celery, carrot, beans,
and potatoes and cook the vegetables for
5 or 6 minutes, or until they are barely
tender. (The vegetables must all be evenly
cubed or they will not be done at the same
time.) Drain the vegetables and run them
under cold water to stop further cooking,
then drain again until they are completely
cool. Set aside.

2. In a mixing bowl combine the vegetable
mixture, peas, and enough mayonnaise
to bind it well. Season the mixture with
salt and pepper and spoon it into a
rectangular serving dish. Chill.

3. At serving time, roll 2 to 3 asparagus
stalks in each slice of ham. Place the ham
and asparagus rolls close together, in one
layer, on top of the vegetable salad.
Garnish each roll with a strip of pimiento
and a sprig of parsley and serve chilled,
accompanied by thinly sliced, buttered
pumpernickel.

Ham and tongue salad

Serves: 4 to 6
Preparation time: 30 minutes

Ingredients

2   cups baked or cooked ham, cut into
    ½-inch strips
2   cups cooked tongue, cut into 1½-inch
    julienne strips
½   cup minced dill gherkins
4   tablespoons finely minced green
    pepper
1   tablespoon finely minced fresh parsley
3   tablespoons finely minced scallion
2   tablespoons finely minced pimiento-
    stuffed olives
1   cup Mayonnaise (see page 208)
Salt and freshly ground black pepper
1   teaspoon hot prepared mustard
    (preferably Colman's)

Garnish:
Cherry tomatoes
Finely sliced green pepper rings
Dill gherkins, sliced lengthwise

Preparation

1. In a glass serving bowl combine the
ham, tongue, gherkins, green pepper,
parsley, scallions, and olives. Set aside.

2. Season the mayonnaise (made with 1
whole egg) with salt and pepper, then add
the mustard. Taste and correct the seasoning; the mayonnaise should be highly
seasoned. Add the mayonnaise to the
bowl, toss the salad lightly, season with
salt and pepper, and chill.

3. Thirty minutes before serving, bring the
salad back to room temperature. Surround
with cherry tomatoes and green pepper
rings. Make a decorative pattern with the
sliced gherkins and serve the salad
accompanied by thinly sliced black
bread and sweet butter.

hors d'oeuvres and salads

Viennese sausage salad

Serves: 4 to 6
Preparation time: 10 minutes
Cooking time: 5 minutes

Here is a salad that is popular all over Austria and Hungary, where it is served mostly in simple *Bierstuben* as a staple of the appetizer table. Well prepared it is an economical yet delicious appetizer.

Ingredients

4   German knockwurst or 4 to 6 frank-
    furters
1½ tablespoons cider vinegar
½   teaspoon granulated sugar
5   tablespoons olive oil
1   small red onion, thinly sliced
1   tablespoon well-drained capers
2   tablespoons finely chopped pimiento
1   small green pepper, diced
1   small dill pickle, thinly sliced
4   Italian plum tomatoes, quartered
Salt and freshly ground black pepper
1 to 2 tablespoons minced parsley

Preparation

1. Drop the knockwurst into fast-boiling water and cook for 5 minutes. Drain. As soon as the sausages are cool enough to handle remove the skins, slice thin and set aside.

2. In a serving bowl combine the vinegar, sugar, and oil and whisk until the sugar is dissolved, then add the sausages, onion, capers, pimiento, green pepper, pickle, and tomatoes. Season the salad with salt and pepper and toss lightly. Marinate for 2 to 4 hours.

3. Just before serving, correct the seasoning and sprinkle with the parsley. Serve chilled but not cold.

Shrimp salad mikado

Serves: 6 to 8
Preparation time: 25 minutes
Cooking time: 15 minutes

Ingredients

2   small zucchini
1   tablespoon butter
1   tablespoon vegetable oil
2   tablespoons finely minced shallots or
    scallion
2   large, ripe tomatoes, peeled, seeded,
    and chopped
Salt and freshly ground black pepper
1½ to 2 cups Mayonnaise (see page 208)
2   teaspoons to 1 tablespoon curry
    powder
1   large clove garlic, mashed
½   pound shrimp, cooked and peeled
2   hard-boiled eggs, chopped
½   cup finely diced green pepper
½   cup finely diced red pepper

Garnish:
Thinly sliced sweet red pepper rings
Black Greek olives
2   tablespoons well-drained capers

Preparation

1. Bring salted water to boil in a large saucepan. Add the zucchini and poach them over medium heat for 5 to 8 minutes; they should still be crisp. Remove and run under cold water to stop further cooking, then drain on paper towels. As soon as they are cool enough to handle, cube them and set aside.

2. Heat the butter and oil in a heavy, 10-inch skillet. Add the shallots and tomatoes and cook until the mixture is thick and all the tomato juices have evaporated. Season with salt and pepper and set aside to cool.

Shrimp salad à la toulonnaise

Serves: 6
Preparation time: 30 minutes
Cooking time: 20 to 30 minutes

Several years ago I found an amusing old cookbook in a shop in Toulon. The recipes were given without measurements, some of the ingredients were added as an "afterthought," and there was no index. I adapted a shrimp salad from this gem.

Ingredients

3   tablespoons vinegar
⅔   cup olive oil
Juice of 1 large lemon
1   teaspoon Dijon mustard
1   teaspoon hot prepared mustard
     (preferably Colman's)
1   large clove garlic, mashed
Salt and freshly ground black pepper
Pinch of cayenne pepper
4 to 6 small new potatoes
½   pound mushrooms, thinly sliced and
     stems removed
1   bay leaf
1   large sprig fresh parsley
1   pound small shrimp
½   cup thinly sliced pimiento
1   cup small black olives (preferably
     Niçoise)
2   large green peppers, roasted, peeled,
     and sliced (see page 31)
Finely minced fresh parsley

Preparation

1. In a small screwtop jar combine 2 tablespoons of the vinegar, ½ cup of the olive oil, 1 tablespoon of the lemon juice, the mustards, garlic, salt, and pepper. Add the cayenne, then cover the jar and shake until the dressing is smooth and well blended. Set aside.

3. In a mixing bowl combine the mayonnaise, curry powder, tomato mixture, and garlic. Blend thoroughly, then correct the seasoning, adding a little more curry powder if you wish, and set aside.

4. In a serving bowl combine the shrimp, eggs, zucchini, and diced peppers. Add the curry mayonnaise and blend the salad carefully. Correct the seasoning and chill for 2 to 4 hours before serving.

5. Just before serving, garnish with red pepper rings, olives, and capers.

Notes

hors d'oeuvres and salads

Turkey salad niçoise

Serves: 4 to 6
Preparation time: 15 minutes

2. Bring salted water to boil in a saucepan. Add the potatoes and cook until barely tender, then drain, cool, and peel. Slice the potatoes thin and place them in the bottom of a large serving dish. Season with salt and pepper, sprinkle with the mushrooms, and pour the dressing over. Toss lightly and set aside.

3. In a saucepan combine salted water with the remaining lemon juice, bay leaf, and parsley sprig. Bring to a boil, then add the shrimp and cook until they just turn pink. Remove the saucepan from the heat and let the shrimp cool in the poaching liquid. Peel the shrimp, then dice.

4. Add the shrimp to the salad bowl, together with the pimiento, olives, and green pepper. Toss the salad again, being careful not to break the potatoes; taste and correct the seasoning. Chill for 2 hours.

5. At serving time, bring the salad back to room temperature. Taste again and add the remaining vinegar and oil; both mushrooms and potatoes absorb a great quantity of oil and vinegar. Sprinkle with parsley and serve with French bread and a bowl of sweet butter.

Remarks

For an excellent variation, add 1 small, finely cubed fennel bulb to the salad and garnish with finely minced greens instead of parsley.

Leftover roast turkey is one of those morsels I always look forward to but usually find dry and disappointing. This salad from the south of France is usually made with leftover roast chicken. Turkey, after being marinated in oil and vinegar overnight, is an excellent substitute.

Ingredients

3   cups cold roast turkey, cut into fine julienne
2   tablespoons well-drained capers
1   dill gherkin, finely minced
7   tablespoons olive oil
3½ tablespoons tarragon vinegar
1   clove garlic, mashed
1   tablespoon finely minced fresh tarragon
1   teaspoon Dijon mustard
Salt and freshly ground black pepper
1   romaine lettuce heart, cut into fine julienne
1   small red onion, thinly sliced
½   cup small black olives (preferably Niçoise)
6 to 8 rolled anchovy fillets

Preparation

1. In a bowl combine the turkey, capers, and gherkins. Add 2 tablespoons of the olive oil and 2 tablespoons of the vinegar. Toss the mixture lightly and chill overnight.

2. In a small screwtop jar combine the remaining oil and vinegar, the garlic, tarragon, and mustard. Season with salt and pepper, cover, and shake until the dressing is thick and well blended. Pour it into a glass serving bowl and top with

the lettuce. Add the turkey and garnish with onion rings, olives, and anchovies. Sprinkle with a heavy grinding of black pepper.

3. Toss the salad at the table and serve accompanied by thinly sliced, buttered pumpernickel.

Remarks

Roast capon or chicken can also be used for making this salad.

Notes

Cheese salad italienne

Serves: 4 to 6
Preparation time: 5 minutes

Ingredients

3 cups mozzarella or Swiss cheese cut into 2-inch matchsticks
1 small white onion, thinly sliced
½ cup thinly sliced green olives
1 green Italian pepper, seeded and finely sliced
2 tablespoons tiny, well-drained capers
1 cup finely cubed celery
2 to 3 anchovies, finely mashed
1 clove garlic, mashed
1½ tablespoons white wine vinegar
½ cup olive oil
Salt and freshly ground black pepper
1 tablespoon minced fresh parsley

Garnish:
8 slices Italian salami

Preparation

1. In a mixing bowl combine the cheese, onion, olives, green pepper, capers, and celery. Set aside.

2. In a small jar combine the anchovies, garlic, vinegar, and olive oil. Close the jar tightly and shake to blend the dressing, then pour it over the cheese mixture and toss lightly. Season the salad with salt and a generous grinding of black pepper and chill for 2 to 3 hours.

3. Thirty minutes before serving, bring to room temperature, correct the seasoning, and place in a rectangular serving dish. Sprinkle with the parsley and arrange the salami slices in an overlapping line down the center of the salad. Serve as a luncheon salad or as part of an hors d'oeuvre table.

vegetables

For anyone growing up in a Mediterranean country, it would be hard to imagine life without an open market. This is where the basic inspiration for the day's meal comes from. Stalls filled with shiny green and red peppers, eggplants, and artichokes all make their own fresh statement according to the season. When I grew up I did not need the calendar to tell me what time of the year it was—Nature's calendar was always visible at the market. With spring came mountains of fresh peas and baskets of pale green asparagus; with summer an abundance of tomatoes, cucumbers, and peppers appeared; and then with fall came the musty, delicious aroma of wild mushrooms.

The marvelous sensation of picking out your own fresh fruit and vegetables can never be duplicated by choosing from ubiquitous cellophane packages, nor will that box of frozen vegetables ever replace the real thing. I am always astonished when asked what the difference is between frozen and fresh vegetables. The best answer to this question would be to cook a package of frozen green beans simultaneously with some fresh ones, giving each of them the same attention and care and serving them on individual plates side by side. The results will be obvious. The frozen bean will be limp and soggy, the fresh bean crisp and tasty. It's hard to convince people in this country that fresh vegetables are not only better than frozen ones but are just about as easy and fast to prepare. With the right understanding of each vegetable, we can often buy and cook marvelous, fresh produce for less money than the frozen varieties.

For those who do try to cook them, fresh vegetables here have often met with a sad fate. One school of thought has believed in cooking them to death; the other, that two minutes of cooking in very little water is plenty, thereby preserving their nutritional value, but ignoring taste completely. Both are wrong. Undercooked vegetables are as bad as overcooked ones, and all vegetables demand individual attention and care. This lack of attention must be because vegetables are all too often considered as an accompaniment to the main course and seldom benefit from the cook's time and effort.

When we look at the peasant cuisines of Europe and the Middle East, we find that vegetables are handled with great creativity, often replacing meat as the main part of the meal. This is partly due to economics, but also because frozen vegetables were relatively unknown in Europe until a few years ago. The peasant cook gives as much attention to vegetable cooking as to any other part of the meal. Almost every European country has created a vegetable classic over the years, with dishes such as the French *ratatouille* and the Italian *caponata* becoming increasingly popular in this country. Others, such as the Armenian Baked Eggplant or the Gratin Catalan in this book (see pages 63 and 71) deserve equal recognition, since they successfully blend several vegetables into one delicious dish. These days, because of the interest in growing one's own garden, we are rediscovering the delicious taste of fresh produce and its fantastic potential. Although we do not have much of a tradition in the way of vegetable dishes that stand on their own, we should learn to serve them as a separate course, either as an appetizer or as a main dish for a simple supper or lunch.

Cold stuffed artichokes aurora

Serves: 6
Preparation time: 35 minutes
Cooking time: 25 minutes

A good artichoke actually needs little adornment. It must not be overcooked and should not be refrigerated. A simple vinaigrette or lemon-flavored butter is the usual accompaniment to this extremely versatile vegetable. I find this light shrimp sauce makes a welcome change from the ordinary.

Ingredients

6   large globe artichokes
Salt
1   lemon, cut in half
1   pound shrimp
1   cup Mayonnaise (see page 208)
Juice of 1 lemon
1   large clove garlic, mashed
2   tablespoons chili sauce
Freshly ground white pepper

Garnish:
2   tablespoons finely minced chives

Preparation

1. Cut the artichoke stems off at the base. Break off some of the outer leaves, then slice ½ inch off the top of each artichoke. With sharp scissors trim off the sharp points of the outer leaves. Immediately rub the artichokes with the cut side of a lemon.

2. Bring 6 to 8 cups of salted water to boil in a large, flameproof casserole. Add the remaining lemon half and arrange the artichokes upright in the casserole, then cover and cook over medium heat for 15 minutes.

3. With kitchen tongs remove the artichokes. Cool slightly, then spread the leaves gently, pull out the cone, and carefully scrape out the fuzzy "choke" with a grapefruit spoon. Return the artichokes to the casserole and cook for another 10 minutes, or until tender; test by piercing the base with the tip of a sharp knife. Remove the artichokes and let them drain, upside down, on a double layer of paper towels. Set aside.

4. Bring salted water to boil in a 2-quart saucepan. Add the shrimp and cook for 3 minutes, or just until they turn bright pink. Remove the shrimp, cool, peel, and devein. Reserve 6 shrimp for garnish and mince the rest. Set aside.

5. To the mayonnaise in the container of a blender, add the shrimp, lemon juice, garlic, and chili sauce. Blend until the mixture is smooth, then season with salt and pepper and chill.

6. Just before serving, fill the artichokes with some of the shrimp sauce. Garnish with the chives and the reserved shrimp, place on a serving platter, and serve at room temperature.

Notes

Artichokes stuffed alla milanese

Serves: 6 to 8
Preparation time: 45 minutes
Cooking time: 1 hour and 15 minutes

Ingredients

6 to 8 large artichokes
1 lemon, cut in half
Salt
2 tablespoons all-purpose flour
5 tablespoons butter
1 onion, finely minced
½ cup soft, fresh bread crumbs
½ cup milk
¾ pound ground veal or a combination
     of veal and beef
1 egg
2 tablespoons finely minced fresh parsley
2 cloves garlic, mashed
2 tablespoons water
½ teaspoon dried marjoram
Pinch each of ground allspice and
     dried thyme
Freshly ground white pepper
¼ cup finely grated fresh Parmesan
     cheese
¼ cup finely grated Gruyère
2 cups Fresh Tomato Sauce (see
     page 207)

Preparation

1. Preheat the oven to 325 degrees.

2. With a sharp knife cut off the top third
of the artichokes. Remove the tough outer
leaves until they start turning inward into
a cone shape and become pale green in
color. Cut the remaining leaves off at the
base with a sharp knife, and rub the
artichoke bottoms with the cut side of
a lemon. Set aside.

3. In a large, flameproof casserole combine
4 quarts of water with a large pinch
of salt and the flour. Bring the water to a
boil, then add the artichoke bottoms and
cook for 12 to 15 minutes, or until barely
tender. Drain the artichokes and scrape
the "chokes" out carefully with a grapefruit spoon. Place the artichokes on paper
towels to drain.

4. Heat 2 tablespoons of the butter in a
small skillet. Add the onion and cook
until it is soft but not browned, then
remove and set aside.

5. Soak the bread crumbs in the milk for
2 or 3 minutes, then drain and set aside.

6. In a mixing bowl combine the ground
meat, bread crumbs, onion, egg, parsley,
garlic, water, and herbs and spices. Work
the mixture with your hands until it is
well blended, then season with salt and
pepper and set aside.

7. Melt the remaining butter in a flameproof
baking dish. Fill each artichoke bottom
with some of the meat mixture, forming a
dome. Place the artichoke bottoms in the
dish, top them with a mixture of the
Parmesan and Gruyère, and place the
dish in the oven. Bake the artichokes,
covered, for 45 minutes, basting them
often with the butter in the pan, then
uncover the dish and bake for 15 more
minutes. Serve the artichokes hot or at
room temperature, with a side dish of hot
Tomato Sauce.

Cold artichoke hearts mimosa

Serves: 6
Preparation time: 40 minutes
Cooking time: 30 minutes

Ingredients

6   large artichokes
1   lemon, cut in half
Salt
⅓   cup all-purpose flour
1   teaspoon Dijon mustard
½   teaspoon dry mustard
2   tablespoons lemon juice
1   tablespoon wine vinegar
1   large clove garlic, mashed
½   cup olive oil
Freshly ground pepper
18 small shrimp, cooked and peeled
2   small white onions, thinly sliced
2   anchovies, finely minced
2   tablespoons finely diced pimiento
½   cup finely diced black Greek olives
2   hard-boiled eggs
2   tablespoons finely minced fresh parsley

Garnish:
Boston lettuce leaves
6   whole cooked shrimp (optional)

Preparation

1. Cut off the top third part of the artichokes with a sharp knife. Remove the tough outer leaves until the leaves start turning inward into a cone shape and are pale green in color. Cut off the remaining leaves just above the heart with a sharp knife and rub the surface with the cut side of a lemon.

2. Bring 6 to 8 cups of salted water to a boil in a large, flameproof casserole. Add the flour and artichoke bottoms and cook for 25 to 30 minutes, or until tender; test them by piercing them with

the tip of a sharp knife. Drain the artichokes on paper towels, and as soon as they are cool enough to handle, carefully remove the "chokes" with a grapefruit spoon. Set aside.

3. In a bowl combine the mustards, lemon juice, vinegar, garlic, and olive oil. Whisk the mixture until it is well blended, then season with salt and pepper. Dip each artichoke bottom into the dressing and remove to a side dish. Add 18 shrimp, the onion rings, anchovies, pimiento, and olives to the dressing and chill the mixture for 2 to 4 hours.

4. Mince the hard-boiled eggs fine and combine with the parsley. Set aside.

5. Top each artichoke bottom with the shrimp salad and sprinkle with the egg and parsley mixture. Garnish the platter with lettuce leaves and 6 additional shrimp, if desired, and serve chilled but not cold.

Notes

Gratin of asparagus

Serves: 4 to 6
Preparation time: 15 minutes
Cooking time: 35 minutes

If and when you have a bowl of béchamel sauce at hand, there is nothing simpler than combining it with a poached seasonal vegetable to make a delicious appetizer.

Ingredients

2 pounds fresh asparagus
Salt
¼ cup finely grated Swiss cheese
2 tablespoons finely grated fresh Parmesan cheese
1 tablespoon butter
2 to 2½ cups Sauce Béchamel à l'Ancienne (see page 205)
Freshly ground white pepper

Preparation

1. Peel the asparagus with a vegetable peeler and wash them thoroughly under cold running water. Remove 2 inches off the butt of each and tie the asparagus into even bundles, leaving 1 stalk loose for testing.

2. Bring plenty of salted water to a boil in a large, flameproof oval casserole. Add the asparagus bundles. Bring the water back to a boil, then reduce the heat and cook the asparagus, uncovered, for 8 to 10 minutes, or until barely tender. As soon as the asparagus is done, run it under cold water to stop further cooking. Place the bundles on a double layer of paper towels, untie them, and spread the spears to cool.

3. In a small mixing bowl combine the Swiss cheese with the Parmesan, then set aside.

4. Preheat the oven to 350 degrees.

5. Butter a large, rectangular baking dish. Spread a layer of the sauce in the dish and sprinkle with a little of the cheese mixture. Arrange the asparagus in an overlapping pattern and top with the remaining sauce, leaving the tips exposed. Sprinkle with the remaining cheese and a grinding of white pepper. Bake the asparagus for 20 to 25 minutes, or until the sauce is hot and bubbling and the cheese is melted. Serve immediately.

Remarks

The béchamel sauce can be made several days in advance and frozen. It is a good sauce to have on hand, as it goes well with other vegetables, such as broccoli, spinach, and cauliflower.

Notes

Asparagus à la provençale

Serves: 4
Preparation time: 30 minutes
Cooking time: 15 minutes

Asparagus is one of spring's best and most beautiful vegetables. Ideally, it should be allowed to stand on its own as an appetizer, since it seems to lose some of its special quality when eaten with other foods. But this does not mean that asparagus must always be served with either hollandaise or mayonnaise. This is an immensely versatile vegetable, and can be prepared in many interesting ways. Here is an example: asparagus served in the manner of the Midi, with ripe tomatoes and a Provencal bread crumb mixture.

Ingredients

2   pounds fresh asparagus
2   medium-sized, ripe tomatoes
Salt
⅓ cup fresh, white bread crumbs
2   tablespoons finely minced fresh parsley
1   tablespoon finely minced shallots
1   large clove garlic, finely minced
Freshly ground black pepper
6   tablespoons melted, lightly browned
    butter

Preparation

1. Remove the tough ends of the asparagus, leaving the stalks about 4 inches long. Scrape the stalks with a vegetable peeler and tie them into even bundles, leaving one stalk loose for testing. Set aside.

2. Cut each tomato crosswise into 3 to 4 thick slices. Place the sliced tomatoes on a large plate, then sprinkle with salt and let drain for 30 minutes.

3. Bring salted water to boil in a large, flameproof casserole. Add the asparagus bundles and cook them, uncovered, over high heat for 8 to 10 minutes, or until they are almost tender, then drain and run under cold water to stop them from further cooking. Untie the bundles and spread the stalks on a double layer of paper towels.

4. In a small mixing bowl combine the bread crumbs, parsley, shallots, and garlic, then add a pinch of salt and a grinding of black pepper. Set aside.

5. Butter a large, rectangular baking dish. Arrange the asparagus at each end of the dish and place two rows of overlapping tomato slices down the center. Sprinkle the bread crumb mixture over the vegetables and dribble the melted butter over them.

6. Preheat the broiler.

7. Just before serving, run the dish under the broiler and bake for 5 to 6 minutes, or until the tomatoes are just heated through and the bread crumbs are lightly browned. Serve immediately.

Notes

Cold asparagus tyrolienne

Serves: 4 to 6
Preparation time: 15 minutes
Cooking time: 12 minutes

Asparagus, one of the most delicious of vegetables, is spring's gift to the world of food. Since the season is relatively short, I try to take advantage of it as much as possible. Here is a light appetizer that takes only minutes to prepare. It can also be served as an accompaniment to cold roast chicken or poached salmon.

Ingredients

2   pounds fresh asparagus
Salt

Sauce tyrolienne:

1   hard-boiled egg, finely minced, plus
2   hard-boiled egg yolks
½ teaspoon dry mustard
Large pinch of granulated sugar
Salt and freshly ground white pepper
⅔ cup olive oil
¼ cup vinegar
2   tablespoons finely minced chives
1   tablespoon finely minced fresh chervil
    or ½ teaspoon dried

Garnish:
1   cup finely diced, cooked beets

1. Peel the asparagus with a vegetable peeler, and slice off the tough ends of each stalk, leaving them about 5 to 6 inches long. Tie the asparagus into equal bundles; leave one stalk loose for testing.

2. Bring salted water to a boil in a large, flameproof casserole. Add the asparagus bundles and cook them, uncovered, over high heat for 10 to 12 minutes, starting to test for doneness after 8 minutes. Cook until just tender; do not overcook.

3. As soon as the asparagus are done, remove them to a double layer of paper towels, untie them, and spread the stalks out to allow them to cool completely. Place them on a rectangular serving platter and set aside; do not refrigerate.

4. In a mixing bowl mash the 2 egg yolks. Add the mustard, sugar, salt, and pepper, then add a little, about a third, of the oil and whisk the mixture until it is smooth and well blended. Add the vinegar and remaining oil and again whisk until the dressing is very creamy. Add the chives, minced egg, and chervil.

5. Spoon the dressing over the asparagus, sprinkle with the diced beets, and serve immediately.

Remarks

You may vary the dressing by omitting the chives and chervil and replacing it with finely minced fresh dill. A few cooked and shelled shrimp can be added to the platter for a more elaborate presentation.

Avocado halves à l'italienne
Serves: 6
Preparation time: 10 minutes

Notes

The avocado, in its perfect stage of ripeness, is a subtle fruit that lends itself beautifully to the creative touch. It is interesting to see how different countries serve it in various combinations—in addition to the conventional crabmeat filling. The Italians like their avocados teamed with this gutsy sauce made with anchovy fillets and scallions. The result is a delightful, light appetizer.

Ingredients
⅓ cup minced fresh parsley
2 tablespoons minced scallion, green part and all
1 tablespoon minced fresh basil or ½ teaspoon dried
2 anchovy fillets
2 cloves garlic, mashed
2 tablespoons wine vinegar
⅔ cup fruity olive oil
Freshly ground black pepper
3 ripe avocados
Juice of ½ lemon
Salt

Garnish:
2 hard-boiled eggs, finely minced

1. In the container of a blender combine the parsley, scallion, basil, anchovy fillets, garlic, vinegar, and oil. Blend until the mixture is completely smooth, then taste for seasoning, adding a large grinding of black pepper. Set aside.

2. Just before serving, slice the avocados in half lengthwise. Remove the pits and immediately sprinkle with a little lemon

Avocados in sauce verte

Serves: 6
Preparation time: 15 minutes
Cooking time: 5 minutes

juice and a little salt. Fill the cavity of each avocado half with a tablespoon of sauce and sprinkle with finely minced egg. Serve chilled but not cold.

Remarks

For an hors d'oeuvre table presentation, peel the avocados, slice them in half lengthwise and then into very fine slices. Place the slices in an attractive pattern on a round serving platter, sprinkle with the sauce and then with the minced egg. The center of the platter may be filled with cooked and peeled shrimp dressed in a little vinaigrette.

Notes

Ingredients

1½ cups Mayonnaise (see page 208)
1   cup coarsely chopped watercress
     leaves
1   tablespoon minced scallion
¼   cup minced fresh parsley
1   tablespoon minced fresh chervil or
     tarragon or ½ teaspoon dried
Salt and freshly ground white pepper
12 to 14 shrimp, cooked and peeled
3   ripe avocados
Juice of ½ lemon

Garnish:
Sprigs of watercress

Preparation

1. Combine the mayonnaise, chopped watercress, scallion, and parsley in the container of a blender. Blend the mixture at high speed, then add the chervil or tarragon, season with salt and pepper, and pour into a bowl.

2. Finely cube 6 of the shrimp; add to the mayonnaise and chill for 2 to 4 hours. Slice the remaining shrimp in half lengthwise and set aside.

3. Cut the avocados in half lengthwise and remove the pits. Carefully scoop out most of the avocado flesh and cut into fine cubes. Sprinkle both flesh and shells with lemon juice and add the flesh to the mayonnaise and shrimp mixture. Season the shells with salt and pepper, refill with the shrimp and avocado mixture, and garnish with the remaining shrimp.

vegetables

Broccoli parisienne
Serves: 3 to 4
Preparation time: 10 minutes
Cooking time: 35 minutes

4. Place the avocados on a round serving platter, decorate with sprigs of watercress, and serve well chilled, accompanied by thinly sliced, buttered pumpernickel.

Notes

In spite of France's proximity to Italy, it is amazing how long it takes some vegetables to cross borders. Broccoli is one of them. It is a marvelous vegetable that is slowly gaining popularity in France today, to combine successfully with a classic French preparation such as this.

Ingredients
3 cups water
2 tablespoons white wine vinegar
1 bay leaf
1 sprig fresh parsley
1 3-inch stalk celery
1 small carrot, peeled and thinly sliced
1 small onion, thinly sliced
Salt
4 peppercorns
2 pounds fresh broccoli
Beurre Manié (see page 213)
6 tablespoons cold butter
Freshly ground white pepper

Preparation

1. In a heavy, enameled saucepan combine the water, vinegar, bay leaf, parsley, celery, carrot, onion, salt, and peppercorns. Bring to a boil, then reduce the heat and simmer the mixture for 20 minutes, or until the vegetables are tender.

2. Meanwhile, prepare the broccoli. Remove the tough outer leaves and cut 2 inches off the base, then quarter the branches lengthwise. Peel the broccoli stalks with a vegetable peeler all the way to the flower buds and set aside.

3. When the vegetable mixture is done, place a steamer in the saucepan. Arrange the broccoli in it and steam, covered, over medium heat for 8 to 10 minutes, or until tender. Test by piercing the stalks with the tip of a sharp knife.

4. When the broccoli is done, remove it to a double layer of paper towels and set aside. Discard the bay leaf, celery, and parsley sprig. Raise the heat, and with the saucepan uncovered, reduce the liquid to 1 cup. Add the *beurre manié* and whisk the sauce, over the heat, until it thickens. Reduce the heat to a bare simmer and add the cold butter, a tablespoon at a time, whisking constantly until it is just melted and incorporated in the sauce. Taste and correct the seasoning, adding a grinding of white pepper. Set aside.

5. Arrange the broccoli in a serving dish, spoon the sauce over it, and serve immediately.

Remarks

The poaching liquid can be prepared a day or two ahead of time. The finished sauce can be kept warm in a pan of warm water, with the broccoli served at room temperature.

Notes

Cauliflower in emerald sauce

Serves: 4 to 6
Preparation time: 10 minutes
Cooking time: 25 minutes

Ingredients

½ cup olive oil
2 tablespoons red wine vinegar
¼ cup minced fresh parsley
2 tablespoons minced scallion, green part only
2 cloves garlic, mashed
2 tablespoons minced zucchini, skin only
Salt and freshly ground black pepper
2 tablespoons minced green pepper
2 to 4 flat anchovy fillets, minced
1 tablespoon tiny, well-drained capers
1 dill gherkin, minced
1 large head cauliflower

Garnish:
Sprigs of watercress
Black olives
Cherry tomatoes

Preparation

1. In the container of a blender combine the oil, vinegar, parsley, scallions, garlic, zucchini, salt, and pepper. Blend at top speed for 30 seconds, or until the mixture is completely smooth, then pour into a small mixing bowl. Add the green pepper, anchovies, capers, and gherkin, and whisk until the anchovies are completely blended into the dressing. Taste for seasoning and set aside.

2. Bring salted water to a boil in a large, flameproof casserole. Add the cauliflower, whole, and cook, covered, over medium heat until tender; test by piercing the base with the tip of a sharp knife. Do not overcook. Carefully transfer the cauliflower to a round serving platter. Let cool for a

Cauliflower à l'italienne

Serves: 4 to 6
Preparation time: 15 minutes
Cooking time: 40 minutes

few minutes, then wipe away any water
that may have accumulated on the platter.

3. Pour the dressing over the cauliflower,
garnish with sprigs of watercress, black
olives, and cherry tomatoes and serve at
room temperature as part of a buffet or
hors d'oeuvre table.

Notes

Ingredients

Salt
1   tablespoon all-purpose flour
1   large cauliflower, trimmed and broken
    into florets
8   tablespoons (1 stick) butter
Freshly ground white pepper
½   cup coarsely grated fresh Parmesan
    or Romano cheese
1   tablespoon olive oil
8 to 10 Italian plum tomatoes, peeled
1   large clove garlic, crushed
2   tablespoons minced fresh oregano or
    1 teaspoon dried

Garnish:
Sprigs of fresh parsley

Preparation

1. Preheat the oven to 350 degrees.

2. In a large, flameproof casserole combine
3 quarts of water, a large pinch of salt,
and the flour. Bring to a boil, then add the
cauliflower. Reduce the heat and cook,
partially covered, for 6 to 8 minutes, or until
barely tender. Drain and run the cauliflower
under cold running water to stop further
cooking. Dry on a double layer of paper
towels and set aside.

3. In a small saucepan heat 6 tablespoons
of the butter until lightly browned. Pour
a little of the butter into a large baking dish,
then arrange the cauliflower in it and
sprinkle with salt and pepper and the
Parmesan. Dribble with the remaining
butter.

4. Place the dish in the upper part of the
oven and bake for 25 minutes.

5. While the cauliflower is baking, heat the remaining butter and oil in a large, heavy skillet. Add the tomatoes, crushed garlic, and oregano and cook over low heat until the tomatoes are just heated through; they must still retain their shape. Season with salt and pepper, then remove the pan from the heat. Set aside.

6. Preheat the broiler.

7. Run the cauliflower under the broiler for 2 to 3 minutes, or until the top is nicely browned. Remove the dish from the oven, arrange the tomatoes in the baking dish, garnish with parsley sprigs and serve immediately.

Notes

Cucumber boats au roquefort

Serves: 6 to 12
Preparation time: 25 minutes

Here is a "double purpose" appetizer I find especially useful for weekend entertaining. The proportions of the cheese mixture are purposely high, since this appetizer can be served either as a dip or as a filling for cucumber boats or tomatoes. If you are serving the Roquefort mixture as a dip, add 2 more ounces of Roquefort and thin the dip with additional sour cream or lightly whipped heavy cream. Surround the dip with finely sliced endives, zucchini sticks, or other raw vegetables.

Ingredients

1 ounce (2 tablespoons) Roquefort cheese
4 ounces cream cheese
1 cup sour cream
¼ cup lemon juice
2 tablespoons well-drained capers
¾ cup finely minced fresh parsley
2 tablespoons finely minced scallion
2 cloves garlic, mashed
½ cup finely minced pimiento
½ cup finely minced green pepper
3 to 6 small cucumbers
Salt

Preparation

1. In a bowl combine the Roquefort, cream cheese, sour cream, and lemon juice. Mash the mixture with a fork until it is well blended and quite smooth, then add the capers, ½ cup parsley, the scallion, garlic, pimiento and green pepper. Blend well. Taste carefully for seasoning, as Roquefort is often salty and may not need additional seasoning, and chill the mixture until serving time.

2. Peel the cucumbers, cut them in half lengthwise, and scoop out the seeds carefully with a grapefruit spoon. Sprinkle the cucumber boats with salt and let them drain, upside down, on paper towels for 30 minutes to 1 hour.

3. Wipe the "boats" dry with additional paper towels and fill with the Roquefort mixture. Place on a serving platter and sprinkle with the remaining finely minced parsley. Serve chilled, with finely sliced, buttered pumpernickel.

Remarks

Thinly sliced, cooked beets flavored with lemon juice and olive oil are a perfect garnish for the platter.

Notes

Baked eggplant genovese
Serves: 4
Preparation time: 10 minutes
Cooking time: 45 minutes

One of the simplest ways to prepare eggplant, this method is equally good for zucchini and tomatoes. A proof of the ingenuity in Italian peasant cooking . . .

Ingredients

2 medium-sized eggplants
Salt
¼ cup fresh, unflavored bread crumbs
2 tablespoons minced fresh parsley
2 to 3 cloves of garlic, finely minced
6 tablespoons finely minced fresh basil
1 tablespoon finely minced fresh oregano
    or ½ teaspoon dried
Freshly ground black pepper
2 tablespoons water
½ cup olive oil, approximately
2 medium-sized, ripe tomatoes

Preparation

1. Cut the eggplants in half lengthwise. Cut deep, long slits in each half, sprinkle with salt, and let them drain, upside down, for an hour, on a double layer of paper towels.

2. While the eggplants are draining, combine the bread crumbs, parsley, garlic, ¼ cup of the basil, and the oregano in a mixing bowl. Add salt and pepper and set aside.

3. Wipe the eggplants thoroughly with paper towels. Spread a little of the bread-crumb mixture on each eggplant half, pressing it well into the slits. Set aside.

4. Combine the water with ¼ cup of the oil in a large, rectangular baking dish.

Baked eggplants parma

Serves: 4 to 6
Preparation time: 35 minutes
Cooking time: 55 minutes

Arrange the eggplants, cut side up, in the dish.

5. Preheat the oven to 375 degrees.

6. Cut the tomatoes crosswise into ¼-inch slices. Place them in an overlapping pattern lengthwise over the eggplants, dribble with a little more oil, and bake for 45 minutes, basting two or three times with the oil in the pan.

7. When the eggplants are done, remove them carefully to a serving platter. Cool to room temperature, and just before serving, sprinkle with the remaining minced basil and a little more oil.

Notes

I often wonder why one of the best eggplant dishes has met such a sad fate! To many people baked eggplant is synonymous with eggplant Parmigiana, a wonderful dish. Sadly though, the version of this dish served in most Italian restaurants in this country is a dreary concoction that hardly resembles the great dish it should be. Here is a version of the dish as it is served in and around Parma.

Ingredients

3 medium eggplants
Salt
½ to ¾ cup olive oil
3 to 4 slices baked or smoked ham
2 large sweet red peppers, roasted, peeled, seeded, and sliced (see page 31)
2 tablespoons finely minced fresh oregano or 1 teaspoon dried
½ cup freshly grated Parmesan cheese
Freshly ground black pepper
1½ cups Fresh Tomato Sauce (see page 207)

Preparation

1. Slice the eggplant, unpeeled, lengthwise into thick slices (discard the end pieces). Sprinkle the slices with salt, place on a double layer of paper towels, and drain for 2 to 4 hours. Dry the eggplant slices thoroughly in a kitchen towel and set aside.

2. Heat ¼ cup of the oil in a large, heavy skillet. Add a few eggplant slices and cook until nicely brown on both sides, then remove to a double layer of paper towels.

vegetables

Armenian baked eggplant

Serves: 4
Cooking time: 30 to 40 minutes
Preparation time: 10 minutes

Add more oil to the pan and continue
sautéing until all the slices are done.
Set aside.

3. Preheat the oven to 350 degrees.

4. Make a layer of eggplant slices in a
rectangular baking dish. Top with a layer
of ham, then sprinkle with the peppers,
oregano, and half the Parmesan and
season with salt and freshly ground black
pepper. Spoon half the tomato sauce over
the mixture, then top with another layer
of eggplant and the remaining tomato
sauce. Sprinkle with the remaining
Parmesan.

5. Bake for 45 minutes, uncovered, and
serve hot or at room temperature.

Remarks

This dish is equally good hot or cold. When
preparing it as a cold appetizer it is best
to omit the Parmesan, since the cheese
gets hard when it cools and gives an
unpleasant texture to the dish.

Notes

Ingredients

2   eggplants
2   tablespoons olive oil
Juice of ½ lemon
Salt and freshly ground black pepper
1   cup sour cream
1   large clove garlic, mashed
3   tablespoons minced scallion

Garnish:
Black olives
Cherry tomatoes

Preparation

1. Preheat the broiler.

2. Place the eggplants on a baking sheet
6 to 8 inches from the heat. Bake for 25 to
30 minutes, or until the skins are almost
charred and the eggplants are tender; test
with the tip of a sharp knife. Remove
from the oven and cool.

3. Peel the eggplants, cut into large
chunks, and arrange in a shallow serving
dish. Sprinkle with the olive oil, lemon
juice, salt, and pepper and set aside.

4. In a bowl combine the sour cream,
garlic, and scallion, then fold the mixture
into the eggplant. Taste and correct the
seasoning. Chill.

5. Thirty minutes before serving, bring the
salad back to room temperature. Garnish
with black olives and cherry tomatoes
and serve as part of an hors d'oeuvre table.

Sardinian baked eggplant

Serves: 4 to 6
Preparation time: 30 minutes
Cooking time: 1 hour

Ingredients

2   medium-sized eggplants or 4 to 6
    tiny ones
Salt
½ cup olive oil
½ to ¾ cup fresh, white bread crumbs
2   tablespoons minced fresh parsley
3   large cloves garlic, mashed
4 to 6 flat anchovy fillets, finely minced
2   tablespoons finely minced fresh
    marjoram or oregano or 1 teaspoon
    dried
Freshly ground black pepper

Garnish:
Finely sliced pimiento
2   tablespoons well-drained capers

Preparation

1. Preheat the oven to 350 degrees.

2. Cut the eggplants in half lengthwise.
Make 2 to 3 slits in each half, sprinkle
with salt, and place, cut side down, on a
double layer of paper towels. Let the
eggplants drain for an hour.

3. Heat 6 tablespoons of the oil in a large
skillet. Add the eggplants, thoroughly
dried, and cook, cut side down, over low
heat until they are browned and very soft
when tested with the tip of a sharp knife.
Remove the eggplant to a chopping board.
As soon as they are cool enough to handle,
scoop out the flesh without breaking the
skin. Place the shells in a well-oiled baking
dish and set aside.

4. Mince the eggplant pulp fine. Combine
it in a mixing bowl with ½ cup of the
bread crumbs, the parsley, garlic, anchovies, and marjoram and blend thoroughly with a fork. (Add the remaining ¼
cup bread crumbs if the mixture seems too
soft.) Season with salt and pepper.

5. Fill the shells with the eggplant mixture
and dribble with olive oil. Place the baking
dish in the center of the oven and bake
for 20 minutes. Remove the dish, cool the
eggplants completely, and transfer to a
serving platter. Garnish with pimiento,
sprinkle with capers, and serve at room
temperature.

Notes

vegetables

Braised endives à la polonaise

Serves: 6
Preparation time: 10 minutes
Cooking time: 30 minutes

Ingredients

12 medium-sized endives
10 tablespoons sweet butter
Juice of ½ lemon
Pinch of granulated sugar
Salt and freshly ground white pepper
1 cup water
4 tablespoons fresh, white bread crumbs
2 hard-boiled eggs, finely minced
2 tablespoons minced fresh parsley

Preparation

1. Trim the endives, removing any wilted outer leaves.

2. Melt 4 tablespoons of the butter in a heavy skillet. Add the lemon juice, a pinch of sugar, and the endives. Season with salt and pepper and roll them in the butter. Add the water, then cover the skillet and simmer the endives for 20 to 30 minutes, shaking the pan several times to ensure even cooking. Test the endives; they are done if they can easily be pierced with the tip of a sharp knife. Remove the endives to a serving platter and keep warm.

3. Heat the remaining butter in a small, heavy skillet until it is lightly browned, then add the bread crumbs and sauté for 2 minutes until they are nicely browned. Pour the bread crumb and butter mixture over the endives and sprinkle with minced egg and parsley. Add a heavy grinding of pepper and serve immediately.

Cold endives in herb vinaigrette

Serves: 6
Preparation time: 10 minutes
Cooking time: 25 to 30 minutes

Unfortunately, many vegetables seem almost doomed to be served in only one or two ways. Few cooks dare to be creative when it comes to their preparation. This seems to be especially the case with endives. They are almost always served raw in a mixed salad or maybe, once in a while, braised. Here is a new approach: the endive is poached and served cold, dressed in a well-flavored herb vinaigrette.

Ingredients

6 Belgian endives
Salt
1½ tablespoons tarragon vinegar
½ cup olive oil
⅓ cup finely minced fresh parsley
1 tablespoon minced scallion, green part only
¼ teaspoon dry mustard
½ teaspoon Dijon mustard
Freshly ground black pepper
Juice of ½ lemon

Garnish:
2 tablespoons minced chives
2 to 3 medium-sized beets, cooked and finely cubed (optional)

Preparation

1. Select endives of equal size. Trim the bases carefully, remove any wilted outer leaves, and wash under cold running water. Do not soak.

2. Place the endives in a large casserole. Cover with water, add a large pinch of salt, and bring to a boil, then reduce the

Fried leeks à l'arlesienne

Serves: 6
Preparation time: 10 minutes
Cooking time: 15 minutes

heat and simmer, partially covered, for
20 to 30 minutes, or until the endives are
tender when tested with the tip of a sharp
knife. Drain the endives on a double layer
of paper towels and set aside.

3. In the container of a blender combine
the vinegar, olive oil, parsley, scallion, and
mustards. Blend the mixture at high speed
for 30 seconds, then add salt and a heavy
grinding of black pepper. Set aside.

4. Cut the endives in half lengthwise and
arrange them, cut side down, on a rectangular serving platter. Sprinkle with
lemon juice and pour the dressing over,
then garnish with minced chives and chill
for 6 hours or overnight.

5. An hour before serving, bring the endives
back to room temperature. Arrange the
cubed beets, if desired, along the platter
and serve accompanied by thinly sliced,
buttered pumpernickel or as part of an
hors d'oeuvre table.

Notes

Here is one of the best ways of serving
leeks I know. They make a delicious
appetizer either by themselves or with a
side platter of finely sliced prosciutto or
they can be served as an accompaniment
to roast veal or chicken.

Ingredients

12 leeks of even size (about 1 inch in
    diameter)
Salt
2 eggs, beaten
All-purpose flour for dredging
Freshly ground black pepper
½ cup olive oil
1 bay leaf
Juice of 1 lemon
¼ cup finely minced fresh parsley
1 large clove garlic, finely minced
1 tablespoon finely minced fresh thyme
    or ¼ teaspoon dried

Preparation

1. Trim the leeks and remove any wilted
outer leaves. Remove the greens, leaving
the leeks 6 inches long. Cut a cross in the
green part and rinse them thoroughly
under cold running water.

2. Bring salted water to a boil in a large
saucepan. Add the leeks and cook for
7 to 8 minutes, or until barely tender. Drain
and dry on a double layer of paper towels,
then dip in beaten egg and then roll them
in flour. Season with salt and pepper
and set aside.

Cold leeks in mustard sauce

Serves: 4
Preparation time: 10 to 15 minutes
Cooking time: 10 to 12 minutes

3. Heat the oil in a large, heavy skillet. Add the bay leaf and leeks and cook over low heat until the leeks are nicely browned on both sides. Add the lemon juice, 2 tablespoons of the parsley, the garlic, and thyme and cook for 1 more minute. Remove the pan from the heat.

4. Arrange the leeks on a rectangular serving platter and spoon the cooking oil over them. Cool to room temperature and serve sprinkled with the remaining parsley and a grinding of black pepper.

Notes

Ingredients

6 to 8 medium-sized leeks
Salt

Mustard sauce:
1   hard-boiled egg
1   raw egg yolk
1½ teaspoons Dijon mustard
½   cup olive oil
1½ tablespoons white wine vinegar
2   teaspoons well-drained capers
Freshly ground white pepper

Garnish:
1   tablespoon finely minced pimiento
2   tablespoons minced fresh parsley

Preparation

1. Trim the roots off the leeks and cut off all but an inch of the green part (use the tops for stocks and soups), leaving the leeks about 5 to 6 inches long. Cut the green part of the stalks lengthwise, then wash thoroughly under cold running water to remove sand.

2. Place the leeks in a large saucepan, cover with 3 inches of salted water, and bring to a boil. Reduce heat and simmer the leeks until the white part is tender when pierced with the tip of a sharp knife. (If the leeks are not of uniform size they must be tested several times, as some may be done before the others.)

3. As soon as the leeks are done, remove them to a double layer of paper towels to drain.

4. Separate the hard-boiled egg, reserving the yolk and mincing the white fine.

Cold leeks niçoise

Serves: 4 to 6
Preparation time: 10 minutes
Cooking time: 15 minutes

5. In a small stainless steel bowl combine the hard-boiled egg yolk, the raw yolk, and the mustard, mashing the mixture with a fork until it is perfectly smooth.

6. Slowly add the olive oil, beating the mixture with a small electric mixer or wire whisk until it is thick and smooth. Add the wine vinegar, capers, salt, and pepper and correct the seasoning.

7. Place the leeks in a rectangular hors d'oeuvre dish and spoon the sauce over them; sprinkle with the minced white of egg, the pimiento, and parsley and serve chilled but not cold.

Notes

In recent years in this country, leeks have been gaining a well-deserved popularity. In France, where leeks are both economical and plentiful, they are called the poor man's asparagus. In the United States, unfortunately, leeks are usually expensive, but are well worth it, since they are one of the tastiest and most versatile of vegetables.

Ingredients

8 to 10 leeks of even size (about 1½ inches in diameter)
2 ripe tomatoes
Salt
½ cup olive oil
1 bay leaf
2 cloves garlic, peeled
2 tablespoons finely minced fresh basil or 1 teaspoon dried
2 tablespoons finely minced fresh oregano or 1 teaspoon dried
Juice of 1 lemon
8 black Greek olives, pitted and cut in half
Freshly ground black pepper

Garnish:
2 tablespoons finely minced fresh parsley
½ cup crumbled feta cheese (optional)

Preparation

1. Clean the leeks by trimming the root ends and removing the wilted leaves and the greens, leaving the leeks about 6 to 7 inches long. Cut a deep cross into the green part of the leeks and rinse them thoroughly under cold running water. Set aside.

Sweet and sour onions à la provençale

Serves: 6 to 8
Preparation time: 20 minutes
Cooking time: 2 hours

Though mostly served in Provence as part of an hors d'oeuvre table or as an accompaniment to pâtés and sausages, this delicious garnish is also found in northern Italian and Spanish cooking, where the onions are served as an accompaniment to a roast duck or pork.

Ingredients

Salt
2 to 2½ pounds tiny white onions
⅓ cup olive oil
2 tablespoons wine vinegar
¾ cup water
1½ tablespoons granulated sugar
2 teaspoons tomato paste
1 cup dark raisins
1 large clove garlic, thinly sliced
1 bay leaf
Freshly ground black pepper

Preparation

1. Preheat the oven to 275 degrees.

2. Bring salted water to boil in a 4-quart casserole. Add the onions and cook for 2 to 3 minutes, then drain and peel. Trim them, but do not remove the root end or they will fall apart during cooking.
Set aside.

3. Heat the oil in a shallow, enameled baking dish or casserole where the onions can remain in one layer. Add the onions and roll them in the oil for 1 or 2 minutes. Add the vinegar, ½ cup of the water, the sugar, tomato paste, raisins, garlic, bay leaf, salt, and pepper, and bring to a boil

2. Quarter the tomatoes, sprinkle with salt, and let them drain in a colander for 30 minutes.

3. Combine the oil, bay leaf, garlic, and leeks in a large, heavy skillet. Cover the skillet and simmer over low heat for 10 to 15 minutes, or until the leeks are tender but not browned. Add the tomatoes, herbs, lemon juice, and olives, then season with salt and pepper and simmer for another 3 to 4 minutes, or until the tomatoes are heated through. Remove the pan from the heat, pour the mixture into a serving bowl, and cool.

4. Before serving, taste and correct the seasoning, sprinkle with parsley and the optional feta cheese, and serve, slightly chilled, as part of an hors d'oeuvre table.

Notes

Cold baked onions

Serves: 6
Preparation time: 10 minutes
Cooking time: 45 minutes to 1 hour

on top of the stove. Place the dish in the center of the oven.

4. Cook the onions for 1½ to 2 hours, depending on their size, basting them several times with the pan juices. Test the onions for doneness by piercing them with the tip of a sharp knife; they must be very soft but not falling apart.

5. Remove the dish from the oven, place over direct heat, and add the remaining water. Cook for 2 more minutes; the pan juices must be thick and syrupy.

6. Transfer the onions into an earthenware or glass serving bowl and serve at room temperature.

Remarks

The onions will keep for several weeks. Refrigerate them in a covered jar and bring them back to room temperature before serving. Tiny pearl onions are often hard to find on the East Coast. In the spring I usually find them in nurseries catering to the home gardener, where they are sold by the pound.

Notes

Ingredients

6 medium to large yellow onions
¾ cup olive oil
Salt and freshly ground black pepper
2 tablespoons red wine vinegar
2 tablespoons finely minced fresh parsley

Preparation

1. Preheat the oven to 375 degrees.

2. Peel the onions. Cut a ¼-inch slice off the bottom of each one, then cut off the pointed end and stand the onions in a well-oiled baking dish. Season with salt and pepper, dribble the remaining oil over, and bake in the upper part of the oven for 45 minutes, or until tender and lightly browned, basting several times with the oil in the pan.

3. Run the onions under the broiler until they are nicely browned (do not let them burn), then remove the dish from the oven.

4. Transfer the onions to a serving platter, dribble with the oil in the pan and the vinegar. Sprinkle with parsley and serve at room temperature or slightly chilled, as part of a buffet or hors d'oeuvre table.

Notes

Cold gratin à la catalane

Serves: 4 to 6
Preparation time: 25 minutes
Cooking time: 25 minutes

Ingredients

3 to 4 green peppers
3 to 4 sweet red peppers
½ cup olive oil (preferably a fruity oil,
    such as Plagniol)
4 onions, thinly sliced
Salt and freshly ground pepper
2 to 3 tomatoes
2 tablespoons finely minced fresh thyme
    or 1 teaspoon dried
¼ cup fresh, white bread crumbs
2 tablespoons finely minced fresh parsley
2 large cloves garlic, finely minced

Garnish:
Rolled anchovy fillets

Preparation

1. Preheat the broiler.

2. Arrange the peppers on a baking sheet, place 6 to 8 inches from the source of heat and grill until their skin is blistered, turning them once or twice. Remove the peppers, and as soon as they are cool enough to handle peel them under cold running water. Cut into thick strips and set aside.

3. Heat 3 tablespoons of the oil in a large, heavy skillet. Add the onions and cook for 5 minutes over low heat, or until they are soft but not browned. Set aside.

4. Put a layer of peppers in a rectangular baking dish. Top with a layer of the onions and season with salt and pepper. Add another layer of peppers. Cut the tomatoes into ¼-inch slices, then arrange them, slightly overlapping, in the dish. Sprinkle with salt, pepper, and thyme and set aside.

5. Add 3 more tablespoons of oil to the skillet. When the oil is hot, add the bread crumbs, parsley, and garlic and cook the mixture for 1 or 2 minutes, then spoon it over the tomatoes. Dribble with the remaining oil and run the dish under the broiler for 3 to 4 minutes, or until the tomatoes are just heated through and the bread crumb mixture is nicely browned. Do not let it burn. Remove the dish from the oven and cool.

6. Garnish with rolled anchovy fillets and serve at room temperature, right out of the baking dish.

Remarks

The dish can be made a day ahead of time. It does not need to be refrigerated.
For an excellent variation cut a medium-sized eggplant into ¼-inch slices, sauté in olive oil, and add to the baking dish. Alternate the eggplant slices with the peppers and onions.

Notes

Spinach à l'andorrana

Serves: 6
Preparation time: 20 minutes
Cooking time: 10 minutes

Although Spanish food usually goes hand in hand with garlic, it is amusing to find in northern Spanish cooking dishes made with raisins and nuts without so much as a hint of garlic!

Ingredients

3 pounds fresh spinach
Salt
¾ cup dark raisins
4 tablespoons butter
½ cup pine nuts
1 tablespoon olive oil
1 cup finely cubed prosciutto or smoked ham
Freshly ground black pepper

Garnish:
Slices of French bread fried in olive oil

Preparation

1. Remove the tough stems from the spinach leaves, then wash thoroughly under cold running water.

2. Bring 6 quarts of salted water to a boil in a large casserole. Add the spinach and cook it over low heat for 3 to 5 minutes, then drain in a colander and run under cold water to stop further cooking. When the spinach is cool enough to handle, squeeze out the remaining moisture, a little at a time.

3. In a small saucepan combine the raisins with 2 cups of warm water. Bring to a boil, then reduce the heat and simmer the raisins for 3 to 5 minutes. Drain and set aside.

4. Heat 2 tablespoons of the butter in a large heavy skillet. Add the pine nuts and cook over low heat until lightly browned, then remove them to a side dish with a slotted spoon. Put the remaining butter and oil in the pan, then add the prosciutto or smoked ham and heat through. Stir in the spinach, raisins, salt, and pepper and continue stirring the spinach over low heat until it is well heated and all the moisture has evaporated.

5. Add the pine nuts, correct the seasoning, and serve immediately, accompanied by a side dish of fried bread.

Notes

Middle eastern stuffed tomatoes

Serves: 6 to 8
Preparation time: 35 minutes
Cooking time: 25 to 30 minutes

Eggplants and tomatoes have always been happily "married" in the world of food. Since the eggplant originated in Asia and the tomato in America, it would be interesting to know who first thought of combining these two marvelous vegetables.

Ingredients

6 to 8 medium-sized, ripe tomatoes
Salt
2   large eggplants
2   small cloves garlic, mashed
2   tablespoons finely minced chives
2   tablespoons finely minced Italian
    parsley
2 to 3 tablespoons Mayonnaise
    (see page 208)
Freshly ground black pepper

Garnish:
6 to 8 black Greek olives
Strips of pimiento

Preparation

1. Cut the tops off the tomatoes. With a sharp knife carefully remove the tomato pulp and seeds (reserve the pulp for stews and sauces), then sprinkle the tomato shells with salt and place them, upside down, on paper towels to drain for 30 minutes to 1 hour.

2. Place the eggplants on a hot charcoal grill; they can be placed directly on the coals, or under the broiler. Cook the eggplants until the skin is completely charred on all sides. Watch them carefully and turn them once or twice, being careful not to pierce the skin.

3. Remove the eggplants to a cutting board. Cut them in half lengthwise and scoop out the eggplant pulp with a spoon, being careful not to include any of the charred skin. Place the pulp in a small strainer and sprinkle lightly with salt. Drain the pulp for 30 minutes, then chop it fine and place in a mixing bowl.

4. Add the garlic, chives, and parsley to the eggplant pulp and fold in the mayonnaise. Season the mixture with salt and pepper and chill for 30 minutes.

5. Fill the well-drained tomatoes with the eggplant mixture. Roll a strip of pimiento around each olive and top each tomato with an olive. Place the tomatoes on a round serving platter and serve chilled but not cold.

Remarks

These tomatoes are an excellent accompaniment for grilled steaks or shish kebab.

Notes

Stuffed tomatoes florentine

Serves: 6
Preparation time: 45 minutes
Cooking time: 35 minutes

Ingredients

2   pounds fresh spinach
6   medium-sized ripe tomatoes
Salt
4   tablespoons butter
3   tablespoons finely minced scallion
1   large clove of garlic mashed
Freshly ground white pepper
Hollandaise (see page 206)

Preparation

1. Preheat the oven to 325 degrees.

2. Wash the spinach thoroughly under cold running water, then remove the stems and any wilted leaves. Place the spinach in a colander or wire salad basket and let it drain over a bowl.

3. Cut a ¼-inch slice off the top of each tomato and carefully scoop out the pulp and seeds with a sharp knife (reserve the pulp for sauces and stews). Salt the tomatoes and let them drain, upside down, on a platter for 30 minutes.

4. Bring 6 quarts of salted water to a boil in a large casserole. Add the spinach and cook it, uncovered, for about 5 minutes, then drain the spinach in a colander. Run cold water over it to refresh it and let it cool. As soon as the spinach is cool enough to handle, chop it fine and set aside.

5. Heat the butter in a large skillet. Add the scallion and garlic and cook until tender, without browning. Add the chopped spinach and cook the mixture until all the moisture has evaporated, then season with salt and pepper, cover, and simmer for 5 minutes. Set aside.

6. Place the tomatoes in a buttered baking dish. Fill them with the spinach mixture, then cover them with foil. Place the dish in the middle of the oven and bake for 10 minutes, or until the tomatoes are just heated through. Remove the dish from the oven, top each tomato with a little hollandaise, and serve immediately.

Notes

Stuffed tomatoes printanier

Serves: 6
Preparation time: 20 minutes (plus 30 minutes to 1 hour draining time)
Cooking time: 20 minutes

For an informal dinner or family entertaining, an appetizer can be of the utmost simplicity. Here is one of my spring favorites. It can also be served with roast chicken or sautéed veal scallops.

Ingredients

6   medium-sized, ripe tomatoes
Salt
6   tablespoons butter
2   tablespoons water
1   teaspoon granulated sugar
1½ pounds fresh peas, shelled
¾ cup finely diced baked or cooked ham
All-purpose flour
Freshly ground white pepper
1   tablespoon finely minced fresh parsley
2   teaspoons finely minced fresh mint
     (optional)

Preparation

1. Cut the tops off the tomatoes. Carefully scoop out the pulp and seeds with a sharp knife (reserve the pulp for sauces or stews), being careful not to break the skin. Sprinkle the tomato shells with salt and let them drain, upside down, on a double layer of paper towels for 30 minutes to 1 hour.

2. Preheat oven to 350 degrees.

3. Melt the butter in a small, heavy saucepan. Add the water, sugar, and peas and cook, covered, over low heat for about 8 to 12 minutes, then remove the peas to a side dish, with a slotted spoon. Reduce the liquid in the saucepan to 2 tablespoons,

then add the ham and heat it through. Return the peas to the saucepan, dust lightly with flour, and season with salt and pepper. Toss the peas over low heat until the flour is completely incorporated and the mixture becomes slightly creamy. Add the parsley and optional mint.

4. Fill the tomatoes with the pea and ham mixture and place them in an oiled baking dish. Bake the tomatoes for 7 to 8 minutes, or until well heated through. (Do not overcook the tomatoes or they will fall apart.) Serve immediately.

Notes

Stuffed zucchini florentine

Serves: 4
Preparation time: 35 minutes
Cooking time: 35 minutes

Ingredients

4 to 6 medium zucchini
Salt
1   package fresh spinach, well washed
     and drained
5½ tablespoons butter
2   tablespoons finely minced scallion
1   clove garlic, mashed
Freshly ground white pepper
2   tablespoons all-purpose flour
½   cup milk, heated to boiling
3   tablespoons finely grated fresh
     Parmesan cheese

Preparation

1. Wash the zucchini under cold running water. Cut off the stems and discard.

2. Bring salted water to boil in a large, flameproof casserole. Add the zucchini and cook over medium heat for 8 minutes, then remove with a slotted spoon and cool.

3. Add the spinach to the boiling water and cook over high heat for 5 minutes. Drain thoroughly, pressing out the moisture with your hands. Chop the spinach fine and set aside.

4. Cut a ¼-inch strip lengthwise off each zucchini; mince the strips fine and set aside. Carefully scoop out the flesh without breaking the shell. Discard the flesh (or reserve for another use).

5. Melt 2 tablespoons of the butter in a heavy skillet. Add the scallion and minced zucchini skin and cook over low heat for 3 to 4 minutes, or until the scallion is

soft but not browned. Add the spinach and garlic, season with salt and pepper, and cook the mixture for another 5 minutes, partially covered. Set aside.

6. Melt 1½ tablespoons of the butter in a small, heavy saucepan. Add the flour and cook for 1 or 2 minutes, stirring constantly without browning. Remove the pan from the heat, add the milk all at once, and whisk the mixture until completely smooth. Return to the heat and cook until very thick, then season with salt and pepper and set aside.

7. Add the spinach mixture to the sauce and blend well. Taste and correct the seasoning, then spoon the mixture into the zucchini "boats."

8. Melt the remaining butter in a rectangular flameproof baking dish. Arrange the zucchini in the dish, sprinkle with Parmesan, and set aside.

9. Preheat the oven to 350 degrees.

10. Bake the zucchini for 15 minutes in the upper part of the oven, then put under the broiler for another 3 to 4 minutes, or until the top is nicely browned. Serve hot.

Remarks

The zucchini can be prepared well in advance and baked at the last moment. The spinach filling can be served by itself as a base for poached or fried eggs, or as an accompaniment to grilled sausages or hamburgers.

Zucchini alla piemontese

Serves: 6
Preparation time: 25 minutes
Cooking time: 30 minutes

Ingredients

6   medium-sized zucchini
Salt
6   tablespoons olive oil
3   tablespoons minced scallion
3   cloves garlic, mashed
1   tablespoon minced fresh parsley
1   tablespoon minced fresh basil or ½
    teaspoon dried
6   flat anchovy fillets, finely minced
6   tablespoons fresh, white bread crumbs
Freshly ground black pepper

Preparation

1. Preheat the oven to 350 degrees.

2. Wash the zucchini thoroughly under
cold running water. Remove the stems.

3. Bring salted water to boil in a large
saucepan. Add the zucchini and cook over
medium heat for 10 minutes, then drain
and cool.

4. Cut a ¼-inch lengthwise slice off each
zucchini; mince the strips fine and set
aside. Carefully scoop out the flesh without
breaking the skin. Discard the flesh (or
reserve for another purpose).

5. Heat 3 tablespoons of the olive oil in
a large, heavy skillet. Add the scallion and
minced zucchini skin, cover, and cook
the mixture over low heat for 5 minutes, or
until tender. Add the garlic, parsley, basil,
anchovies, ¼ cup of the bread crumbs,
salt, and pepper. Blend thoroughly and
cook for another 2 minutes, then taste
and correct the seasoning.

6. Fill the zucchini "boats" with the mixture
and set aside.

7. Heat 2 tablespoons of the oil in a flameproof rectangular baking dish and arrange
the zucchini in the dish. Sprinkle with the
remaining bread crumbs, dribble with
the remaining oil, and bake for 10 minutes,
then place the dish, 6 to 8 inches from the
source of heat, under the broiler and cook
for 2 to 3 minutes longer, or until the top
is nicely browned.

8. Remove the zucchini to a serving platter
and serve at room temperature.

Notes

Zucchini alla romana

Serves: 4 to 6
Preparation time: 25 minutes
Cooking time: 40 minutes

Ingredients

4 to 6 small zucchini
Salt
2   tablespoons butter
2   large shallots, finely minced
1   tablespoon minced fresh parsley
½   pound sausage meat
Freshly ground black pepper
2   large cloves garlic, mashed
1   teaspoon dried marjoram
½   teaspoon dried oregano
Large pinch of ground allspice
½   cup milk
⅓   cup fresh, white bread crumbs
¼   cup freshly grated Parmesan
3   tablespoons water
3   tablespoons olive oil

Garnish:
Sprigs of fresh parsley
Italian plum tomatoes, quartered

Preparation

1. Wash the zucchini thoroughly and cut off the stems. With a sharp knife cut a ¼-inch lengthwise slice off each zucchini and set aside. Carefully scoop out the flesh without breaking the shell, then mince both the flesh and the reserved slices fine and set aside. Sprinkle the "boats" with salt and place, upside down, on a double layer of paper towels to drain.

2. Heat the butter in a small, heavy skillet. Add the shallots and minced zucchini and cook over low heat for 3 to 4 minutes, or until soft but not browned. Add the parsley and cook for another 2 minutes, then remove the pan from the heat and set aside.

3. In a mixing bowl combine the sausage meat, salt, pepper, garlic, marjoram, oregano, and allspice. Add the zucchini and shallot mixture and blend thoroughly.

4. Combine the milk and bread crumbs in a small bowl, then squeeze the moisture out of the bread crumbs and add to the meat mixture, together with 2 tablespoons of the Parmesan. Work the filling with your hands until it is well blended, then add 1 tablespoon of the water to loosen it. Taste and correct the seasoning.

5. Combine the oil with 2 tablespoons of water in a rectangular baking dish. Fill the zucchini boats with the meat mixture, arrange them in the dish, and sprinkle with the remaining Parmesan.

6. Preheat the oven to 350 degrees.

7. Place the dish in the center of the oven and bake for 30 minutes, basting the zucchini several times with the pan juices, then run the zucchini under the broiler until the tops are browned. Remove from the oven and cool.

8. Arrange the zucchini on a serving platter and garnish with sprigs of parsley and quartered plum tomatoes. Serve at room temperature as an appetizer or part of an hors d'oeuvre table.

I often remember my childhood in Spain, a large, black stock pot tucked away on the corner of the stove, brimming with bones and vegetables. It simmered away day after day, filling the air with a tempting aroma. The result was a hearty, wonderful stock used as the base of all our soups. Since those days, eating good homemade soup has always been an important part of my life as a cook. Unfortunately, I came to realize that such homemade soup is an unexpected, even rare pleasure in this country. Soups here just do not play the major role they still do in European countries. Whatever tradition might have developed in America literally died on the shelf with the soup can. But soups make a hearty and delicious family meal, and are also a simple, satisfying, and economical way to entertain.

Most European countries boast national soups that over the years have become world renowned. The Spanish invented *gazpacho,* a refreshing cold, garlic-flavored tomato soup garnished with finely minced cucumber, green pepper, and onion. It is rivaled by the cool Scandinavian cucumber and dill soup and the Greek *avgolemono,* a light, lemon-flavored soup that is an absolute triumph when made with homemade stock. Austria has given us its goulash soup, a gutsy, highly spiced meat soup actually borrowed from the Hungarian cuisine. As for Russia, borscht is by far the best winter soup I know!

France probably has more soups in its repertory than any other country, but is particularly famous for its *bouillabaisse,*

a wonderful Mediterranean seafood soup that, sadly enough, is slowly disappearing due to the scarcity and high cost of the rock-type fish essential to its success.

In Europe, in general, cooks have developed marvelous soups using plentiful local produce. They work with what is available from their gardens or fresh vegetable markets rather than with what is sitting on the supermarket shelf or lying in the frozen food department. The best example of such a soup is Italian *minestrone,* which can be made with combinations of various fresh vegetables, and as fresh as the garden itself, is hearty and filling as well.

Although some soups can be made successfully with water, like *minestrone* or other vegetable soups where a strong herb such as basil is added, even a light stock is usually preferable. Stock gives a great deal of body and flavor to any soup. Today, when most produce does not have the rich taste of yesteryear, it is best always to use a stock as the base for soups. A stock can be made quickly by doctoring an ordinary commercial bouillon with a few meat bones and vegetables.

The three basic homemade soup stocks—white, chicken, and fish—can be prepared quite easily (see pages 201, 203, and 204). They are definitely the soul and secret to great soups. While chicken and white stocks involve long, slow simmering of scraps of meat, bones, and vegetables, fish stock is the simplest to make. It requires only 40 minutes of simmering, and usually the fish trimmings can be obtained free at an obliging fish market. Astonishingly, however, fish soups have never achieved great popularity in this country. People's adventurous spirit seems to end with the Manhattan and New England clam chowders, two classics that, when well prepared, certainly deserve their popularity. But America has a graet variety of fish that lend themselves readily to good soups and provide the versatility that we all need in our menus. A good fish market will give you cod necks for practically nothing, if not free. Several delicious fish soups can be made from these, such as the Galician cod soup in this book (Fish Soup à la Gallega, page 92).

Although it is not necessary to have a large number of soups in your repertory, I think it's a good idea to have at least two for each season, choosing the least expensive and most available vegetables each season offers. Aside from the pleasure of looking forward to a soup you have not served for several months and the joy of rediscovering the taste of a fresh herb or of fresh, young peas, this seasonal approach is also the only way to get the maximum flavor out of each vegetable. If you are going to go to the trouble of making a homemade soup, it ought to be the best of its kind.

We are fortunate enough in America to get carrots, potatoes, leeks, turnips, and onions all year round. With this abundance, we can learn from the peasant cuisines of Europe, where soups are made from inexpensive ingredients. The classic French Garbure and the Catalan Cabbage Soup are both soups featuring combinations of potatoes, carrots, cabbage, and dry legumes.

No matter what kind of soups you choose to make, you should remember that the soup pot is not a catchall for everything. Soups call for vegetables with an affinity for one another. The different vegetables cannot be tossed into the pot all at the same time, but must be added with careful consideration of the cooking time each requires. This way, the best flavor of each will be preserved. Also, while cooking, a soup must be carefully seasoned and tasted.

Since soups are freezable, you can enjoy them throughout the year. A perfectly flavored tomato soup is lovely in winter when tomatoes are out of season. Nor should you arbitrarily label a soup "hot" or "cold." A hearty vegetable soup is delicious when slightly chilled and served on a cool summer evening, while a zucchini and tomato soup that is ordinarily served cold makes a good hot soup for a chilly fall day. All the soups in this book are of a simple, peasant character. They are generous soups suitable for one-dish meals, to be eaten along with good bread and a bowl of sweet butter, and followed by a salad. Soup making is truly an art, and a great soup can be as memorable as any other dish you can serve.

Soupe julienne
Serves: 6
Cooking time: 2 hours
Preparation time: 20 minutes

There are literally no limits to the preparation of vegetable soups. They quickly set the mood of a meal, and can be served either hot and comforting or cold and refreshing. Every season brings us a new vegetable addition for the soup pot. This one combines a wide variety of vegetables and is served hot and hearty.

Ingredients
4   tablespoons soft butter
2   tablespoons finely minced fresh parsley
2   cloves garlic, mashed
Salt and freshly ground white pepper
8 to 10 cups Light White Stock (see page 201) or Chicken Stock (see page 203)
2 to 3 potatoes, peeled, and cut into 1-inch matchsticks (enough to make 2 cups)
1 to 2 turnips, peeled and cut into 1-inch matchsticks (enough to make 1 cup)
2   stalks celery, cut into 1-inch matchsticks (enough to make 1 cup)
2   cups finely shredded cabbage
2   carrots, peeled and cut into 1-inch matchsticks (enough to make 1 cup)
5   peppercorns
1   cup green beans, trimmed and cut into 1-inch pieces
1   cup shelled fresh peas

Preparation
1. In a small mixing bowl combine the butter, parsley, garlic, salt, and pepper. Mash the mixture with a fork until it is well blended. Chill until serving time.

2. In a large, flameproof casserole combine the stock, potatoes, turnips, celery, cabbage, and carrots. Add a large pinch of salt and the peppercorns. Bring to a boil, then reduce the heat and simmer the soup, covered, for 1½ hours. Add the beans and peas and continue cooking the soup for another 30 minutes. Taste and correct the seasoning.

3. Spoon the soup into individual soup dishes, top each with a teaspoonful of herb butter, and serve piping hot, accompanied by black bread and a bowl of sweet butter.

Remarks
All soups improve greatly when made with a light stock instead of water. A few chicken giblets and some meaty soup bones will do the trick. All you really need is 10 more minutes of preparation time and the result is well worth the effort.

Notes

Soupe jardinière

Serves: 6 to 8
Preparation time: 20 minutes
Cooking time: 1½ hours

For a summer lunch I recently served a large basket of raw vegetables fresh from my garden as part of an hors d'oeuvre table. When I found myself with many good leftovers, I decided to combine them all in a garden soup.

Ingredients

6   tablespoons olive oil
1   large onion, finely minced
4   cloves garlic, minced
2   tablespoons finely minced fresh
     oregano or 1 teaspoon dried
2   large ripe tomatoes coarsely chopped
2   tablespoons tomato paste
2   cups cubed, peeled potatoes
1   cup peeled, diced carrots
1   cup cubed celery
2   cups finely shredded cabbage
10 cups of water
Salt and freshly ground black pepper
1   cup diced green beans
1   cup diced zucchini
3   tablespoons minced fresh parsley
2   cups fresh basil leaves
⅓   cup freshly grated Parmesan cheese

Preparation

1. Heat 2 tablespoons of the oil in a large, heavy, flameproof casserole. Add the onion, 2 cloves garlic, and oregano and cook over medium heat for 5 minutes, or until onion is soft but not browned. Add tomatoes and tomato paste and cook for 5 more minutes, stirring two or three times, until most of the tomato juices have evaporated. Add the potatoes, carrots,

celery, and cabbage. Add the 10 cups of water, salt, and pepper. Bring the mixture to a boil, then reduce the heat and simmer the soup for 1 hour. Add the green beans and zucchini and simmer for another 30 minutes, or until all the vegetables are tender. Remove the soup from the heat and cool to room temperature.

2. In the container of a blender combine the parsley, the remaining garlic, the basil, and the remaining oil. Blend at high speed until smooth, then season with salt and pepper and add the Parmesan. Whisk the mixture into the soup and taste and correct the seasoning.

3. Serve the soup cool, with black bread and a bowl of sweet butter.

Notes

Potage delphine

Serves: 4 to 6
Preparation time: 15 minutes
Cooking time: 50 minutes

Many soups in French cuisine have classic names and immediately call to mind a particular vegetable. This is the case with *potage Crécy* (carrot soup) and *potage Parmentier* (leeks and potatoes). *Potage Delphine*, however, is an unusual soup that does not have the distinct flavor of any one particular vegetable. I have never been able to discover its origin; it's just a marvelous soup with a lovely name.

Ingredients

3   tablespoons butter
2   leeks, finely sliced
1   onion, peeled and diced
3   large tomatoes, peeled and seeded
2   all-purpose potatoes, peeled and cubed
1   cup finely diced celery
3   cups sliced sorrel leaves
6   cups Light Chicken Stock (see page 204)
1   Bouquet Garni (see page 214)
Salt and freshly ground white pepper
1   cup Crème Fraîche (see page 206)
    or sour cream

Preparation

1. Heat the butter in a large, flameproof casserole. Add the leeks and onion, cover, and cook over low heat for 5 minutes, or until the vegetables are soft but not browned. Chop 2 of the tomatoes and add to the casserole, then raise the heat and cook, uncovered, until all the tomato juices have evaporated. Add the potatoes, celery, 2 cups of the sorrel leaves, the stock, and the *bouquet garni*. Season with salt and pepper and bring to a boil, then reduce the heat and simmer, covered, for 45 minutes. At the end of that time, discard the *bouquet garni* and cool the soup completely.

2. Puree the soup in the blender, pour it back into the casserole, and set aside.

3. When ready to serve, reheat the soup until piping hot. Add the *crème fraîche* or sour cream and whisk until well blended, then taste and correct the seasoning. (Do not let the soup come back to a boil if you have used sour cream.)

4. Just before serving, remove from the heat and stir in the remaining tomato, diced, and the remaining sorrel leaves, cut into julienne. Serve in individual soup bowls or a soup tureen, accompanied by thinly sliced, buttered pumpernickel.

Notes

Potage printanier

Serves: 4 to 6
Preparation time: 10 minutes
Cooking time: 20 minutes

What could be more springlike than a soup using all of that season's marvelous greens! Here is one I adapted from an old Provençal cookbook. I consider it a treasure.

Ingredients

6   cups Light Chicken Stock
    (see page 204)
2   cups fresh spinach leaves
1   cup watercress leaves
1   cup sorrel leaves or a small Boston
    lettuce heart
6   tablespoons butter
3   tablespoons all-purpose flour
1   cup shelled fresh peas
Salt and freshly ground white pepper

Garnish:
2   tablespoons finely minced fresh parsley
    or mint

Preparation

1. Bring the stock to a boil in a large, heavy-bottomed saucepan. Add the spinach, watercress, and sorrel or Boston lettuce heart, all finely shredded. Bring the mixture to a boil, then reduce the heat and simmer for 5 minutes, or until the vegetables are wilted. Cool, then puree in the blender. Set aside.

2. Melt 3 tablespoons of the butter in the saucepan. Add the flour and cook, stirring, for 2 minutes, without letting the mixture brown. Remove the pan from the heat, add the vegetable puree all at once, and whisk until the soup is smooth and well blended.

3. Return the saucepan to the heat. Bring the soup to a boil, add the peas, then reduce the heat and simmer, covered, for 15 to 20 minutes, or until the peas are tender. Season with salt and pepper.

4. Just before serving, whisk in the remaining butter, sprinkle with parsley or mint, and serve, accompanied by French bread and a bowl of sweet butter.

Remarks

The lettuce is by no means a substitute for the sorrel, which has a slightly sour taste. It will, however, give the soup the consistency you are looking for. A dollop of sour cream or Crème Fraîche (see page 206) on each plate will give the soup a finishing touch.

Notes

Creole black bean soup

Serves: 8 to 10
Preparation time: 25 minutes (plus over-
night soaking time)
Cooking time: 3 to 4 hours

Ingredients

3   cups dried black beans
1½ cups 2-inch pieces slab bacon
1 or 2 smoked pig's knuckles
6   tablespoons butter
3   large onions, finely minced
4   cloves garlic, finely minced
3   leeks, some green included, thinly
    sliced
2   bay leaves
1   large sprig fresh thyme or 1 teaspoon
    dried
1   teaspoon dried oregano
1   teaspoon freshly ground coriander
Freshly ground black pepper
10 to 12 cups White Stock (see page 201)
    or bouillon
Salt, if necessary
1   cup Madeira or ½ cup rum
2 to 3 tablespoons lemon juice

Preparation

1. Place the beans in a large casserole,
cover them with cold water, and let them
soak overnight. Drain the beans the next
day and set aside.

2. Bring 2 quarts of water to a boil in a
large saucepan. Add the bacon and pig's
knuckles and cook for 10 minutes, then
drain and set aside.

3. Melt the butter in a large, heavy, flameproof casserole. Add the bacon cubes
and cook until almost crisp, then remove
with a slotted spoon and set aside.

4. To the fat remaining in the pot add the
onions, garlic, and leeks. Cook the mixture
until soft and lightly browned, then add
the bay leaves, thyme, oregano, beans,
pig's knuckles, bacon, coriander, and a
large pinch of pepper. Add the stock and
bring the mixture to a boil, then reduce
the heat and cover the casserole tightly.
Simmer at very low heat for 3½ to 4 hours.
After the soup has been simmering for
an hour, taste for seasoning and add salt
if necessary.

5. When the soup is done, cool it slightly.
Puree half the soup in the blender or pass
it through a food mill, then return it to the
casserole, together with the Madeira or
rum. Heat the soup, but do not let it come
to a boil. Add lemon juice, taste and
correct the seasoning.

6. Serve as a one-dish meal in a large
tureen, with a side dish of cooked rice,
or as a soup in individual soup plates,
topping each serving with a large spoonful
of sour cream.

Notes

Ukrainian beet soup

Serves: 8
Preparation time: 45 minutes
Cooking time: 3 to 4 hours

Borscht is synonymous with Russian cooking. But people do not realize that there are as many versions of this soup as of Italian *minestrone* or any other national soup. Almost every province in Russia makes the soup according to its own traditions and availability of produce. I particularly like the Ukrainian borscht, which is a meal in itself when accompanied by black bread and sweet butter.

Ingredients

Garnish:

1½ cups sour cream
½ cup finely minced fresh dill
2 to 3 pounds beef rib bones
2 pounds veal knuckle bones
2 carrots, scraped and cut in half
2 stalks celery
2 leeks, well washed
1 parsnip, peeled
1 parsley root, scraped, or 2 to 4 large sprigs of fresh parsley
12 to 14 cups water
Salt
4 tablespoons butter
2 cups finely minced onions
1 teaspoon minced garlic
3 large tomatoes, peeled, seeded, and chopped
1 teaspoon tomato paste
1 teaspoon granulated sugar
¼ cup red wine vinegar
Pepper
4 cups peeled and coarsely grated fresh beets
1 small savoy cabbage, coarsely sliced

Preparation

1. In a small bowl combine the sour cream and dill and chill until serving.

2. In a large, flameproof casserole combine the rib and knuckle bones, carrots, celery stalks, leeks, parsnip, and parsley root. Add the water and a good pinch of salt. Bring to a boil, then reduce the heat and simmer the stock, partially covered, for 1½ to 2 hours, or until the meat is tender, skimming the stock carefully several times during the cooking. When tender, remove the meat and bones with a slotted spoon to a side plate and reserve. Strain the stock through a fine sieve, degrease it carefully, and set aside.

3. Melt the butter in a large, heavy, flame-proof casserole. Add the onions and cook, partially covered, over low heat for 10 minutes, or until soft but not browned. Add the garlic, tomatoes, and tomato paste and cook the mixture for 5 minutes, stirring several times. Add the sugar, vinegar, a good dash of salt and a heavy grinding of pepper, and then the beets, cabbage, and stock. Bring the mixture to a boil, then reduce the heat and cook, partially covered, for 40 to 50 minutes. Taste and correct the seasoning, then cut the meat into serving pieces and return it to the pot. Simmer the soup until the meat is well heated through.

4. Spoon the soup into individual bowls, and serve with the sour cream on the side.

White bean and basil soup

Serves: 4 to 6
Preparation time: 30 minutes
Cooking time: 40 minutes

Ingredients

⅔ cup olive oil
1   large onion, finely minced
4   cloves garlic, finely minced
½   cup finely minced fresh parsley
3   ripe tomatoes, peeled, seeded, and
     chopped
2   tablespoons tomato paste
½   teaspoon dried oregano
4 to 5 cups Cooked White Beans
     (see page 210)
4 to 5 cups Light Chicken Stock
     (see page 204)
Salt and freshly ground black pepper
⅓   cup broken up, uncooked thin spaghetti
1   cup tightly packed fresh basil leaves
½   cup freshly grated Parmesan cheese
1   cup thinly sliced garlic sausage,
     chorizo, or Polish sausage

Preparation

1. Heat 3 tablespoons of oil in a large,
heavy, flameproof casserole. Add the
onion, 2 cloves of the garlic, and the
parsley and cook for 2 or 3 minutes, or
until the onion is soft but not browned.
Add the tomatoes, tomato paste, and
oregano and continue cooking until all the
tomato juices have evaporated. Add 2
cups of the beans and 1 cup of the stock,
then season with salt and pepper, cover,
and simmer for 10 minutes.

2. Remove the casserole from the heat
and let the bean and tomato mixture cool,
then place it in the container of a blender
and puree until completely smooth. Pour
the puree into the casserole, add the
remaining stock and beans, and season

with salt and pepper. Add the spaghetti
and simmer the soup for 10 to 12 minutes,
or until the spaghetti is done. The soup
must be quite thick, but add a little more
stock or some of the bean cooking liquid
if the soup seems *too* thick.

3. In the container of a blender combine
the remaining garlic, the basil, the remaining olive oil, and the Parmesan. Blend
the mixture until it is smooth, then set
aside.

4. When the soup is done, whisk in the
basil mixture. Taste and correct the seasoning, then add the sliced sausages and
heat through. Serve the soup hot, with a
side bowl of freshly grated Parmesan
cheese and black bread.

Remarks

This soup is really a one-dish meal; you
can start or follow it with a well-seasoned
salad and finish with a bowl of fruit and
ripened Brie. Perfect for Sunday nights
and simple suppers.

Notes

Balkan bean and oxtail soup

Serves: 6 to 8
Preparation time: 30 minutes
Cooking time: 3 hours

Nourishing, inexpensive, and available in many supermarkets, oxtails, unfortunately, are rarely used creatively. They make an excellent ragoût or a hearty winter soup that is almost a meal in itself.

Ingredients

1 cup dried white beans (preferably Great Northern)
1½ pounds oxtails, cut into 2-inch pieces
2 stalks celery
1 large carrot, peeled and cut in half
1 onion, peeled and stuck with 1 whole clove
3 to 4 sprigs of parsley
2½ quarts water
Salt
2 tablespoons butter
1 onion, finely minced
1 teaspoon paprika
2 large, ripe tomatoes, peeled, seeded, and chopped
2 cloves garlic, mashed
1 hot chili pepper
Freshly ground black pepper
2 tablespoons vegetable oil
2½ tablespoons all-purpose flour

Garnish:
Thinly sliced French bread sautéed in olive oil

Preparation

1. Soak the beans in cold water to cover overnight. The next day drain and set aside.

2. In a large, flameproof casserole combine the oxtails, celery, carrot, onion, and parsley. Add the cold water and a good pinch of salt. Bring to a boil, then reduce the heat and simmer, covered, for 1½ hours.

3. Preheat the oven to 325 degrees.

4. Carefully degrease the oxtail stock then add the beans. Place the casserole in the oven and cook the beans for 1½ to 2 hours, or until they are very tender.

5. While the beans are cooking, heat the butter in a heavy skillet. Add the onion and cook over low heat until it is soft but not browned, then add the paprika, tomatoes, garlic, and chili pepper. Raise the heat and cook the mixture until all the tomato juices have evaporated and the mixture is thick. Season with salt and pepper and set aside.

6. When the beans are done, discard the stock vegetables, cool the soup, and degrease it carefully. Set aside.

7. Heat the oil in a small, heavy saucepan. Add the flour and cook over low heat, stirring, until the flour turns a hazelnut brown. Add the tomato mixture and a ladle of the bean stock. Bring the mixture to a boil, stirring constantly, then pour it into the bean soup. Simmer the soup for 15 more minutes, then discard the chili pepper and correct the seasoning.

8. Serve very hot, with a side dish of thinly sliced French bread sautéed in olive oil.

Remarks

If you cannot get oxtails, you can make an equally good soup with soup bones and 1 cracked pig's knuckle.

Cabbage soup à la paysanne

Serves: 4 to 6
Preparation time: 45 minutes
Cooking time: 2 hours and 30 minutes

An authentic peasant dish, this is not actually a soup but rather an "all in the pot" dish. It is excellent for a fall or winter supper accompanied by black bread and a cold glass of beer....

Ingredients

4   tablespoons butter
1   large onion, thinly sliced
1   carrot, scraped and finely sliced
1   stalk celery, diced
5   cups White Stock (see page 201)
    or beef bouillon
2   pig's knuckles, cut in half crosswise
3 to 4 small marrow bones
1   Bouquet Garni (see page 214)
1   onion, finely minced
1   pound finely ground pork
¾   cup cooked rice (preferably Italian rice)
2   tablespoons finely minced fresh parsley
2   small cloves, garlic, mashed
1   whole egg
2   tablespoons water
Salt and freshly ground black pepper
1   head savoy cabbage
2 to 3 medium-sized potatoes, peeled
    and cubed

Preparation

1. Melt 2 tablespoons of the butter. Add the sliced onion, carrot, and celery. Cook the vegetables over low heat, in a large, flameproof casserole, stirring, them until they are slightly soft but not browned. Add the stock, pig's knuckles, bones, and bring to a boil; skim carefully. Add the *bouquet garni* and simmer, covered, over low heat for 30 minutes.

2. While the stock is simmering, melt the remaining butter in a small heavy skillet. Add the minced onion and sauté until it is soft but not browned.

3. In a mixing bowl combine the pork, rice, parsley, garlic, and sautéed onion. Add the egg and water and work the mixture with your hands until it is well blended. Add a large pinch of salt and freshly ground black pepper; the mixture should be highly seasoned; then set aside.

4. Bring salted water to a boil in a large, flameproof casserole. Add the savoy cabbage, top down, and poach it for exactly 5 minutes, then drain and run it under cold water to stop further cooking. Dry the cabbage carefully with a clean kitchen towel and place on a board. Carefully separate the leaves and place a little of the meat mixture between each leaf. Re-form the cabbage and tie it with kitchen string. Place it in the stock and cover the casserole tightly.

5. Preheat the oven to 350 degrees.

6. Braise the cabbage for 1½ hours, basting it every 20 minutes with the stock. Add the cubed potatoes and continue braising the cabbage until the potatoes are tender. Discard the *bouquet garni* and skim the fat off the soup. Carefully remove the string and transfer the cabbage to a deep tureen, pouring the soup around it.

7. Serve piping hot with black bread, a crock of good mustard, and a bowl of tiny dill gherkins.

Cabbage soup au roquefort

Serves: 8
Preparation time: 35 minutes
Cooking time: 2 to 2½ hours

This is essentially a peasant soup that I like to serve just as soon as I see the first savoy cabbage in the market. It makes a good, hearty fall and winter meal that is relatively inexpensive and ages well.

Ingredients

2   pounds chuck, in one piece
2 to 3 pounds soup bones, including marrow bones
1   parsnip
4   carrots, peeled and left whole
2   leeks, cleaned
2   stalks celery
½   head garlic, unpeeled
3   quarts water
Salt
6   peppercorns
4   tablespoons butter
3   tablespoons vegetable oil
2   onions, thinly sliced
1   small head savoy cabbage, roughly sliced
3   potatoes, peeled and cubed
4   medium turnips, peeled and cubed
Freshly ground black pepper
8   slices French bread
1   ounce Roquefort cheese (2 tablespoons)
3   tablespoons minced fresh parsley

Preparation

1. In a large, flameproof casserole combine the meat, bones, parsnip, 2 of the carrots, the leeks, celery, and garlic. Add the water and season with salt and peppercorns. Bring the mixture to a boil, skim carefully, and simmer, partially covered, for 1½ to 2 hours, or until the meat is tender. Skim the soup from time to time.

2. While the stock is cooking, cube the remaining carrots.

3. When the meat is tender, remove to a side dish; cut it into small chunks and set aside. Discard the bones (if you have used marrow bones, extract the marrow and set aside). Strain the stock through a fine sieve, degrease thoroughly, and set aside.

4. Melt 2 tablespoons of the butter and 1 tablespoon of the oil in a 6-quart, flameproof casserole. Add the onions and cook over low heat until they are soft and lightly browned, then add the reserved stock, the cabbage, potatoes, turnips, and cubed carrots. Season the soup with salt and pepper. Bring to a boil, then reduce the heat and simmer, partially covered, for 30 to 45 minutes.

5. While the soup is simmering, heat the remaining butter and oil in a 10-inch skillet. Add the bread slices and brown them over medium heat on both sides, then remove to a double layer of paper towels and drain.

6. When the soup is done, return the meat to the casserole, together with the marrow, and heat thoroughly. Place a slice of the fried bread in each soup bowl, top with a little Roquefort, and ladle the soup over. Garnish with the parsley and serve very hot.

Remarks

You may serve the soup in a soup tureen, with a side dish of Roquefort and fried bread.

Clam soup à la martegal

Serves: 6 to 8
Preparation time: 25 minutes
Cooking time: 50 minutes

Ingredients

2   dozen littleneck clams
1   tablespoon all-purpose flour
½   cup white wine
3   cups Fish Stock (see page 204) or water
1   Bouquet Garni (see page 214)
Salt
3   tablespoons butter
2   leeks, cleaned and thinly sliced
2   cloves garlic, finely minced
3   potatoes, peeled and cubed
1   cup heavy cream
Cayenne pepper

Garnish:
2   tablespoons finely minced herbs
    (parsley, chives, and chervil)

Preparation

1. Thoroughly scrub the clams under cold running water. Place in a large bowl and cover with cold water, then add the flour and let the clams soak for 2 hours.

2. In a large, heavy, flameproof casserole combine the clams, wine, fish stock, and *bouquet garni.* Add a pinch of salt and bring to a boil, then reduce the heat and steam the clams, partially covered, for 10 minutes, or until they open. As they open, remove them to a side dish and reserve.

3. Shell the clams, mince them, and set aside. Strain the broth through a double layer of cheesecloth and reserve.

4. Melt the butter in a large, heavy, flame-proof casserole. Add the leeks and garlic and simmer, covered, for 5 minutes, or until the leeks are soft but not browned. Add the potatoes and clam broth and bring to a boil, then reduce the heat and cook, covered, for 30 minutes. Cool the soup.

5. Puree the cooled soup in the blender. Pour it back into the casserole, add the clams and heavy cream, and reheat. Taste and correct the seasoning, adding a good pinch of cayenne.

6. Pour the soup into a soup tureen, garnish with the minced herbs, and serve very hot, accompanied by French bread.

Remarks

This soup freezes very successfully. For a variation, cook 1 large, finely sliced leek in 2 tablespoons of butter until soft but not browned and add to the finished soup. It gives the soup an interesting texture.

Notes

Fish soup à la gallega

Serves: 4
Preparation time: 20 minutes
Cooking time: 1 hour

Some of the best fish dishes and soup come from Galicia, a province at the northern Atlantic tip of Spain where the quantity, variety, and quality of the seafood is staggering. Most of the dishes are robust but quite simple, relying entirely on the quality of the fish. Here is a soup that can be served as a main course for a family supper.

Ingredients

Garnish:
4   slices of Italian bread rubbed with garlic

4   small cod steaks, cut ¾ inch thick
Salt and freshly ground black pepper
3   tablespoons olive oil
1½ pounds onions, thinly sliced
3   cloves garlic, finely minced
1   dried hot chili pepper
4   tablespoons all-purpose flour
1   Bouquet Garni (see page 214)
2   quarts Fish Stock (see page 204)

Preparation

1. Preheat the oven to 375 degrees.

2. Place the bread slices on a baking sheet and toast in the oven until nicely browned. Remove from the oven and set aside.

3. Season the fish steaks with salt and pepper. Set aside.

4. Heat the oil in a large, heavy, flame-proof casserole. Add the onions, garlic, and chili pepper, season with salt and pepper, and cook, covered, over low heat for 40 minutes, stirring frequently.

5. Add the flour and stir the mixture for 2 minutes. Add the stock, all at once, and whisk until the soup is smooth, then bring to a boil. Reduce the heat and add the fish steaks and *bouquet garni*. Simmer the soup, covered, for 15 minutes. (Do not let it come to a boil, or the fish will fall apart.) Remove the *bouquet garni*. Taste the soup and correct the seasoning, adding a heavy grinding of black pepper.

6. Place a slice of bread in deep, individual soup plates. Carefully transfer a fish steak to each plate and spoon the hot soup over it.

Notes

Galician corn and spinach soup

Serves: 4
Preparation time: 25 minutes
Cooking time: 25 minutes

Corn is rarely found in Mediterranean cooking. I was therefore intrigued by this light fish soup from northern Spain, which was given to me by a Galician market woman. If you have made the fish stock with cod necks, flake them and add to the finished soup.

Ingredients

8 to 10 littleneck clams
4   cups Fish Stock (see page 204)
3   tablespoons olive oil
1   cup thinly sliced onion
2   large cloves garlic, finely minced
½   pound shrimp, peeled, deveined, and diced
Salt and freshly ground black pepper
1½ cups fresh corn kernels
    (approximately 3 large ears)
2   cups fresh spinach

Preparation

1. Scrub the clams thoroughly under cold running water.

2. In a saucepan combine 1 cup of the fish stock and the clams. Cook the clams, covered, over low heat. As they open, remove them to a side dish with a slotted spoon. As soon as the clams are cool enough to handle, shell and dice them, then set them aside. Strain the stock through a double layer of cheesecloth and combine with the remaining fish stock.

3. Heat the oil in a heavy-bottomed, flame-proof casserole. Add the onion and cook over low heat until very soft and lightly browned, then add the garlic and shrimp and cook until the shrimp turn pink. Season lightly with salt and pepper. Add the stock and corn, then bring the mixture to a boil. Reduce the heat and simmer, covered, for 10 minutes.

4. Add the clams and spinach to the soup and cook for 2 more minutes, or until the spinach is just wilted. Remove the soup from the heat, correct the seasoning, and serve immediately.

Notes

Lentil soup à la paysanne

Serves: 6 to 8
Preparation time: 30 minutes
Cooking time: 2¼ hours

Ingredients

½   pound salt pork, cut into 1-inch cubes
2   tablespoons butter
1   tablespoon vegetable oil
2   onions, finely chopped
2   leeks, including some of the green, finely sliced
1   stalk celery, thinly sliced
1   carrot, peeled and thinly sliced
2   tomatoes, peeled, seeded, and chopped
1   tablespoon tomato paste
Salt and freshly ground black pepper
1   cup dried lentils
2   quarters White Stock (see page 201) or beef bouillon
1   Bouquet Garni (see page 214)
1   two-pound piece of beef chuck (optional)

Preparation

1. Bring 4 cups of water to a boil in a saucepan. Add the cubed salt pork and cook for 5 minutes over medium heat, then drain and dry thoroughly on paper towels.

2. Heat the butter and oil in a large, heavy, flameproof casserole. Add the pork cubes and cook until lightly browned, then spoon off all but 2 tablespoons of fat from the casserole. Add the onions and leeks and cook until soft and lightly browned. Add the celery, carrot, tomatoes, tomato paste, salt, and pepper. Bring the mixture to a boil and cook for 5 minutes, stirring frequently. Add the lentils, stock, *bouquet garni*, and optional piece of beef. Cover the casserole and simmer the soup for 2 hours, skimming it several times.

3. Cool the soup and degrease it carefully. Taste, correct the seasoning, and discard the *bouquet garni*.

4. Just before serving, reheat the soup and serve, accompanied by black bread and a bowl of sweet butter.

Remarks

This soup is at its best when prepared 1 day ahead of time.

Notes

soups

Mussel soup à la marseillaise

Serves: 6
Preparation time: 20 minutes
Cooking time: 1 hour 5 minutes

Mussels are a staple of southern French cooking. The best come from an area close to Marseilles called Sete sur Mer. It is here that the mussel soup is at its finest. It can, however, easily be duplicated with our own mussels, as long as they are not too large and are of the utmost freshness.

Ingredients

1   cup white wine
2   onions, finely minced
1   Bouquet Garni (see page 214)
5   peppercorns
6   pounds small mussels, well scrubbed and cleaned
¼   cup olive oil
1   carrot, peeled and finely minced
2   leeks, white part only, finely minced
3   cloves garlic, minced
¼   cup minced fresh parsley
3   large, ripe tomatoes, peeled, seeded, and diced
1½ teaspoons crushed saffron
Salt and freshly ground black pepper
6   cups Fish Stock (see page 204)
Cayenne pepper

Preparation

1. In a large saucepan combine the wine, half the minced onion, the bouquet garni, peppercorns, and mussels. Bring to a boil, then partially cover the saucepan and steam the mussels open over medium heat. Set aside to cool in their liquid.

2. Heat the oil in a large, heavy, flame-proof casserole. Add the remaining onion, the carrot, leeks, garlic, and 2 tablespoons of the parsley. Cook the mixture, partially covered, over low heat for 5 minutes, or until it is soft but not browned. Add the tomatoes, saffron, salt, pepper, and stock. Bring to a boil, then reduce the heat and simmer, covered, for 45 minutes.

3. While the stock is simmering, shell the mussels and set aside. Pass the poaching liquid through a double layer of cheesecloth and set aside as well.

4. Add the mussels and reserved stock to the casserole, then add a pinch of cayenne. Taste the soup and correct the seasoning, cover, and simmer for another 10 minutes.

5. Ladle into individual soup bowls, sprinkle with the remaining parsley, and serve with thinly sliced French bread sautéed in olive oil.

Notes

Basque pumpkin soup

Serves: 6 to 8
Preparation time: 30 minutes
Cooking time: 4 hours

The pumpkin is considered one of the most "American" of vegetables, yet, surprisingly, it is used extensively for the flavoring of soups in both Spanish and Central European cooking. In European markets, a piece of pumpkin is always included in the bundle of soup greens. It was a surprise, however, to come across this old Basque recipe in which pumpkin is used as a main ingredient. This is a perfect fall soup. I find the result delicious.

Ingredients

1   cup dried white beans
Salt
1½ pounds slab bacon
2   tablespoons bacon fat or lard
2   onions, finely minced
2   large leeks, well cleaned and thinly
     sliced
4   large cloves garlic, minced
1   large carrot, peeled and cubed
2   stalks celery, finely cubed
1   large sprig fresh parsley
1   teaspoon dried thyme
1   bay leaf
6   peppercorns
8 to 12 cups Light White Stock
     (see page 201)
1½ pounds fresh pumpkin, peeled and
     cubed
2   frankfurters or small garlic sausages,
     thinly sliced (optional)

Preparation

1. Put the beans in a large, flameproof casserole, along with enough water to cover them by 2 inches. Bring the beans to a boil over high heat and cook for 1 minute, then remove from the heat. Cover and let the beans stand for 1 hour.

2. Preheat the oven to 325 degrees.

3. Add more water to the beans to cover again by 2 inches. Season with a good pinch of salt and set the casserole in the oven. Cook the beans for 2 hours, or until very tender, then remove the casserole from the oven, drain the beans, and set aside.

4. Bring 6 cups of water to a boil in a large saucepan. Add the bacon and cook for 3 minutes over high heat, then drain and cut into ½-inch slices. Set aside.

5. Heat the bacon fat or the lard in a large, heavy, flameproof casserole. Add the onions, leeks, and garlic and cook until soft and lightly browned, then add the carrot, celery, parsley, thyme, bay leaf, peppercorns and a good pinch of salt and cook for another 5 minutes. Add the stock and bacon and bring the mixture to a boil. Add the pumpkin and simmer, covered, for 1½ hours. Add the drained beans and cook for another 20 to 30 minutes, then taste the soup and correct the seasoning. Discard the parsley sprig and bay leaf. Add the optional frankfurters and heat through.

6. Serve the soup in a large tureen, accompanied by thinly sliced French bread sautéed in olive oil.

Russian sorrel soup

Serves: 6 to 8
Preparation time: 20 minutes
Cooking time: 30 minutes

In the last few years, sorrel has become the most "fashionable" green on Parisian menus. It deserves its popularity, since it is an exquisite vegetable. In Russian cooking, however, sorrel has always been popular. Here is that country's version of sorrel soup.

Ingredients

6 to 8 cups Light Chicken Stock
    (see page 204)
3   medium-sized all-purpose potatoes,
    peeled and cubed
1½ pounds fresh sorrel
Salt and freshly ground white pepper

Garnish:
1   cup Crème Fraîche (see page 206) or 1
    cup sour cream
2   tablespoons finely minced chives

Preparation

1. Bring the stock to a boil in a large, flameproof casserole. Add the potatoes and cook over medium heat for about 20 minutes, or until they are tender.

2. Clean the sorrel thoroughly under cold running water, removing the stems. Add the sorrel to the stock and continue simmering for another 10 minutes.

3. Cool the soup slightly, then puree it in a blender until it is completely smooth. Pass the soup through a fine sieve, return to the casserole, and reheat. Taste for seasoning, adding salt and freshly ground pepper.

4. Combine the *crème fraîche* and chives in a bowl and set aside.

5. Pour the soup into individual soup bowls and top each serving with a spoonful of the cream and chive mixture. Serve the soup hot, accompanied by French bread.

Remarks

For an interesting variation, add 1 cup of packed sorrel leaves, cut into fine julienne, to the hot soup. Let the leaves melt in the soup for 1 or 2 minutes; don't let the soup return to a boil. Serve out of a soup tureen with the *crème fraîche* and chives on the side.

Notes

Chilled cream of sorrel soup

Serves: 6 to 8
Preparation time: 20 minutes
Cooking time: 30 minutes

For a light summer dinner, serve this
Russian sorrel soup creamed and chilled.

Ingredients

6 to 8 cups Russian Sorrel Soup
   (see page 97)
1 to 2 small cloves garlic, mashed
1 cup heavy cream
Salt and freshly ground white pepper
2 tablespoons finely minced fresh herbs
   (chives, parsley, and chervil)

Preparation

1. Bring the soup to a boil in a large,
flameproof casserole. Add the garlic and
cream and stir, then correct the seasoning
with salt and pepper. Chill the soup for
2 to 4 hours.

2. Just before serving, add the minced
herbs and serve chilled, but not cold, with
thinly sliced, buttered pumpernickel and
a bowl of radishes.

Notes

Seafood soup à la parisienne

Serves: 6
Preparation time: 45 minutes
Cooking time: 1 hour

Ingredients

5 cups Fish Stock (see page 204)
1 pound cod steak or other firm white fish
½ pound sea scallops, cubed
¾ cup white wine
1 small onion, finely minced
1 Bouquet Garni (see page 214)
12 to 16 small mussels, scrubbed and
   cleaned
4 tablespoons butter
2 white onions, thinly sliced
3 tablespoons all-purpose flour
Salt and freshly ground white pepper
2 egg yolks
1 cup heavy cream
Juice of ½ lemon

Garnish:
1 tablespoon finely minced fresh parsley
1 tablespoon finely minced fresh tarragon
   or fennel tops

Preparation

1. Heat the fish stock in a large saucepan.
Add the cod steak and poach it, covered,
for 8 minutes over low heat, then carefully
remove to a side dish and set aside.
Add the scallops to the stock and simmer
for 4 to 5 minutes, or until the scallops
turn an opaque white. Remove them with
a slotted spoon to a side dish and reserve.
Keep the stock warm.

2. In a saucepan combine the wine,
minced onion, and bouquet garni, then
add the mussels and steam them open
over medium heat for 5 to 6 minutes.
Remove the mussels and shell them,
removing the black edge. Add them to the

scallops. Strain the mussel cooking liquid through a fine sieve and add it to the fish stock.

3. Heat the butter in a large, heavy, flame-proof casserole. Add sliced onions, cover, and cook until they are soft but not browned. Add the flour and cook, stirring constantly, for 2 minutes, without browning. Add the hot stock all at once, whisking constantly until the soup is thick and smooth. Season with salt and pepper, then reduce the heat and simmer for 30 minutes.

4. In a small bowl combine the egg yolks and heavy cream. Season with salt and pepper and set aside.

5. Break the fish steak into small pieces, carefully removing the bones. Add, along with the scallops and mussels, to the soup and heat through.

6. Add the cream and yolk mixture to the soup and reheat without letting it come to a boil. Taste and correct the seasoning, then add the lemon juice.

7. Pour the soup into a tureen, garnish with the minced herbs, and serve hot, accompanied by French bread and a chilled white wine.

Notes

Tomato and zucchini soup alla genovese

Serves: 4 to 6
Preparation time: 20 minutes
Cooking time: 50 minutes

The marvelous affinity of basil, tomatoes, and zucchini inspired me to make this light soup. It had to be a success. After all, what can go wrong when you are using the best of your garden's summer crop?

Ingredients

6   large, very ripe tomatoes
6   tablespoons butter
5 to 6 tablespoons olive oil
1   onion, peeled and finely minced
2   cloves garlic, peeled and finely minced
1   tablespoon tomato paste
2   tablespoons finely minced fresh
    oregano or 1 teaspoon dried
Salt and freshly ground black pepper
3   cups Light Chicken Stock
    (see page 204)
1   large sprig fresh parsley
1   zucchini, finely cubed
1   cup tightly packed basil leaves
2   tablespoons all-purpose flour

Preparation

1. Core the tomatoes and cut into small cubes.

2. Heat 2 tablespoons of the butter and 1 tablespoon of the oil in a heavy, 3-quart saucepan. Add the onion and garlic and cook, partially covered, for 5 minutes, or until the onion is soft but not browned. Add the tomatoes, tomato paste, and oregano, season with salt and pepper and cook the mixture for 2 to 3 minutes longer. Add the stock and parsley sprig. Bring to a boil, then reduce the heat and simmer for 30 minutes.

3. In the meantime, melt 2 tablespoons of the butter in a small, heavy skillet. Add the zucchini, salt, and pepper, then cover and cook over low heat for 5 minutes. Remove the pan from the heat and set aside.

4. In the container of a blender combine the basil leaves with the remaining oil. Blend until the mixture is reduced to a fine puree. (You may need 1 or 2 more table-spoons oil.) Set aside.

5. Strain the soup through a food mill or rub it through a coarse sieve. Set aside.

6. Melt the remaining butter in a large heavy saucepan. Add the flour and cook, stirring with a wire whisk, for 2 minutes, without browning. Add the soup and continue whisking constantly until the mixture is smooth. Bring to a boil, then reduce the heat and simmer for 10 minutes. Add the basil puree and the zucchini, then taste and correct the seasoning.

7. Serve the soup hot, accompanied by crusty French bread.

Remarks

This soup is equally good cold. It will thicken considerably in the refrigerator, but you can thin it out with a little chicken stock. For a variation omit the zucchini and add finely diced green and red peppers to the soup.

The one-dish meal has always played a major role in peasant cooking. This was true not only for reasons of economics, but also because the one-dish meal was a great time saver for housewives who had to serve their families both lunch and dinner. They also made hearty and nourishing meals. But then, for a while, the one-dish meal began to disappear. Eating habits changed in favor of light lunches of sandwiches, salads, or omelets. One-dish meals started coming off the cook's lunch repertory even in countries like France and Italy, where the traditions of one-dish meals had always been strong.

In the last few years there has been an exciting renaissance of composite peasant dishes to be found on the menus of top restaurants in France, Italy, and Spain, as well as other parts of the world. No longer are the pig's knuckles, stuffed cabbage, or braised oxtails reserved for the small bistro or country restaurant. These dishes have been rediscovered by great chefs as well as by the family cook. Now the one-dish meal has been given a major role at the dinner table.

Actually, there is nothing heartier and more satisfying than a casserole of different meats and vegetables slowly braised and carefully flavored. Nor is there anything lighter on the family budget. One-dish meals can be made from inexpensive ingredients such as ground meats, oxtails, and dried legumes, and are also wonderful for last-minute entertaining. They can be prepared several days ahead of time and successfully refrigerated and frozen, and will only get better and tastier when reheated.

The variety of this kind of cooking is virtually unlimited. A good *cassoulet*—the casserole of white beans, pork, goose, and lamb that is the pride of the Toulouse region of France—is truly robust and delicious. Nor can anything be more satisfying than a well-flavored *choucroute,* the staple of Alsatian cooking. Other countries also boast delicious one-dish meals: the Spanish *paella*; the Italian *bollito misto* (close cousin to the French *pot-au-feu*); the Hungarian goulash, spicy beef braised with sauerkraut or potatoes and heavily flavored with paprika.

These are just a few. Almost every European country, and every province within it, has its own version of a particular dish, usually depending on the availability of fresh produce and on the family budget. America too has produced some fine composite dishes, including chili con carne and Southern black bean soup with rice.

The dishes in this chapter are suitable for simple dinners and Sunday suppers. They are mostly of the robust peasant variety, and should be served on their own with nothing other than a cold glass of beer or a light table wine. Follow with a well-flavored salad and a piece of fruit.

Ragoût of white beans toulousaine

Serves: 4 to 6
Preparation time: 20 minutes (plus over-
night soaking time)
Cooking time: 2½ hours

The *cassoulet*, a savory dish of meats and
beans from the southwestern part of
France, has been gaining popularity in
this country in recent years. It is both an
expensive and time-consuming dish to
make authentically, but the flavor can
nevertheless be duplicated in this "poor
man's" version, which is both hearty and
inexpensive.

Page

Ingredients

2   cups dry white beans (preferably
     Great Northern)
Salt
2   pig's knuckles, split in half
1   large carrot, peeled and cut in half
1   stalk celery
1   onion stuck with 1 whole clove
1   Bouquet Garni (see page 214)
2   garlic sausages or knockwurst
1   tablespoon butter
1   tablespoon vegetable oil, lard, or
     chicken fat
1½ cups cubed, blanched bacon
1   large onion, finely sliced
2   cloves garlic, minced
4   tablespoons minced fresh parsley
3   large tomatoes, peeled, seeded, and
     chopped
½   teaspoon dried marjoram
1   teaspoon meat glaze (optional)
Tomato paste (optional)
Freshly ground black pepper

Garnish:
2   tablespoons finely minced parsley
2   tablespoons thinly sliced pimiento

Preparation

1. Soak the beans in cold water overnight.
The next day drain and set aside.

2. Preheat the oven to 350 degrees.

3. Bring 3 quarts of salted water to boil
in a large, heavy, flameproof casserole.
Add the pig's knuckles, carrot, celery,
onion stuck with the clove, and the *bouquet
garni*. Cook over medium heat for 5
minutes, skimming carefully, then add
the beans. Cover the casserole, set in the
oven, and braise the beans for 2 hours,
or until they are tender. Twenty minutes
before the beans are done, add the
sausages to the casserole.

4. While the beans are cooking, melt the
butter and oil in a large, heavy skillet.
Add the bacon and cook until almost crisp,
then remove it to a side dish with a slotted
spoon.

5. Discard all but 2 tablespoons of fat
from the pan. Add the sliced onion and
cook over low heat until it is soft and
lightly browned, then add the garlic,
2 tablespoons parsley, the tomatoes,
and marjoram. Cook the mixture over high
heat until all the tomato juices have
evaporated and the mixture is thick. Add
the optional meat glaze and tomato paste
and season with salt and pepper. Return
the bacon to the pan and set aside.

6. When the beans are done, pour them
into a colander placed over a bowl,
discarding the vegetables and *bouquet
garni*. Cube the meat from the pig's

knuckles, slice the sausages, and add, together with the beans, to the tomato mixture. Add 1 cup of the bean cooking water and place the skillet in the oven. Bake the "ragoût" for 30 minutes, or until most of the bean water has evaporated; it must not be dry.

7. Remove from the oven, sprinkle with the remaining parsley and the sliced pimiento, and serve right out of the skillet, accompanied by a well-seasoned salad and French bread.

Notes

Red cabbage ragoût

Serves: 6
Preparation time: 35 minutes
Cooking time: 3 hours

Red cabbage makes a hearty dish, good for fall and winter meals. It should be made a day ahead of time and reheated slowly before serving. Aside from sausages, you can add a 2-pound piece of smoked pork butt to the casserole and garnish the platter with new potatoes cooked in their skins.

Ingredients

1   pound slab bacon, cut into 3 chunks
3   tablespoons butter
2   large onions, finely minced
2   large cloves garlic, minced
2 to 3 pounds red cabbage, finely
      shredded
3   large baking apples, peeled and cubed
2   cloves
2   cups red wine
2   cups White Stock (see page 201) or
      bouillon
Salt and freshly ground white pepper
Freshly grated nutmeg
1   two-pound piece smoked pork butt
      (optional)
3   tablespoons brown sugar
½   cup vinegar
2   tablespoons vegetable oil
2   tablespoons all-purpose flour
6   frankfurters or 6 smoked sausages

Garnish:
8 to 10 small new potatoes

Preparation

1. Preheat the oven to 350 degrees.

2. Bring water to a boil in a 2-quart saucepan. Add the bacon pieces and

cook for 3 minutes, then drain thoroughly on paper towels. Melt the butter in a large, heavy, flameproof casserole. Add the bacon and cook until almost crisp, then remove to a side plate.

3. Discard all but 2 tablespoons of fat from the casserole. Add the onions and garlic and cook over low heat until the onion is soft and lightly browned. Add the cabbage, apples, cloves, wine, and stock. Bring to a boil, adding a good pinch of salt, freshly ground white pepper, and a good pinch of freshly grated nutmeg. Return the bacon to the casserole, cover tight, and set in the center part of the oven. Cook for 1½ hours, then add the optional smoked pork to the casserole and continue cooking for another 1½ hours.

4. While the red cabbage is braising, combine the brown sugar and vinegar in a small bowl. Whisk until the sugar is completely dissolved and set aside.

5. Twenty minutes before the cabbage is done, remove the casserole from the oven. Heat the oil in a small, heavy skillet and add the flour and cook, stirring constantly, until it turns a nutty brown. Add the flour mixture to the casserole, together with the vinegar and sugar mixture. Stir the cabbage until well blended, then return the casserole to the oven and finish braising.

6. Bring water to a boil in a 3-quart saucepan. Add the sausages and cook for 5 minutes, then drain and add to the red cabbage for 10 or 15 minutes.

7. Remove the casserole from the oven. Taste the cabbage and correct the seasoning; it should have a sweet and sour taste. Spoon the cabbage onto a serving platter, then cut the pork butt into thin slices and arrange them over the cabbage. Arrange the sausages around the platter, with the small new potatoes cooked in their skins. Serve very hot.

Remarks

This is a good-natured dish that does not demand exact cooking time. You may leave the finished dish in a warm oven for 1 to 2 hours before serving, or leave it overnight in a cool place and reheat slowly on top of the stove the next day. For a sharper flavor add the juice of ½ lemon before serving.

Notes

Stuffed cabbage provençale

Serves: 6
Preparation time: 45 minutes
Cooking time: 1 hour and 45 minutes

Some dishes are classics of the peasant cuisines of many countries. Stuffed cabbage is one of these. Different countries have interpreted the dish in different ways; for example, in Hungarian cooking, sauerkraut is added to the sauce, and in Viennese cooking a sweet and sour taste is given to it. Here is the Mediterranean version of this classic peasant dish. It should be prepared two or three days in advance, since it is particularly good when reheated. It can also be served cold as part of a Sunday lunch or simple supper.

Ingredients

1   cup cubed salt pork
4   tablespoons butter
2   medium onions, peeled and finely minced
½   pound ground pork
½   pound ground beef
2   tablespoons raw rice
2   eggs
1   pound spinach or Swiss chard, cooked, drained, and chopped (optional)
3   large garlic cloves, finely minced
4   tablespoons finely minced fresh parsley
½   teaspoon thyme
Large pinch of allspice
½   teaspoon marjoram
Salt
Freshly ground black pepper
1   large savoy cabbage
1   cup finely minced carrots
1   stalk celery, finely minced
4 to 5 ripe tomatoes, peeled, seeded and chopped
½   cup white wine
1   Bouquet Garni (see page 214)

2 to 3 cups Brown Stock (see page 202) or White Stock (see page 201)
Beurre Manié (see page 213)

Garnish:
2   tablespoons minced fresh parsley

Preparation

1. Bring 2 cups water to boil in a small saucepan, add the salt pork and cook for 5 minutes. Drain and reserve.

2. Melt 2 tablespoons of butter in a 10-inch heavy iron skillet, add the onion and cook until soft and lightly browned. Set the pan aside.

3. In a large mixing bowl combine the meats, rice, eggs, sautéed onion, and optional spinach or chard. Add 1 clove of garlic, 2 tablespoons of parsley, the thyme, allspice, and marjoram. Season with salt and pepper. Work the mixture with your hands until well blended. Taste and correct the seasoning. Reserve.

4. In a large casserole bring 2 quarts salted water to boil, add the cabbage and cook it upside down for 5 minutes. Drain and, when cool enough to handle, separate the leaves.

5. With a sharp knife cut out a 2-inch wedge from the hard core. Place a spoonful of stuffing on each leaf and roll it up, tucking in the ends. Repeat until all the stuffing is used. Set the rolls aside. Slice the rest of the cabbage fine and reserve.

6. Preheat the oven to 350 degrees.

7. Heat the remaining butter in a large, heavy oval casserole, add the salt pork and cook until it is almost crisp. Spoon off all but 2 tablespoons of fat, add the carrot, celery and remaining garlic and cook until soft and lightly browned. Add the sliced cabbage, tomatoes, wine, and salt and pepper to taste. Bring the mixture to a boil and cook until most of the wine has evaporated. Arrange the cabbage rolls in the casserole, add the *bouquet garni* and stock, and bring to a boil. Cover the casserole tightly and place in the oven. Bake for 1 hour and 30 minutes.

8. Remove the casserole from the oven. Carefully remove the cabbage rolls to a deep serving platter; discard the *bouquet garni*. Place the casserole over medium heat and add bits of *beurre manié* until the pan juices are thick. Taste and correct the seasoning. Spoon the pan juices over the cabbage rolls, sprinkle with remaining parsley and serve with black bread and a bowl of sweet butter.

Notes

Cold cabbage rolls à la monegasque

Serves: 6
Preparation time: 45 minutes
Cooking time: 1 hour and 45 minutes

Stuffed cabbage leaves make a wonderful cold appetizer or simple supper dish. In the south of France they are often featured as part of an hors d'oeuvre table garnished with sliced tomatoes and finely sliced onions and black olives.

Ingredients

6 tablespoons fruity olive oil
12 Stuffed Cabbage Provençale (see page 106)
1 Bouquet Garni (see page 214)
2 cups Brown Stock (see page 202) or beef bouillon
2 tablespoons finely minced fresh parsley
2 tablespoons lemon juice
1 clove of garlic, finely minced

Preparation

1. Preheat the oven to 375 degrees.

2. Heat 2 tablespoons of oil in a large, rectangular baking dish and arrange the cabbage rolls in one layer in the dish. Bury the *bouquet garni* among them, and pour the stock over the cabbage rolls. Cover the dish, set in the middle part of the oven and bake for 45 minutes to an hour.

3. Uncover the dish and continue cooking the rolls for another 45 minutes, basting them with the pan juices every 10 minutes. By the end of the cooking time the pan juices should be well reduced and the cabbage rolls nicely browned. Remove the dish from the oven, discard the *bouquet garni*, sprinkle with parsley, the remaining olive oil and the lemon juice. Serve right from the dish at room temperature accompanied by French bread and a simple red table wine.

Ratatouille basquaise

Serves: 8 to 10
Preparation time: 1 hour, 15 minutes
Cooking time: 45 minutes

The ratatouille, a vegetable stew from the south of France, has gained enormous popularity in this country in recent years. It is a well-deserved popularity, since I can think of nothing more delicious and refreshing than this excellent potpourri of vegetables that have such a marvelous affinity to one another. Personally, I prefer this somewhat spicy Basque version of the ratatouille. The leftovers can be used successfully in combination with eggs and crêpes, and as a filling for a quiche.

Ingredients

2   medium unpeeled eggplants, cubed
Salt
2 to 3 small zucchini, cubed
8 to 10 tablespoons olive oil
2   large onions, peeled and finely sliced
1   dry hot chili pepper
2   green peppers, seeded and finely sliced
2   garlic cloves, finely minced
3   tablespoons minced fresh parsley
1   red pepper, seeded and finely sliced,
    or 1 cup finely sliced pimientos
2   teaspoons tomato paste
4   large ripe tomatoes, peeled, seeded
    and chopped
Freshly ground black pepper
2   tablespoons finely minced basil or 1
    teaspoon Basil Paste (see page 210)
1   cup diced proscuitto
½   cup pitted black olives (preferably the
    Greek or Niçoise kind)

Garnish:
2   tablespoons finely minced fresh parsley
1   tablespoon well-drained capers

Preparation

1. Place the eggplant in a colander, sprinkle with salt and let drain for 30 minutes to an hour. Sprinkle the zucchini with salt, place on a double layer of paper towels and let drain for an hour. Dry the vegetables thoroughly and reserve.

2. Heat 4 tablespoons of oil in a large heavy skillet, add the eggplant and sauté until nicely browned on all sides. Remove to a side dish and reserve. Add more oil to the skillet, add the zucchini and cook until nicely browned. Mix with the eggplant and set aside.

3. Add a little more oil to the pan if necessary, add the onions, chili pepper, green peppers, and garlic and cook until the onions are soft and lightly browned. Add the parsley and the red pepper or pimientos. Cover the skillet and cook for 10 minutes or until the peppers are soft.

4. Uncover the skillet, raise the heat, add the tomato paste and tomatoes, and cook for 5 or 6 minutes or until most of the tomato juice has evaporated.

5. Return the eggplant and zucchini to the pan; season lightly with salt and pepper, and add the basil or basil paste. Cook the mixture over low heat for another 10 minutes. Add the prosciutto and olives, heat through and pour into a serving bowl. Let the ratatouille cool. Serve it at room temperature garnished with finely minced parsley and capers and accompanied by French bread.

one-dish meals

Sardinian stuffed peppers

Serves: 6 to 8
Preparation time: 30 minutes
Cooking time: 50 minutes to 1 hour

Remarks

Do not season the ratatouille too heavily as both the prosciutto and olives will add saltiness to the dish. For variety, omit the prosciutto and add 1 cup of flaked tuna in olive oil.

Notes

Ingredients

1 medium eggplant, peeled and cubed
Salt
½–¾ cup olive oil
1 small onion, finely minced•
3 large, ripe tomatoes, peeled, seeded, and finely chopped
½ cup finely minced celery
1 tablespoon tomato paste
Freshly ground black pepper
1 tablespoon finely minced fresh oregano or ½ teaspoon dried
1 tablespoon finely minced fresh basil or ½ teaspoon dried
1 can (7½ ounces) tuna in olive oil
3 hard-boiled eggs, finely minced
½ cup finely minced green olives
2 cloves garlic, mashed
2 tablespoons finely minced fresh parsley
¾ to 1 cup fresh, white bread crumbs
6 to 8 small green peppers

Preparation

1. Place the eggplant cubes in a colander. Sprinkle with salt and let drain for 1 to 2 hours.

2. Dry the eggplant cubes thoroughly with paper towels. Heat 3 tablespoons of oil in a heavy, iron skillet. Add the eggplant and sauté over high heat until nicely browned on all sides, adding more oil if necessary. Remove to a double layer of paper towels to drain.

3. Heat 3 more tablespoons of oil in the skillet. Add the onion and cook until soft but not browned, then add the tomatoes, celery, tomato paste, salt, and pepper.

Cook the mixture over high heat until it is thick and all the tomato juices have evaporated, then add the oregano, basil, tuna, eggplant, eggs, olives, garlic, and parsley and cook for 2 minutes longer. Fold ¾ cup bread crumbs into the mixture; taste and correct the seasoning. (The filling must be quite thick; if it seems loose, add the remaining bread crumbs.) Set aside.

4. Preheat the oven to 375 degrees.

5. Cut a thin slice from the stem end of each pepper, remove the core and seeds. Stuff the peppers with the filling. Arrange them in a well-oiled rectangular baking dish, dribble with the remaining oil, and bake for 25 to 30 minutes, or until the peppers are tender. Do not overcook. Cool the peppers and serve at room temperature.

Remarks

Large peppers can be cut in half length-wise, cored, and filled. Bake them for 20 minutes, sprinkle with minced parsley, and serve right from the baking dish.

Notes

Viennese spinach roulade

Serves: 8
Preparation time: 30 minutes
Cooking time: 35 minutes

Ingredients

The "Cake":
4   tablespoons butter
6   tablespoons all-purpose flour
2   cups warm milk
4   eggs, separated
Salt and freshly ground white pepper
Pinch of granulated sugar

The Filling:
1   package fresh, thoroughly washed
    spinach
2   tablespoons butter
2   tablespoons finely minced scallion
Salt and freshly ground white pepper
1   cup sour cream
6   ounces cream cheese, softened
2   tablespoons finely minced fresh dill
1   large clove garlic, mashed
1   tablespoon finely grated fresh Par-
    mesan cheese

Garnish:
Watercress leaves
8   broiled mushrooms or cherry tomatoes

Preparation

1. Start by making the filling. In a large saucepan combine the spinach with ½ cup cold water. Bring to a boil, then reduce the heat and simmer for 4 to 5 minutes, or until the spinach is completely wilted. Remove the spinach to a colander and let drain for 15 to 20 minutes, then squeeze with your hands to extract all the moisture, chop fine, and set aside.

2. Heat the butter in a small, heavy skillet. Add the scallion and cook over low heat until soft but not browned, then add the

spinach, season with salt and pepper, and cook the mixture for 2 minutes. Set aside.

3. In a bowl combine the sour cream and cream cheese. Mash the mixture with a fork until it is smooth and well blended; then add the spinach mixture, dill, garlic, and Parmesan and blend thoroughly. Correct the seasoning and set aside.

4. Preheat the oven to 325 degrees.

5. Butter a jelly-roll pan, then line it with waxed paper. Butter the paper and dust it with flour, shaking off the excess. Set aside.

6. Now prepare the batter for the "cake." Melt the butter, over low heat, in a heavy-bottomed, 2-quart saucepan. Add the flour and cook, stirring constantly, for 2 minutes, without browning.

7. Remove the pan from the heat, then add the warm milk all at once and whisk the mixture until it is smooth and well blended. Set the saucepan over moderate heat and whisk until the batter is very thick. Remove the pan from the heat and incorporate the egg yolks, one at a time, then season with salt, pepper, and the pinch of sugar. Set aside.

8. Beat the egg whites until stiff in a copper or stainless steel bowl. Delicately fold them into the batter then spread the mixture evenly into the prepared jelly-roll pan and bake for 30 to 35 minutes, or until the "cake" is lightly browned and a tooth-pick comes out clean.

9. Invert the pan over a sheet of foil. Lift it off, then peel the waxed paper off carefully, with the help of a sharp knife. Cool for 3 or 4 minutes, then spread with the spinach mixture and roll up the roulade lengthwise.

10. With 2 large spatulas transfer the roll to a rectangular serving platter. Garnish with watercress leaves and broiled mush-rooms or cherry tomatoes and serve immediately.

Remarks

The roulade can be made several hours in advance. Wrap it in foil and set it on a baking sheet over a pan of warm water. It can also be made with the following filling.

Notes

Filling bernoise

Ingredients

4 tablespoons butter
½ pound chicken livers, well cleaned
Salt and freshly ground white pepper
3 tablespoons finely minced shallots
½ pound mushrooms, finely minced
¾ cup sour cream
6 ounces cream cheese, softened
1 large clove garlic, mashed
2 tablespoons finely minced fresh parsley

Preparation

1. Heat 2 tablespoons of the butter in a heavy skillet. Add the chicken livers, and cook them over high heat until they are nicely browned on both sides. Season with salt and pepper, then scrape into a bowl and set aside.

2. Heat the remaining butter in the pan. Add the shallots and mushrooms and cook for 4 to 5 minutes, or until all the moisture has evaporated and the mixture is quite dry. Season with salt and pepper and set aside.

3. Dice the chicken livers fine and add them to the mushroom mixture.

4. In a mixing bowl combine the sour cream and cream cheese. Mash the mixture with a fork until it is smooth and well blended, then add the garlic, parsley, and the chicken liver and mushroom mixture and blend thoroughly. Taste and correct the seasoning, then cool for 15 to 20 minutes before filling the roulade.

Boulettes à la bayonnaise

Serves: 3 to 6
Preparation time: 30 minutes
Cooking time: 1 hour and 45 minutes

"*Boulettes*" are actually French meat balls. They should be highly seasoned, and are usually prepared in a spicy tomato and pepper sauce. The *boulettes* can be made small, and served as part of a buffet table, or large, and served with a side dish of curry-flavored rice for a simple family supper. Follow with a salad and a selection of good dessert cheeses and red table wine.

Ingredients

1½ pounds ground chuck or a mixture of beef and pork
2 tablespoons minced fresh parsley
1 whole egg
1 teaspoon ground cumin
½ teaspoon dried marjoram
Salt and freshly ground black pepper
⅛ teaspoon hot Spanish paprika
¼ teaspoon dried thyme
2 large cloves garlic, mashed
2 tablespoons butter
1 onion, finely minced
3 tablespoons water
½ cup bread crumbs soaked in milk and drained
All-purpose flour
6 to 8 tablespoons olive oil
2 large onions, thinly sliced
1 dried hot chili pepper
1 green pepper, thinly sliced
1 red pepper, thinly sliced
1 tablespoon tomato paste
4 large tomatoes, peeled, seeded, and chopped
1 bay leaf
2 medium zucchini, cubed

spinach, season with salt and pepper, and cook the mixture for 2 minutes. Set aside.

3. In a bowl combine the sour cream and cream cheese. Mash the mixture with a fork until it is smooth and well blended; then add the spinach mixture, dill, garlic, and Parmesan and blend thoroughly. Correct the seasoning and set aside.

4. Preheat the oven to 325 degrees.

5. Butter a jelly-roll pan, then line it with waxed paper. Butter the paper and dust it with flour, shaking off the excess. Set aside.

6. Now prepare the batter for the "cake." Melt the butter, over low heat, in a heavy-bottomed, 2-quart saucepan. Add the flour and cook, stirring constantly, for 2 minutes, without browning.

7. Remove the pan from the heat, then add the warm milk all at once and whisk the mixture until it is smooth and well blended. Set the saucepan over moderate heat and whisk until the batter is very thick. Remove the pan from the heat and incorporate the egg yolks, one at a time, then season with salt, pepper, and the pinch of sugar. Set aside.

8. Beat the egg whites until stiff in a copper or stainless steel bowl. Delicately fold them into the batter then spread the mixture evenly into the prepared jelly-roll pan and bake for 30 to 35 minutes, or until the "cake" is lightly browned and a tooth-pick comes out clean.

9. Invert the pan over a sheet of foil. Lift it off, then peel the waxed paper off carefully, with the help of a sharp knife. Cool for 3 or 4 minutes, then spread with the spinach mixture and roll up the roulade lengthwise.

10. With 2 large spatulas transfer the roll to a rectangular serving platter. Garnish with watercress leaves and broiled mushrooms or cherry tomatoes and serve immediately.

Remarks

The roulade can be made several hours in advance. Wrap it in foil and set it on a baking sheet over a pan of warm water. It can also be made with the following filling.

Notes

Filling bernoise

Ingredients

4   tablespoons butter
½   pound chicken livers, well cleaned
Salt and freshly ground white pepper
3   tablespoons finely minced shallots
½   pound mushrooms, finely minced
¾   cup sour cream
6   ounces cream cheese, softened
1   large clove garlic, mashed
2   tablespoons finely minced fresh parsley

Preparation

1. Heat 2 tablespoons of the butter in a heavy skillet. Add the chicken livers, and cook them over high heat until they are nicely browned on both sides. Season with salt and pepper, then scrape into a bowl and set aside.

2. Heat the remaining butter in the pan. Add the shallots and mushrooms and cook for 4 to 5 minutes, or until all the moisture has evaporated and the mixture is quite dry. Season with salt and pepper and set aside.

3. Dice the chicken livers fine and add them to the mushroom mixture.

4. In a mixing bowl combine the sour cream and cream cheese. Mash the mixture with a fork until it is smooth and well blended, then add the garlic, parsley, and the chicken liver and mushroom mixture and blend thoroughly. Taste and correct the seasoning, then cool for 15 to 20 minutes before filling the roulade.

Boulettes à la bayonnaise

Serves: 3 to 6
Preparation time: 30 minutes
Cooking time: 1 hour and 45 minutes

"Boulettes" are actually French meat balls. They should be highly seasoned, and are usually prepared in a spicy tomato and pepper sauce. The boulettes can be made small, and served as part of a buffet table, or large, and served with a side dish of curry-flavored rice for a simple family supper. Follow with a salad and a selection of good dessert cheeses and red table wine.

Ingredients

1½   pounds ground chuck or a mixture of beef and pork
2   tablespoons minced fresh parsley
1   whole egg
1   teaspoon ground cumin
½   teaspoon dried marjoram
Salt and freshly ground black pepper
⅛   teaspoon hot Spanish paprika
¼   teaspoon dried thyme
2   large cloves garlic, mashed
2   tablespoons butter
1   onion, finely minced
3   tablespoons water
½   cup bread crumbs soaked in milk and drained
All-purpose flour
6 to 8 tablespoons olive oil
2   large onions, thinly sliced
1   dried hot chili pepper
1   green pepper, thinly sliced
1   red pepper, thinly sliced
1   tablespoon tomato paste
4   large tomatoes, peeled, seeded, and chopped
1   bay leaf
2   medium zucchini, cubed

Garnish:
2   tablespoons finely minced parsley
6   pimiento-stuffed olives, cut in half

Preparation

1. Preheat the oven to 350 degrees.

2. In a mixing bowl combine the meat, 2 tablespoons parsley, the egg, cumin, marjoram, salt, pepper, paprika, thyme, and garlic. Work the mixture with your hands until it well blended, then set aside.

3. Heat the butter in a small, heavy skillet. Add the minced onion and cook over medium heat until it is soft but not browned, then add to the meat mixture, together with the water and the bread crumbs. Work the mixture again, then taste and correct the seasoning. Form the meat into slightly oval balls the size of a small fist. Dredge them lightly in flour on all sides and set aside.

4. Heat 2 tablespoons of the oil in a large, flameproof casserole or deep, heavy skillet. Add the meat balls, a few at a time; do not crowd. Cook the balls over medium heat until they are well browned on both sides, then carefully remove to a side dish.

5. When all the meat balls are done, discard all but 2 tablespoons of fat (if the oil has burned, discard it completely and add 2 more tablespoons of oil to the pan). Add the sliced onions and cook until they are soft and lightly browned, then add

the chili pepper and green and red peppers and cook for 2 to 3 minutes longer, scraping the bottom of the pan well with a wooden spoon. Add the tomato paste, tomatoes, salt, and pepper and bring to a boil. Reduce the heat, then return the meat balls to the pan in one layer. Add the bayleaf, cover, and set in the oven. Braise the *boulettes* for 1½ hours, basting them several times with the pan juices.

6. While the meat is braising, heat the remaining oil in a heavy skillet. Add the zucchini cubes and cook until they are well browned on all sides. Season with salt and pepper and set aside.

7. Fifteen minutes before the meat is done, add the zucchini cubes to the casserole and continue braising until they are well heated through.

8. When the meat is done, arrange it in a deep, oval serving dish. Pour the sauce and vegetables around it, sprinkle with parsley, and pimiento-stuffed olives and serve, accompanied by crusty bread.

Remarks

The entire dish can be made several hours ahead of time and reheated slowly in a 250-degree oven.

Ragoût of oxtails bourguignonne

Serves: 6
Preparation time: 45 minutes
Cooking time: 3 hours

■○

Although oxtails are both a delicious and inexpensive cut of meat, few people seem to recognize their marvelous potential. I particularly like to combine them in this classic method, the addition of good fresh vegetables resulting in a delicious one-dish meal. It is always best to make this kind of dish one or two days ahead of time and slowly reheat it in the oven before serving. Serve accompanied by French bread and a full-bodied red wine.

Ingredients

1½ cups cubed salt pork
2   tablespoons butter
1   tablespoon vegetable oil
4 to 5 pounds lean oxtails, cut into 2-inch
     pieces
Salt and freshly ground black pepper
1   cup finely minced onion
1   cup finely minced carrot
½   cup finely minced celery
2   large cloves garlic, minced
1½   tablespoons tomato paste
3   cups full-bodied Burgundy
3   cups beef bouillon or White Stock
     (see page 201), approximately
1   Bouquet Garni (see page 214)
12 to 16 small white onions, peeled
12 to 16 small new potatoes, peeled
12 to 16 pieces of carrot, scraped and
     cut into 2-inch matchsticks
12 to 16 tiny turnips balls, peeled

Optional:

1   tablespoon cornstarch mixed into a
     paste with a little cold stock

Preparation

1. Preheat the oven to 350 degrees.

2. Bring water to a boil in a small sauce-pan. Add the salt pork cubes and cook for 5 minutes, then drain and dry thoroughly on paper towels. Set aside.

3. Heat the butter and oil in a large, heavy, flameproof casserole. Add the salt pork cubes and sauté over medium heat until almost crisp; then remove with a slotted spoon to a side dish and set aside.

4. Discard all but 2 tablespoons of fat from the casserole. Add the oxtails, a few pieces at a time, brown on all sides, and season with salt and pepper. Remove to a side dish and reserve.

5. Discard all but 3 tablespoons of fat out of the casserole, add the onion, carrot, celery, and garlic, and cook the mixture for 3 to 4 minutes, until nicely browned. Add the tomato paste and salt and pepper to taste. Return the salt pork and oxtails to the casserole. Add the wine and stock, bring to a boil, and bury the *bouquet* among the oxtails. Cover the casserole and place in the oven.

6. Braise the oxtails for 2 hours or until almost tender. Remove the casserole from the oven. Carefully degrease the pan juices. Add the onions, potatoes, carrots, and turnips. Return the casserole to the oven and continue cooking until all the vegetables are tender.

Pig's knuckles à la lyonnaise

Serves: 2 to 3
Preparation time: 10 minutes
Cooking time: 2 hours

7. Remove the casserole from the oven. With a slotted spoon transfer the oxtails and vegetables to a deep dish. Place the casserole over high heat and reduce the pan juices by a third. For a thicker sauce, beat in the cornstarch mixture—the sauce must heavily coat the spoon. Taste and correct the seasoning. Pour the sauce over the oxtails and vegetables and serve accompanied by French bread; follow it by a well-seasoned salad.

Notes

Pig's knuckles are rarely used creatively in the American kitchen, but they are both inexpensive and flavorful. They add flavor and body to bean soup, or they can be roasted or grilled. I particularly like them cooked and served hot with a well-flavored vinaigrette.

Ingredients

2   quarts of water or Light Chicken Stock (see page 204)
4   pig's knuckles
1   stalk celery
1   carrot, peeled and cut in half
1   large onion, peeled and stuck with 1 whole clove
Salt
5   peppercorns
1   bay leaf
1   large sprig fresh parsley

The vinaigrette:

2   tablespoons red wine vinegar
¾   cup olive oil
½   teaspoon Dijon mustard
½   teaspoon dry mustard (preferably Colman's)
Freshly ground pepper
1   tablespoon finely minced dill gherkin
2   tablespoons finely minced green pepper
1   tablespoon well-drained capers
2   tablespoons finely minced scallion
1   tablespoon minced fresh parsley

Preparation

1. Combine the water or stock, pig's knuckles and vegetables in a large flame-

proof casserole. Add a good pinch of salt, the peppercorns, bay leaf, and parsley. Bring to a boil, then reduce the heat and simmer, partially covered, for 1½ to 2 hours, or until the knuckles are very tender.

2. Remove the knuckles to a cutting board. Cut off and discard the fat and bones, and cut the meat into serving pieces. Set aside and keep warm.

3. In a small glass screwtop jar combine the wine vinegar, olive oil, mustards, salt, and pepper. Shake the jar until the mixture is smooth and well blended. Add the minced gherkin, green pepper, capers, scallion, and parsley and whisk. Taste for seasoning.

4. Pour the dressing over the knuckles and serve, accompanied by black bread and a bowl of sweet butter.

Remarks

You may use the broth for cooking white beans or chick-peas. If the knuckles are not to be served right away, keep them in the broth and heat through just before serving.

Sausages à la campagnarde

Serves: 4
Preparation time: 35 minutes
Cooking time: 15 to 20 minutes

Pork link sausages are available in almost every good supermarket. They are inexpensive and suitable to many preparations other than as the usual partner to fried eggs. I often prepare them in this Basque country way for family suppers or Sunday brunch. Needless to say, the better the sausages the better the dish will be.

Ingredients

3   ripe tomatoes, coarsely cubed
Salt
¼   cup fruity olive oil
4 to 6 pairs pork sausages
2   tablespoons white wine
1   large onion, thinly sliced
1   teaspoon finely minced garlic
½   pound mushrooms, stems removed and thinly sliced
2   green peppers, roasted, peeled, seeded, and finely sliced (see page 31)
Freshly ground black pepper
½   teaspoon Spanish paprika
¼ to ½ teaspoon crushed hot pepper
¼   teaspoon dried thyme
¼   teaspoon dried rosemary

Garnish:
½   cup finely cubed pimiento
2   tablespoons finely minced garlic
2   tablespoons finely minced parsley

Preparation

1. Place the tomatoes in a colander over a bowl. Sprinkle with salt and let them drain for 30 minutes.

2. Heat 2 tablespoons of the oil in a large, heavy skillet. Add the sausages and wine,

Brochettes of chicken livers in sage butter

Serves: 6
Preparation time: 10 minutes
Cooking time: 15 minutes

cover, and cook over low heat until the sausages are nicely browned on both sides. Remove to a side plate and reserve.

3. Discard all the fat remaining in the pan. Add the remaining oil, and when it is hot add the onion and garlic and cook until soft and lightly browned. Add the mushrooms and green peppers, season with salt and pepper, and cook for 3 to 4 minutes longer, or until the mushrooms are lightly browned.

4. Add the paprika, hot pepper, thyme, rosemary, and tomatoes, then return the sausages to the pan and continue cooking over medium heat until all the tomato juices have evaporated. Taste and correct the seasoning.

5. Sprinkle with the pimiento, garlic and parsley and serve directly out of the skillet, accompanied by French bread and a bowl of sweet butter.

Notes

Few cooks seem to be aware of our good fortune in this country in having chicken livers readily available in quantity at most butchers' and supermarkets. In Europe, where you can only get one or two chicken livers with every chicken you buy, it is considered quite a delicacy. Here is an inexpensive yet delicious appetizer that can easily be turned into a main course by serving the brochettes on a bed of curry-flavored risotto.

Ingredients

1   pound chicken livers
18 small mushrooms
2 to 4 tablespoons olive oil
Salt and freshly ground white pepper
4   tablespoons sweet butter
18 bread slices cut into 1½ inch squares

Sage butter:
6   tablespoons softened sweet butter
2   tablespoons finely minced fresh sage
2   tablespoons finely minced fresh parsley
2   shallots finely minced
Salt
Freshly ground white pepper

Preparation

1. Clean the chicken livers and carefully remove any green or dark spots, cut the livers in half and set aside.

2. For the sage butter, combine the 6 tablespoons butter, the sage, parsley, shallots, salt, and pepper in a mixing bowl. Mash the mixture thoroughly with a fork and set aside.

3. Place the mushrooms on an oiled baking dish, then season with salt and pepper, dribble with a little olive oil, and place under the broiler for 2 minutes. Remove and set aside.

4. Heat the butter with 1 tablespoon of the oil in a large, heavy skillet. Add the chicken livers and cook over high heat until they are nicely browned on both sides. (Do not overcook; the chicken livers must still be pink inside.) Season with salt and pepper, then remove to a side plate with a slotted spoon.

5. Add the remaining oil to the pan. Add the bread squares and sauté on both sides until nicely browned, then remove from the pan and set aside.

6. Preheat the broiler.

7. Thread the bread squares, chicken livers, and mushrooms, alternating them, on small wooden skewers, using three of each to a skewer. Arrange the skewers in a baking dish, top with bits of the sage butter, and place the dish under the broiler. Cook for 3 minutes. turning the skewers once, then serve immediately on individual plates.

Remarks

Herb butters can be prepared several days in advance, and they freeze successfully. The brochettes can be prepared an hour or two ahead of time. Do not refrigerate. Place further away from the broiler heat to ensure that the brochettes have sufficient time to heat through.

Chicken livers à la vonnasienne

Serves: 4 to 6
Preparation time: 30 minutes
Cooking time: 15 to 20 minutes

Vonnas is a tiny village in the Bresse province of France famous for its chickens. They are remarkably different in taste and usually more expensive than commercially grown farm chickens. By not being artificially fed and grown they have a distinct quality and flavor. Here is a specialty of the province given to me by M. Blanc, the chef and owner of the restaurant Chez la Mère Blanche in Vonnas.

Ingredients

½   cup finely minced shallots
1   cup white wine
½   cup Clarified Butter (see page 213) plus
     2 tablespoons vegetable oil
4 to 6 slices white bread, cut ½ inch
     thick and crusts removed
1   pound chicken livers
4   tablespoons butter plus 1 tablespoon oil
Salt and freshly ground pepper
1   teaspoon meat glaze
3   tablespoons Madeira
¾   cup Concentrated Brown Stock
     (see page 203)
½   cup Crème Fraîche (see page 206)
Beurre Manié (see page 213), if necessary

Garnish:
Sprigs of fresh parsley

Preparation

1. Combine the shallots and white wine in a small bowl and let marinate overnight. Drain and set aside.

2. Heat the clarified butter and oil in a large skillet. Sauté the bread slices on both

Chicken livers à la valoise

Serves: 4 to 6
Preparation time: 45 to 50 minutes
Cooking time: 35 minutes

■■●

sides until they are nicely browned, and
set aside.

3. Carefully clean the chicken livers,
removing any green spots. Cut each liver
into 2 or 3 pieces, dry thoroughly on paper
towels. Heat the butter and oil in a large,
heavy iron skillet. Add the chicken livers
(without crowding the pan, or the livers
will steam instead of browning) and cook
over high heat until they are well browned
on all sides. Season the livers with salt
and pepper and remove with a slotted
spoon to a side dish.

4. To the fat remaining in the pan add the
well-drained shallots. Cook them for 1 or 2
minutes, without browning, then lower
the heat. Add the meat glaze and Madeira
and reduce the liquid to 1 tablespoon.
Add the stock, bring it to a boil, and
reduce it by ¼ cup. Add the *crème
fraîche* and cook the sauce for 5 minutes,
or until it heavily coats a spoon, then add
bits of *beurre manié* if the sauce seems
to lack body. Return the chicken livers to
the pan and simmer them in the sauce for
1 or 2 minutes. Taste the sauce for seasoning, adding a heavy grinding of black
pepper. Set the pan aside.

5. Place the sautéed bread on a serving
platter and top each piece with a little of
the chicken liver mixture. Garnish the
platter with sprigs of fresh parsley. Serve
immediately.

Ingredients

4   tablespoons unsalted butter or
     rendered chicken fat
2   pounds fresh spinach, well washed
     and trimmed
Salt and freshly ground white pepper
½   cup Clarified Butter (see page 213)
4 to 6 slices white bread, cut ½-inch
     thick and crusts removed
1   pound well-cleaned fresh chicken livers
1   tablespoon finely minced shallots
1   teaspoon meat glaze
¾   cup Concentrated Brown Stock
     (see page 203)

Béarnaise sauce:

½   cup tarragon vinegar
2   tablespoons finely minced shallots
2   tablespoons finely minced fresh tar-
     ragon or ½ teaspoon dried
3   egg yolks
1   tablespoon cold butter
¾   to 1 cup melted butter
Salt and freshly ground white pepper

Preparation

1. Start by making the sauce. Combine the
vinegar, shallots, and tarragon in a small,
heavy enameled saucepan. Bring the
mixture to a boil and cook over high heat
until all the liquid has evaporated. Remove
the saucepan from the heat and let it cool
until you can touch the bottom of the pan.

2. Add the yolks and the tablespoon of
cold butter to the cooled pan and whisk
well. Return the saucepan to very low
heat and beat with a small electric hand

beater until the yolks become thick and
creamy. Add the melted butter gradually,
beating constantly until the sauce is thick
and smooth, then remove the saucepan
from the heat. Season the sauce with
salt and pepper. Place the saucepan in
a pan of warm water and set aside.

3. Heat 2 tablespoons of the butter or
fat in a heavy, 10-inch skillet. Add the
well-drained spinach and cook it over
low heat for 6 to 8 minutes, or until all the
moisture has evaporated. Season with
salt and pepper and set aside.

4. Heat the clarified butter in a large
skillet. Add the bread slices and brown
them on both sides, then remove them to a
double layer of paper towels.

5. Melt the remaining butter or fat in a
10-inch skillet. Add the chicken livers and
cook over high heat until they are lightly
browned, then add the shallots and continue cooking until the shallots are soft
and lightly browned. Season the mixture
with salt and pepper, add the meat glaze
and stock, and continue cooking the
mixture over low heat, scraping up the
coagulated juices well until the sauce is
reduced by half. Remove from the heat
and set aside.

6. Place the sautéed bread slices on a
rectangular serving platter. Put a little of
the spinach on each slice, covering the
bread completely, then top with chicken
livers. Add a little of the pan juices to
the sauce, blend well, and spoon the sauce
over. Serve immediately.

Chicken wings à la hongroise

Serves: 4 to 6
Preparation time: 15 minutes
Cooking time: 50 minutes

The chicken wing is a delicious morsel
that is both inexpensive and extremely
versatile. I often serve them for a simple
supper or as an appetizer, followed by
grilled or baked fish.

Ingredients

12 to 14 chicken wings, cut in half and
    with tips removed
Salt and freshly ground white pepper
All-purpose flour
2   tablespoons butter
2   tablespoons vegetable oil
2   medium onions, thinly sliced
2   ripe tomatoes, coarsely chopped
1   teaspoon imported paprika
1   teaspoon dried marjoram
1   bay leaf
1   dried hot chili pepper
1   green pepper, thinly sliced
1   red pepper, thinly sliced, or ½ cup
    sliced pimiento
2   frankfurters, sliced

Garnish:
2   tablespoons minced fresh parsley
2   tablespoons minced pimiento

Preparation

1. Wash and dry the chicken wings thoroughly with paper towels. Season with
salt and pepper and dredge lightly in
flour.

2. Heat the butter and oil in a large, heavy
skillet. Add the wings, a few at a time;
do not crowd the pan. Cook, partially
covered, over medium heat until the wings

are nicely browned on all sides, then remove from the skillet and set aside.

3. Add the onions to the pan and cook over medium heat until lightly browned. Add the tomatoes, paprika, marjoram, bay leaf, chili pepper, and green and red peppers. Season with salt and pepper, then raise the heat and cook the mixture for 1 or 2 minutes, scraping the bottom of the pan well. Return the wings to the skillet, reduce the heat, and simmer, covered, for 25 to 30 minutes, or until tender but not falling apart. Add the sliced frankfurters, correct the seasoning, and heat through.

4. Place the wings in a rectangular serving dish. Top with the frankfurter and vegetable mixture, sprinkle with the parsley and pimiento, and serve with French bread and a chilled red table wine.

Notes

Chicken wings in lemon sauce

Serves: 4 to 6
Preparation time: 15 minutes
Cooking time: 35 to 40 minutes

Every cook needs some dishes in her repertory that are both simple and inexpensive to prepare. Chicken wings fill that need. They can be sautéed, grilled, or as here, braised in lemon sauce. Serve them accompanied by French bread and a curry-flavored rice.

Ingredients

12 to 16 chicken wings, cut in half and
    with tips removed
Salt and freshly ground white pepper
5   tablespoons butter
1   tablespoon vegetable oil
4   shallots, finely minced
¼   cup white wine
1   cup Chicken Stock (see page 203)
1   Bouquet Garni (see page 214)
½   pound mushrooms, finely sliced
1   teaspoon cornstarch
Juice of 1 lemon
2   egg yolks
¾   cup heavy cream or Crème Fraîche
    (see page 206)

Garnish:
2   tablespoons finely minced fresh parsley

Preparation

1. Season the chicken wings with salt and pepper and set aside.

2. Heat 3 tablespoons of the butter and the oil in a large, heavy skillet. Add the wings, a few at a time (do not crowd the pan), and cook, partially covered, over medium heat until nicely browned on all sides.

Sautéed chicken wings niçoise

Serves: 4 to 6
Preparation time: 35 minutes
Cooking time: 40 minutes

3. When all the wings are done, remove them to a side dish. Add the shallots to the pan and cook for 1 or 2 minutes, or until they are soft and lightly browned. Add the wine and stock, and bring the mixture to a boil, then add salt, pepper, and the *bouquet garni*. Scrape the bottom of the pan well. Reduce the heat, and return the wings to the skillet, cover, and simmer for 20 to 25 minutes, or until tender but not falling apart.

4. While the wings are cooking, heat the remaining butter in a small heavy skillet. Add the mushrooms and cook over high heat until they are lightly browned. Season with salt and pepper and set aside.

5. In a small mixing bowl combine the cornstarch, lemon juice, egg yolks, and cream. Whisk the mixture until it is smooth and well blended, then season with salt and pepper and set aside.

6. As soon as the chicken wings are done, with a slotted spoon remove them and the mushrooms to a serving dish. Add the egg yolk and cream mixture to the pan juices. Whisk the sauce over low heat without letting it come to a boil. Taste and correct the seasoning. Spoon the sauce over the chicken wings, sprinkle with parsley and serve immediately.

Remarks

If prepared in advance, the chicken wings can be returned to the sauce and the dish may be kept warm over a pan of warm (not boiling) water.

Ingredients

5   tablespoons olive oil
2   pounds chicken wings, cut in half and
    tips removed
Salt and freshly ground black pepper
2   onions, finely minced
2½ teaspoons finely minced garlic
½   cup finely minced celery
½   cup peeled, finely cubed carrot
¼   pound bacon, finely cubed
½   cup dry white wine
2   pounds ripe tomatoes, peeled, seeded,
    and chopped
1   cup Chicken Stock (see page 203)
1   Bouquet Garni (see page 214)
2   tablespoons unsalted butter
4   chicken livers, cut in half
1   cup small, oil-cured olives

Optional:
2   teaspoons cornstarch, blended into a
    paste with a little stock

Garnish:
2   tablespoons finely minced fresh
    parsley

Preparation

1. Heat 3 tablespoons of the oil in a large, heavy skillet. Add the wings, a few at a time (do not crowd the pan), and cook until they are nicely browned on all sides. Remove from the skillet and season with salt and pepper. Set aside.

2. Discard the fat remaining in the pan, then add the remaining oil. When the oil is hot, add the onions, 1 teaspoon of the garlic, the celery, carrot, and bacon. Cook the mixture over medium heat until

Frogs' legs in garlic sauce

Serves: 4
Preparation time: 10 minutes
Cooking time: 35 minutes

◾⊕

soft and lightly browned. Add the wine,
then raise the heat and cook until the
wine is reduced to 2 or 3 tablespoons. Add
the tomatoes, stock, salt, pepper, and
bouquet garni. Return the wings to the
skillet, cover tight, and simmer for 30
minutes, or until tender.

3. While the wings are cooking, heat the
butter in a small skillet. Add the chicken
livers and cook over high heat until they
are nicely browned on both sides. Remove
the skillet from the heat, season the
livers with salt and pepper, and set aside.

4. When the wings are done, remove them
to a serving platter with tongs. Raise the
heat and reduce the pan juices until they
heavily coat a spoon. (If the sauce seems
too thin add a little of the cornstarch
mixture.) Add the olives and livers and
heat through; do not let the sauce boil.
Taste and correct the seasoning. Discard
the *bouquet garni*, then pour the sauce
over the wings, sprinkle with the parsley
and the remaining minced garlic and
serve, with French bread and plenty of
napkins.

Notes

Ingredients

2 dozen frogs' legs
2 tablespoons wine vinegar
1 large head garlic
Milk
All-purpose flour
Salt and freshly ground white pepper
½ cup Clarified Butter (see page 213) or
    4 tablespoons butter and 2 tablespoons
    olive oil
2 tablespoons finely minced shallots
¾ cup Light Chicken Stock (see page 204)
1 cup heavy cream
Beurre Manié (see page 213)
Juice of 1 lemon

Garnish:
2 tablespoons finely minced fresh
    parsley (or parsley and chives)

Preparation

1. Put the frogs' legs in a large bowl and
cover with ice water. Add the vinegar
and let soak for 2 hours.

2. Break the garlic head into cloves; do
not peel.

3. Bring water to a boil in a small saucepan. Add the garlic cloves and cook for 2
minutes, or until very tender. Drain, then
press the cloves through a fine sieve into a
small bowl. Set the puree aside.

4. Dry the frogs' legs thoroughly. Dip in
milk and dredge in flour that has been
seasoned with salt and pepper.

5. Heat the butter or mixture of butter and
oil in a large, heavy skillet. Add the frogs'

legs (do not crowd the pan) and cook them over medium heat for 6 to 8 minutes, turning them once or twice to brown evenly. When all the frogs' legs are done, remove them to a serving dish, cover, and keep warm.

6. Discard all but 2 tablespoons of fat from the pan. Add the shallots and cook for 1 to 2 minutes, or until soft but not browned. Add the stock and bring to a boil, scraping the bottom of the pan well. Cook over high heat until the stock is reduced to ¼ cup, then add the cream. Bring back to a boil and add bits of *beurre manié,* just enough to thicken the sauce; it must heavily coat the spoon. Add the garlic puree, lemon juice, salt, and pepper. Taste the sauce and correct the seasoning.

7. Spoon the sauce over the frogs' legs, sprinkle with parsley, and serve immediately, accompanied by French bread.

Remarks

Chicken wings can be prepared in the same manner.

Notes

Frogs' legs in mustard sauce

Serves: 4
Preparation time: 10 minutes
Cooking time: 20 minutes

Though most of the great chefs in France claim never to cook frozen frogs' legs, I believe that in this case we have to work with what is available to us. Fresh frogs' legs are rarely available here. They are without a doubt far superior to the frozen variety, but when served as in this dish, with its highly seasoned sauce, they can be a smashing success.

Ingredients

2 dozen frogs' legs
2 tablespoons vinegar
All-purpose flour
Salt and freshly ground white pepper
Milk
½ cup Clarified Butter (see page 213)
2 tablespoons finely minced shallots
¼ cup white wine
1 cup Crème Fraîche (see page 206)
2 tablespoons Dijon mustard

Optional:
Beurre Manié (see page 213)

Garnish:
2 tablespoons finely minced fresh parsley

Preparation

1. Put the frogs' legs in a large bowl and cover with ice-cold water. Add the vinegar and let soak for 2 hours.

2. In a shallow bowl combine the flour with salt and pepper. Dip the frogs' legs, drained and well dried, in milk and then into the seasoned flour.

3. Heat the butter in a large, heavy skillet. Add the frogs' legs (do not crowd the pan)

and sauté them over medium heat for 8 to 10 minutes, turning them to brown evenly. As soon as the frogs' legs are done, remove them to a serving platter and keep warm.

4. Discard all but 2 tablespoons of fat from the pan. Add the shallots and cook for 1 or 2 minutes, or until soft but not browned. Add the wine, then raise the heat and cook, scraping the bottom of the pan well, until all the wine has evaporated. Add the *crème fraîche* and cook until it is slightly reduced, then add the *beurre manié*, bit by bit, until the sauce is thick and coats a spoon heavily. Lower the heat and whisk in the mustard, salt, and pepper, then whisk the sauce until it is smooth; do not let it come to a boil. Taste and correct the seasoning.

5. Spoon the sauce over the frogs' legs, garnish with the parsley, and serve immediately with fresh French bread.

Remarks

Sea squabs and chicken wings can be prepared in the same manner.

Notes

Lamb shanks à la fermière

Serves: 4
Preparation time: 35 minutes
Cooking time: 1 hour and 45 minutes
◼◯

Ingredients

4   small lamb shanks
3   cloves garlic, cut into slivers
1   teaspoon rosemary, plus 1 small sprig fresh rosemary
Salt and freshly ground black pepper
Flour for dredging
1   cup salt pork, cubed
4 to 6 small turnips, peeled and cubed
6   Brussels sprouts, well cleaned
2 to 3 medium potatoes, peeled and cubed
1   cup carrots, peeled and cut into 1½-inch matchsticks
4   tablespoons olive oil
1½ cups finely minced onions
1   teaspoon sugar
1½ pounds ripe tomatoes, peeled, seeded and chopped
½   teaspoon thyme
1   bay leaf
¼   teaspoon marjoram
2 to 3 cups Brown Stock (see page 202) or beef bouillon

Garnish:
2   tablespoons minced fresh parsley, plus one sprig

Optional:
Beurre Manié (see page 213)

Preparation

1. Preheat the oven to 375 degrees.

2. Cut deep slits into the lamb shanks. Insert slivers of garlic and a little rosemary into each one, season with salt and pepper, dredge lightly in flour and set aside.

3. Bring 3 cups of water to boil, add the salt pork and cook over high heat for 5 minutes. Drain and reserve. In another saucepan bring 8 cups of water to boil, season with salt, and add the turnips, Brussels sprouts, potatoes, and carrots. Cook for 8 minutes; drain and set aside.

4. Heat the oil in a large, heavy casserole, add the salt pork and cook until almost crisp. Add the parboiled vegetables and toss them in the fat until they are lightly browned. Remove vegetables and salt pork with a slotted spoon and place on a side dish.

5. Add a little more oil to the casserole and add the lamb shanks, two at a time. Do not crowd the casserole, but brown them well on all sides. Remove lamb shanks to a side dish.

6. Discard all but two tablespoons of fat from the casserole, add the onions and cook over medium heat for 3 to 4 minutes or until soft. Sprinkle with sugar, salt and pepper and continue browning for another 10 minutes, being careful not to let them burn. Add the tomatoes, thyme, bay leaf, marjoram and a sprig of parsley, bring to a boil and return the shanks to the casserole. If you have fresh rosemary, bury a small sprig in the pan. Add the stock to cover the shanks by at least one inch. Cover the casserole, set in the middle part of the oven and braise for 1 hour to 1 hour and 15 minutes, or until the shanks are almost tender.

7. Add the vegetables and salt pork to the casserole, return to the oven and continue braising until both the vegetables and shanks are done. Taste pan juices and correct the seasoning. Discard the parsley sprig and bay leaf. Place the casserole over direct heat and beat in the *beurre manié* until the sauce is thick and heavily coats the spoon. Serve directly from the casserole or arrange in a deep dish. Sprinkle with parsley and serve with French bread and a bowl of sweet butter.

Notes

fish

For anyone growing up in a Mediterranean country, seafood is an important part of the everyday diet. There is nothing more beautiful than an open marketplace and a fish stand brimming with the catch from the sea, baskets lined with fig leaves and filled with clams, oysters, fish, and crustaceans. The Bouquería Market of Barcelona is the pride of the city. It is there that I learned most of what I know about fish and its incredible versatility. It is here that one understands why the *paella* and the *zarzuella* have become classics. Both combine several kinds of fish and shellfish into one spectacular dish.

In all countries bordering the Mediterranean, fish is the single most important category of food, and the vast supply of different fish has influenced the peasant cuisines of these countries. Fish soups and stews are in abundance, and some classics such as the bouillabaisse have become world famous. In Italy seafood has been combined successfully with pasta and rice.

The Atlantic, so much richer in seafood than the Mediterranean, has influenced the cuisines of Northern Europe as well as northern Spain and Portugal. Scandinavians have made marvelous use of the sea and its offerings. Herrings are prepared in innumerable ways, and smoked fish, such as eel and sturgeon, are delicacies of the haute cuisine. England has also made a worthy contribution to the world of fish by giving us the glorious smoked salmon and trout. As for France, fish, almost more than any other food, has inspired many of its chefs to create great classics, often in combination with elaborate sauces.

America is as rich in seafood as Europe. We have an abundance of both freshwater and saltwater fish, as well as marvelous shellfish. But although we have some good fish dishes, such as clam chowder and creole gumbos, most Americans are not familiar with more than two or three varieties of seafood, and have not inherited the adventurous spirit of European cooks. It is sad to see that the usual fare of a restaurant menu consists mostly of fish prepared in the most basic and unexciting way.

In this meat-and-potato country, many people have been slow to realize that fish is both extremely nutritious and as high in protein as meat. Good fresh fish makes an excellent one-dish meal, and needs no other accompaniment but fresh bread and a glass of wine.

Freshness of fish and shellfish is absolutely essential. Generally, one can tell freshness of fish by its odor, the brightness of the eyes, and the pink color of the gills, as well as by the firmness of the flesh and the high sheen of the scales. When in doubt, place the fish in a large bowl of cold water. Fresh fish will float.

Try to buy fish at a reputable fish market. Do not buy frozen fish. If you have to buy fish at a supermarket, open the package as soon as you get home and refrigerate, lightly covered, letting the air circulate around the fish. It is best to cook fish the same day it is bought. If this is not possible, refrigerate it on a bed of ice and rinse under cold water before using.

Poached bass à l'antiboise

Serves: 4 to 6
Preparation time: 10 minutes
Cooking time: 55 minutes to 1 hour

■●

Ingredients

½ cup olive oil
Juice of 1 large lemon
1 ripe tomato, finely cubed
Salt and freshly ground white pepper
2 tablespoons finely minced fresh chervil
    or 1 teaspoon dried
1 striped bass (2½ to 3 pounds)
4 to 6 cups water
2 to 3 tablespoons white wine vinegar
1 onion, coarsely sliced
1 carrot, peeled and sliced
1 stalk celery, sliced
1 bay leaf
Sprigs of fresh parsley
1 sprig fresh thyme or ½ teaspoon dried
5 peppercorns
Whole coriander seeds
Lemon quarters

Preparation

1. In a small mixing bowl combine the
olive oil, lemon juice, tomato, salt, pepper,
and chervil. Set aside.

2. Season the fish with salt and pepper,
wrap in cheesecloth, and set aside.

3. In a large, flameproof baking dish
combine 4 cups of water with 2 tablespoons
vinegar, the vegetables, bay leaf, a sprig
of parsley, the thyme, peppercorns, and a
pinch of salt. Bring to a boil, reduce the
heat and simmer, partially covered, for
25 minutes.

4. Add the fish in its cheesecloth wrapping;
the liquid must barely cover it. If it doesn't
add more water and vinegar. Cover the

dish with foil and simmer the fish over
low heat for 20 to 25 minutes. Test it for
doneness by piercing it with the tip of a
sharp knife; the fish should flake easily.

5. Remove the pan from the heat and let
the fish cool in the poaching liquid. Carefully unwrap the fish. Transfer it to a
serving platter, wiping away any liquid
that may accumulate on the platter. Pour
the dressing over the fish, sprinkle with a
heavy grinding of coriander (see below)
and garnish with additional sprigs of
parsley and lemon quarters. Serve warm
or at room temperature.

Remarks

Do not use ground coriander. Buy the
whole coriander seeds that look like white
peppercorns. Put them in a peppermill and
grind the coriander over the fish.

Notes

Baked bass alla molinera

Serves: 4 to 6
Preparation time: 20 minutes
Cooking time: 45 minutes

Ingredients

1   striped bass (3 pounds)
Salt and freshly ground black pepper
Finely minced parsley
2   large cloves garlic, finely minced
4 to 5 lemon slices
½ cup olive oil
2   medium onions, peeled and thinly
    sliced
4   medium all-purpose potatoes, peeled
    and thinly sliced
1   bay leaf
1   large sprig fresh thyme or ¾ teaspoon
    dried
½ cup white wine

Optional:
2   ripe tomatoes, quartered

Garnish:
Finely minced parsley

Preparation

1. Preheat the oven to 350 degrees.

2. Have the fish market clean the bass without splitting it open. Rinse the fish out thoroughly, then make 3 vertical incisions on one side about ½ inch deep. Season with salt and pepper and set aside.

3. In a small bowl combine 3 tablespoons of parsley and the garlic. Cut the lemon slices in half, dip into the parsley mixture and place them in the incisions in the fish. Set aside again.

4. Heat the oil in a large, heavy, flameproof baking dish. Add the onions and cook over low heat for 2 or 3 minutes, until soft but not browned. Add the potatoes, toss them with the onions, and season with salt and pepper. Remove the pan from the heat. Arrange the fish in the dish, then add the bay leaf, thyme, and the remaining parsley mixture. Dribble with a little wine.

5. Place the dish in the oven and bake for 35 minutes, adding a little white wine every 10 minutes and basting the fish with the pan juices.

6. Heat the broiler.

7. Arrange the optional tomatoes in the dish, and broil the fish for another 10 minutes, basting it two or 3 times with the pan juices. Remove the pan from the oven, sprinkle with additional minced parsley and a grinding of black pepper.

8. Serve immediately, directly from the baking dish.

Notes

Baked bass al porto

Serves: 6
Preparation time: 45 minutes
Cooking time: 50 minutes to 1 hour

■ ●

Here is a dish that is suitable for an important dinner party or a small buffet party. The dish was created by the chef of Al Porto, a small fish restaurant on the outskirts of Milan, where I spent several days cooking and sampling their marvelous specialties.

Ingredients

18 to 24 fresh, medium-sized mussels
¾ cup Fish Stock (see page 204)
¼ cup olive oil
12 shrimp, cleaned and diced
3 tablespoons finely minced shallots
1 teaspoon finely minced garlic
½ cup finely minced fresh parsley
2 to 3 small squid, cleaned and thinly sliced
2 cups Fresh Tomato Sauce (see page 207)
1 teaspoon dried oregano
2 tablespoons finely minced fresh basil or 1 teaspoon dried
Salt and freshly ground black pepper
1 bass (3 pounds)
All-purpose flour

Optional:
Beurre Manié (see page 213)

Preparation

1. Scrub the mussels thoroughly under cold running water, and place in a large bowl. Cover with cold water, and soak for 2 or 3 hours.

2. Drain and reserve. In a large saucepan, combine the fish stock and drained mussels. Bring the stock to a boil, then reduce the heat and simmer the mussels, partially covered, until they open. Shell the mussels and set aside. Strain the stock through a double layer of cheesecloth and reserve ½ cup.

3. Heat the olive oil in a large, heavy skillet. Add the shrimp and cook them for 2 or 3 minutes, until they turn bright pink. Remove the shrimp to a side dish. To the oil in the pan add the shallots, garlic, and 3 tablespoons of the parsley. Cook until the mixture is soft but not browned, then add the squid and cook them for 2 minutes, or until the flesh turn opaque white. Remove squid to a side dish. Add to the pan the tomato sauce, reserved stock, oregano, basil, salt, and pepper, then reduce the heat and simmer the sauce, covered, for 15 minutes.

4. Preheat the oven to 375 degrees.

5. Season the bass with salt and pepper, then coat with flour on both sides and place in a well-oiled baking dish. Pour the tomato sauce around it and place the dish in the oven. Bake the fish for 35 to 40 minutes, basting it several times with the sauce. Ten minutes before the fish is done, add the mussels, shrimp and squid to the pan.

6. When the fish is done, remove it carefully to a serving platter. (If the sauce seems too thin, place the baking dish over direct heat and reduce the sauce until it coats the spoon thickly. Add little bits of *beurre manié* to thicken the sauce to the right consistency.) Pour the sauce over the fish, sprinkle with the remaining parsley, and serve immediately.

Herbed bass en papillote

Serves: 4 to 6
Preparation time: 15 minutes
Cooking time: 50 minutes

There are innumerable and easy ways to prepare fish, yet somehow it is rarely served at a dinner party. Many hostesses do not consider fish "substantial" enough as a main course, and assume that it is too much work to prepare fish as an appetizer. This is definitely not so, and here is an example.

Ingredients

8   tablespoons softened butter
2   cloves garlic, finely minced
2   tablespoons finely minced fresh parsley
2   tablespoons finely minced shallots
2   tablespoons finely minced fennel tops (optional)
1   bass (2½ to 3 pounds) cleaned but with head and tail left on
Salt and freshly ground white pepper
Juice of 1 lemon
1   tablespoon finely minced fresh thyme or ½ teaspoon dried
1   bay leaf
1   large sprig fresh parsley

Garnish:
2 to 3 lemons, quartered

Preparation

1. In a bowl combine the butter, garlic, minced parsley, and shallots. Add the optional fennel tops, then beat the mixture with a wooden spoon until it is smooth and well blended. Set aside.

2. Preheat the oven to 400 degrees.

3. Dry the fish thoroughly with paper towels. Season it with salt and pepper, sprinkle it with lemon juice, and place the thyme, bay leaf, and parsley sprig inside the cavity.

4. Arrange a large piece of paper or foil in a shallow baking dish. (The paper must be large enough to wrap the entire fish securely.) Rub the paper with half the herb butter, then place the fish on the paper and dot it with the remaining butter. Enclose the fish in the paper or foil, seal the edges of the paper securely, and bake the fish for 50 minutes.

5. Place the fish carefully, in its paper, on a serving platter and serve immediately, right out of the paper, with French bread and a side dish of quartered lemons.

Remarks

You may use 1 tablespoon of finely minced fresh mint in addition to the parsley, shallots, garlic, and butter. The freshness of the herbs is essential to this simple dish; they will permeate the fish and their aroma will envelop your guests when the paper is opened.

Notes

Poached bass à la villefranche

Serves: 4 to 6
Preparation time: 25 minutes (plus 2 to 4
hours "curdling" time)
Cooking time: 1 hour

Villefranche sur Mer in the south of France
is still one of those fishing villages one
dreams about. It is not completely un-
spoilt but it still retains an immense charm
and some good seafood. Here is an adaptation of a sauce that is served with the
famous Mediterranean *loup de mer*, a type
of bass that unfortunately is getting scarce.

Ingredients

1   striped bass (2½ to 3 pounds)

The sauce:
1½ cups heavy cream
Juice of 1 lemon
1   tablespoon all-purpose flour
2   tablespoons butter
3   egg yolks
2   shallots, finely minced
1   tablespoon minced fresh chervil
     or ½ teaspoon dried
1   tablespoon minced fresh parsley
1   tablespoon finely minced fresh tarragon
     or ½ teaspoon dried
Salt and freshly ground white pepper
4 to 6 cups water
2   tablespoons white wine vinegar
1   onion, coarsely sliced
1   carrot, peeled and sliced
1   stalk celery, sliced
1   bay leaf
Sprigs of fresh parsley
1   large sprig fresh thyme or ¾ teaspoon
     dried

Garnish:
5   peppercorns
Lemon quarters
Additional parsley sprigs

Preparation

1. In a mixing bowl combine the cream
and lemon juice and let the mixture stand
at room temperature for 2 to 4 hours.

2. Combine the flour and butter in a small
bowl. Mash with a fork until the mixture
is reduced to a smooth paste, then set
aside.

3. In the top part of a double boiler
combine the egg yolks, butter-flour paste,
and cream and lemon mixture. Place the
saucepan over barely simmering water
and cook, whisking constantly, until the
sauce is thick. (Do not let it come to a boil
or the yolks will curdle.) Add the shallots
and herbs, then season with salt and
pepper. Keep warm.

4. In a large, deep, flameproof baking
dish combine the water, vinegar, vegetables, bay leaf, a large sprig of parsley,
the thyme, peppercorns, and a large pinch
of salt. Bring to a boil, then reduce the
heat and simmer for 25 minutes.

5. Season the fish with salt and pepper
and wrap it in cheesecloth. Place in the
baking dish, cover loosely with foil, and
cook over very low heat for 20 to 25
minutes. Test the fish; it is done when it
flakes easily when tested with the tip of a
sharp knife.

6. Remove the fish carefully to a serving
platter and discard the cheesecloth.
Remove the skin and wipe up any liquid
that may have accumulated on the platter.
Spoon the sauce over the fish, garnish
the platter with parsley sprigs and quartered lemons, and serve immediately.

Clams caesera

Serves: 4
Preparation time: 15 minutes
Cooking time: 1 hour

The clams usually used for this dish are the tiny, slightly oval-shaped clams that are found in abundance in Mediterranean markets but are unfortunately unavailable in this country. Nevertheless, it is extremely successful when made with littleneck clams. Serve it with plenty of French bread for dipping into the sauce.

Ingredients

4   dozen littleneck clams
½   cup olive oil
3   onions, peeled and finely minced
3   large cloves garlic, peeled and sliced
1   dried hot chili pepper, cut in half
Salt and freshly ground black pepper
2   tablespoons finely minced fresh parsley
½   cup white wine

Preparation

1. Scrub the clams thoroughly under cold running water. Set aside.

2. Heat the oil in a large, heavy skillet. Add the onions and cook the mixture over high heat for 2 minutes, then reduce the heat. Add the garlic cloves and chili pepper, season with salt and pepper, and simmer the mixture, covered, for 45 minutes, stirring frequently. After 45 minutes the onions should be "melted" and lightly browned. Add the parsley, uncover the pan, and cook for another 5 minutes. Set aside.

3. In a large, flameproof casserole combine the wine and clams. Bring to a boil, then reduce the heat and steam the clams, partially covered, until they open. Remove the clams and discard the top shells, leaving the clams on the bottoms. Arrange them on a round serving platter and set aside. Strain the broth through a fine sieve and set aside.

4. Reheat the onion mixture. Add 1½ cups of the clam broth, then bring to a boil and reduce the broth by one-fourth. Discard the chili pepper, then taste the sauce and correct the seasoning.

5. Pour the sauce over the clams and serve immediately, accompanied by French bread.

Remarks

The onion mixture can be prepared several hours ahead of time. The sauce should be quite spicy; test it for the first time with one chili pepper, but you may like two.

Notes

Cod steaks à la dijonnaise

Serves: 4
Preparation time: 10 minutes (plus 1 to 2 hours marinating time)
Cooking time: 15 minutes

Ingredients

4 small cod steaks (preferably from the end piece), cut ¾-inch thick
Salt and freshly ground white pepper
Juice of 1 lemon
1 tablespoon Dijon mustard
1½ cups heavy cream
5 tablespoons butter
½ pound fresh mushrooms, stems removed and thinly sliced
All-purpose flour
1 tablespoon olive oil
2 large shallots, finely minced
½ cup dry white wine
Beurre Manié (see page 213)
2 tablespoons finely minced parsley

Preparation

1. Season the cod steaks with salt and pepper. Sprinkle with lemon juice and let them stand in a cool place for 1 to 2 hours.

2. In a small bowl combine the mustard with ½ cup of the heavy cream, blend the mixture thoroughly and set aside.

3. Heat 2 tablespoons of the butter in a small skillet. Add the mushrooms and cook over high heat for 2 or 3 minutes, or until the mushrooms are nicely browned. Remove to a side dish.

4. Dry the fish steaks thoroughly with paper towels, then dredge lightly in flour, shaking off the excess.

5. Heat the remaining butter and oil in a large, heavy skillet until almost brown. Add the steaks and cook over medium heat for 3 to 4 minutes on each side; do not overcook. Remove the fish to a serving platter and keep warm.

6. Discard all but 2 tablespoons of fat from the pan. Add the shallots and cook for 1 to 2 minutes, or until soft but not browned. Add the wine and cook over high heat, scraping the bottom of the pan well, until it is reduced to 1 tablespoon. Add the remaining heavy cream and continue cooking until the cream is reduced by one-third, then add the *beurre manié* and cook, stirring, until the sauce is thick and smooth. Add the mushrooms, salt, and pepper and heat through, then add the mustard and cream mixture and whisk until the mustard is well incorporated in the sauce; do not let the sauce come to a boil. Taste and correct the seasoning.

7. Spoon the sauce over the fish and garnish with the minced parsley. Serve immediately, accompanied by crusty French bread or tiny new potatoes cooked until barely tender.

Notes

Soft-shell crabs rémoulade

Serves: 6
Preparation time: 25 minutes
Cooking time: 6 to 8 minutes

Most people seem to think the soft-shell crab is a distinct species of crab. It is not. Soft-shell crabs are the blue crabs that are found along the Atlantic coast and caught in the spring, after shedding their shell and before growing a new one. The season of soft-shell crabs is rather short, so take advantage of it as much as possible. They are delectable.

Ingredients

Rémoulade sauce:
2   cups Mayonnaise (see page 208)
1   tablespoon wine vinegar
2   tablespoons chili sauce
2   tablespoons finely minced chives
1   clove garlic, mashed
2   tablespoons well-drained capers
2   tablespoons finely minced green
    pepper
3   hard-boiled egg yolks, finely minced
Salt and freshly ground white pepper

12 small soft shell crabs, cleaned
Milk
All-purpose flour
Salt and freshly ground white pepper
Vegetable oil for deep frying

Garnish:
Sprigs of parsley
Lemon quarters

Preparation

1. In a bowl combine the mayonnaise, vinegar, chili sauce, chives, garlic, capers, green pepper, and egg yolks and blend well. Add salt and pepper to taste and chill the sauce until serving time.

2. Dip the crabs in milk, then dredge in flour seasoned with salt and pepper; shake off the excess flour.

3. Heat the oil in a large deep skillet or deep fryer; it should be at least 2 inches deep. Drop the soft-shell crabs into the hot oil and fry them for 2 or 3 minutes, or until they are nicely browned and crisp. Regulate the heat; the crabs should not cook too fast or they will burn.

4. Place the crabs on a round platter and place the sauce in a bowl in the center of the platter. Drop the parsley sprigs into the hot fat for 2 seconds, then remove and drain on paper towels. Top the crabs with the fried parsley and garnish the platter with quartered lemons.

Remarks

This dish requires last-minute preparation, though the sauce can be made one or two days in advance. Electric frying pans are usually the best for quick frying of shellfish or vegetables.

Notes

Soft-shell crabs niçoise

Serves: 4
Preparation time: 15 minutes
Cooking time: 8 to 10 minutes

■◆

Soft-shell crabs are a delicacy that requires the simplest of preparation. But they can be prepared with some creativity, such as with this typically Mediterranean garnish of mushrooms and tomatoes.

Ingredients

12 soft-shell crabs, cleaned
Salt and freshly ground black pepper
All-purpose flour
4   tablespoons butter
½   pound fresh mushrooms, finely sliced
2   tablespoons olive oil
¼   cup white wine
2   tablespoons finely minced shallots
1   cup Provençal Tomato Fondue
    (see page 207)
2   tablespoons finely minced fresh parsley

Garnish:
Lemon quarters

Preparation

1. Dry the crabs thoroughly with paper towels. Season them with salt and pepper, then dredge lightly in flour, shaking off the excess. Set aside.

2. Heat 2 tablespoons of the butter in a small, heavy skillet. Add the mushrooms and cook over high heat until they are lightly browned, then season with salt and pepper and set aside.

3. Heat the remaining butter and the oil in a large, heavy skillet. Add the crabs, a few at a time, and cook them over high heat for 2 or 3 minutes on each side, or until they are nicely browned. Remove the crabs to a side dish.

4. Lower the heat under the skillet and add the wine. Bring to a boil, scraping the bottom of the pan well, and reduce the wine to 1 tablespoon. Add the shallots and cook over moderate heat until soft. Add the tomato fondu and the mushrooms, stir the mixture, and heat through. Correct the seasoning.

5. Pour the tomato and mushroom mixture into the center of a round serving platter. Circle with the sautéed crabs, sprinkle with parsley, and garnish the platter with quartered lemons.

Notes

Grilled mackerel à la meridionale

Serves: 4
Preparation time: 15 minutes
Cooking time: 12 minutes

Mackerel are best in the spring, and should not be used unless perfectly fresh. I find Boston mackerel far superior to Spanish mackerel, which is larger and usually available year round. Because it is an oily fish of strong flavor, mackerel lends itself extremely well to grilling, and sauces for this fish should be highly seasoned.

Ingredients

4   small mackerel (1 pound each), filleted

Marinade:
Salt and freshly ground black pepper
½ cup olive oil
Juice of 1 lemon
1   small onion, thinly sliced
1   bay leaf, crumbled

Sauce:
1   raw egg yolk
1   hard-boiled egg yolk
1   teaspoon Dijon mustard
4 to 6 flat anchovy fillets, minced
1   large clove garlic, mashed
2   tablespoons wine vinegar
½ cup olive oil
1   tablespoon minced chives
1   tablespoon minced fresh parsley
2   tablespoons well-drained capers
1   tablespoon finely minced fresh tarragon
    or ¼ teaspoon fennel seed, crushed
Salt and freshly ground white pepper
2   tablespoons butter plus 1 tablespoon
    vegetable oil

Garnish:
Sprigs of fresh parsley
Lemon quarters

Preparation

1. Place the mackerel fillets in a shallow porcelain baking dish, skin side down. Sprinkle with salt and freshly ground black pepper, ½ cup of olive oil, the lemon juice, onion, and bay leaf. Cover the dish with foil and marinate the fish for 2 to 4 hours in the bottom of the refrigerator, turning it once.

2. In a mixing bowl combine the raw egg yolk, hard-boiled yolks, mustard, anchovies, garlic, and vinegar. Blend the mixture with a small electric hand mixer until it is smooth. Add the oil by droplets, beating constantly until it is thick and smooth. Add the chives, parsley, capers, and tarragon or fennel seed, then season with salt and pepper and chill until serving time.

3. Preheat the broiler.

4. In a large, shallow, flameproof baking dish, heat the butter and oil. Dry the mackerel fillets with paper towels, then arrange them, skin side up, in the dish. Place the dish 3 inches from the heat and cook the fish for 10 to 12 minutes, basting several times with the juices in the pan.

5. Carefully transfer the fish to a serving platter. Garnish with parsley and quartered lemons and serve the sauce on the side.

Cold mackerel à l'andalouse

Serves: 6
Preparation time: 15 minutes
Cooking time: 35 minutes

Ingredients

3   Boston mackerel (1½ pounds each),
    filleted
Salt and freshly ground black pepper
Juice of 1 lemon
3   tablespoons olive oil
2   large cloves garlic, peeled and crushed
1   cup thinly sliced white onion
4   ripe tomatoes, peeled, seeded,
    chopped, and drained
1   cup dry white wine
2   cups Fish Stock (see page 204)
1   Bouquet Garni (see page 214)
1   teaspoon saffron dissolved in 2
    tablespoons warm water
Dash of Tabasco

Garnish:

Thin lemon slices
Sprigs of fresh parsley

Preparation

1. Season the fish with salt and pepper
and sprinkle with lemon juice. Set aside.

2. Heat the oil in a large, enameled baking
dish. Add the garlic and cook until lightly
brown; do not let it burn. Add the onion
and cook until they are soft but not
browned, then add the tomatoes, wine,
stock, *bouquet garni*, saffron, salt, and
pepper. Bring to a boil, then reduce the
heat; cover the pan loosely with foil and
simmer for 15 minutes.

3. Preheat the oven to 350.

4. Add the fish fillets, skin side down.
Cover the dish with buttered waxed paper
and place in the oven. Bake for 12 minutes,
then test with the tip of a sharp knife; the
fish should flake easily. Remove the dish
from the oven, discard the *bouquet garni*,
and remove the fish carefully to a serving
dish. Place the baking dish over direct
heat and reduce the pan juices by one-
third. Taste and correct the seasoning,
adding a dash of Tabasco. Pour the sauce
over the fish and chill.

5. Serve well chilled, garnished with lemon
slices and parsley sprigs.

Notes

Brochettes of mussels au curry

Serves: 4 to 6
Preparation time: 45 minutes
Cooking time: 25 minutes

Since mussels are the least expensive of our shellfish, I am always looking for new ways to prepare them. This is an appetizer I recently discovered around the Marseilles area. Though I realize it is somewhat tedious to shell mussels, I find the result well worth the effort.

Ingredients

36 to 48 mussels, well cleaned and
    scrubbed
All-purpose flour
Salt and freshly ground white pepper
3 eggs, beaten lightly
Soft, fresh bread crumbs or commercial
    unflavored bread crumbs
4 tablespoons butter
3 tablespoons vegetable oil

Curry sauce:

1½ cups Mayonnaise (see page 208)
1 to 2 teaspoons curry powder
1 tablespoon finely minced chives or
    scallion
1 tablespoon finely minced dill gherkin
1 tablespoon finely minced, well-drained
    tiny capers
Pinch of cayenne pepper

Garnish:

Sprigs of fresh parsley
2 lemons, quartered

Preparation

1. Preheat the oven to 325 degrees.

2. Place the mussels in a large heatproof casserole with 1 cup of cold water. Set the casserole in the center of the oven and steam the mussels until they open, about 20 minutes. Shell the mussels carefully, so as not to break them, then let dry on a double layer of paper towels.

3. To make the sauce, combine the mayonnaise, curry powder, chives, gherkin, and capers in a small serving bowl. Add a pinch of cayenne pepper, then blend the mixture well. Taste and correct the seasoning, adding more curry if you like.

4. On a large plate combine flour with a good pinch each of salt and pepper. Coat the mussels first with flour, then drop them into the beaten egg and roll them in bread crumbs. Chill the mussels for at least an hour before frying.

5. Heat the butter and oil in a deep, heavy skillet. Add the mussels, a few at a time, and sauté them over medium heat until they are nicely browned on both sides. With a slotted spoon, carefully remove the mussels as they are done to a double layer of paper towels, and continue sautéing until all the mussels are done.

6. "String" 8 mussels on a wooden skewer and place each skewer on an individual plate. Garnish with a sprig of parsley and a quartered lemon. Serve the sauce on the side.

fish

Cold salmon steaks in cucumber sauce
Serves: 4 to 6
Preparation time: 30 minutes
Cooking time: 15 minutes

Many people consider trout the finest of fish, but personally I find salmon by far the best! Aside from its versatility, it has a remarkable affinity to almost all vegetables, and is equally good cold or hot.

Ingredients
1½ cucumbers
Salt
2   tablespoons white wine vinegar
2   tablespoons butter
1   carrot, thinly sliced
1   onion, thinly sliced
4   cups water
Sprigs of fresh parsley
Sprigs of fresh dill
1   bay leaf
6   peppercorns
4 to 6 salmon steaks (preferably from the
      end piece), cut ¾-inch thick
Freshly ground white pepper
2   cups Mayonnaise (see page 208)
½   cup Crème Fraîche (see page 206)
2   tablespoons finely minced fresh herbs
      (chives, dill, and chervil)

Garnish:
Lemon quarters
Sprigs of fresh dill or parsley

Preparation
1. Peel the 1½ cucumbers, then cut in half lengthwise. With a grapefruit spoon scoop out all the seeds, and finely slice. Place the slices in a strainer. Sprinkle with salt and 1 tablespoon of the vinegar and set aside to drain for 30 minutes to an hour.

Remarks
The sauce can be made several days ahead of time, or leftover sauce can be served as a dip or as an accompaniment to cold poached fish or hard-boiled eggs. The mussels can be cooked a day in advance, but should be served as soon as they have been fried.

Notes

2. Melt the butter in a shallow, flameproof baking dish. Add the carrot and onion and cook the mixture over low heat for 2 or 3 minutes. Add the 4 cups of water, the remaining vinegar, a large sprig each parsley and dill, the bay leaf, and peppercorns. Bring the mixture to a boil, add a pinch of salt, then reduce the heat and simmer the mixture, covered, for 15 minutes.

3. Season the salmon steaks with salt and freshly ground white pepper. Place them, in one layer, in the baking dish, and add enough water to the liquid to cover them. Cover the baking dish with foil and bring the liquid to a boil. Cook over high heat for exactly 2 minutes, then remove the pan from the heat and let the fish steaks cool completely in the poaching liquid. Chill.

4. While the fish is cooling, measure 1 cup of sliced cucumber, reserving the rest, and dry thoroughly in a paper towel. Mince it fine, and set aside.

5. In a mixing bowl combine the mayonnaise, *crème fraîche*, and herbs. Add the minced cucumber, taste the sauce, and correct the seasoning.

6. An hour before serving, remove the salmon steaks from the poaching liquid. Place them on a serving platter, and wipe up any liquid that accumulates on the platter with paper towels. Spoon the cucumber mayonnaise over the salmon steaks, covering them completely with the sauce. Sprinkle with the remaining cucumber slices and garnish the platter with additional sprigs of fresh dill or parsley and quartered lemons.

Remarks

For an interesting variation, substitute ½ cup cooked fresh peas and ½ cup finely diced, cooked carrots for the cucumber.

Notes

Scallops à l'antiboise

Serves: 4 to 6
Preparation time: 30 minutes
Cooking time: 10 minutes

■◕

One or two scallop dishes such as scallops *à la parisienne* (with mushrooms and a white wine sauce) and scallops *à la provençale* (in a garlic and herb butter) have actually become classics over the years, and are featured on the menus of most French restaurants. The delicate flavor of the scallop lends itself to many other excellent preparations. Here is an example:

Ingredients

6   Italian plum tomatoes, peeled and
      seeded, or 4 small garden tomatoes
Salt
1½ pounds sea scallops
Freshly ground white pepper
All-purpose flour
½ cup Clarified Butter (see page 213)
8   small mushrooms, thinly sliced
2   tablespoons finely minced shallots
1   teaspoon finely minced garlic
2   tablespoons finely minced fresh parsley
Freshly ground black pepper

Preparation

1. If you are not using Italian plum tomatoes, seed the garden tomatoes gently so as to retain their shape, then cut each one lengthwise into four pieces. Cut the Italian tomatoes into halves lengthwise. Sprinkle the tomatoes with salt, and let them drain in a colander.

2. Dry the scallops thoroughly on paper towels. Season them with salt and white pepper and dredge them lightly in flour, shaking off the excess.

3. Heat the butter in a large, heavy skillet. Add the scallops and cook them over high heat until they are nicely browned on both sides, then remove from the skillet and set aside. Add the mushroom slices and cook over high heat until they are browned, then reduce the heat, add the shallots, garlic, and tomatoes, and cook until the tomatoes are just heated through; they must retain their shape and not get mushy. Return the scallops to the pan and sprinkle with the parsley and a heavy grinding of black pepper. Heat them through for 1 minute and serve immediately, right out of the skillet, accompanied by French bread and a well-chilled white wine.

Remarks

This dish requires last-minute preparation, but it is well worth the effort.

Notes

Scallops in mustard mayonnaise

Serves: 4
Preparation time: 10 minutes
Cooking time: 30 minutes

I have recently discovered that one of the best ways to prepare scallops is to steam them in a vegetable steamer placed over a court-bouillon of aromatic vegetables. The scallops remain moist and juicy and can be served with different sauces, either hot or cold, such as the mustard mayonnaise given below.

Ingredients

Mustard mayonnaise:
2 whole eggs
1½ teaspoons tarragon vinegar
Salt and freshly ground white pepper
1 teaspoon Dijon mustard
1½ teaspoons to 2 teaspoons hot prepared mustard
¾ to 1 cup vegetable oil

The court-bouillon:
2 cups water
½ cup white wine
1 tablespoon tarragon vinegar
1 onion, thinly sliced
1 carrot, peeled and thinly sliced
½ cup chopped celery
1 bay leaf
1 large sprig fresh parsley
Large pinch of salt
5 peppercorns
1 pound sea scallops
Salt

Garnish:
Quartered lemons

Preparation

1. Start by making the mayonnaise. In the container of a blender combine the eggs, vinegar, salt, pepper, and mustards. Blend the mixture at high speed for 30 seconds, then, still blending, add the oil by driblets, until the sauce is thick and smooth. Correct the seasoning (it must be quite strong), adding a little more hot mustard if the sauce seems bland. Reserve.

2. To make the court-bouillon, combine the water, wine, vinegar, vegetables, bay leaf, parsley, salt, and peppercorns in a flame-proof casserole. Bring to a boil, then reduce the heat and simmer, partially covered, for 25 minutes, or until the carrots are tender.

3. Lower a vegetable steamer into the liquid. Add the scallops in one layer and sprinkle with salt, then cover the casserole and steam the scallops for 3 to 5 minutes, or until they turn an opaque white. Do not overcook.

4. Transfer the scallops to a warm serving dish, wiping off the moisture that accumulates with a paper towel. Take the sliced carrots from the bouillon with a slotted spoon and arrange on the platter. Spoon the sauce over both scallops and carrots. Garnish the platter with quartered lemons and serve immediately, accompanied by French bread.

Notes

Coquilles st. jacques in shallot butter

Serves: 6
Preparation time: 30 minutes
Cooking time: 15 minutes

An excellent if rather expensive appetizer for last-minute entertainment. It is quickly prepared, and the result is both elegant and delicious.

Ingredients

3 large shallots, finely minced
¾ cup dry white wine
10 tablespoons softened butter
2 tablespoons finely minced fresh tarragon
1 tablespoon finely minced fresh chervil
Salt and freshly ground white pepper
36 to 42 bay scallops
½ cup soft, fresh bread crumbs
1 tablespoon finely minced fresh parsley
1 teaspoon finely minced garlic

Preparation

1. Combine the shallots and wine in a small, heavy saucepan. Cook the mixture over high heat until it is reduced to 2 tablespoons, then remove from the heat.

2. In a bowl combine 7 tablespoons of the butter with a little of the shallot mixture. Add the tarragon, chervil, salt, and pepper and blend well.

3. Rub the inside of 6 scallop shells or dishes with the tarragon butter. Top with 6 to 7 scallops, sprinkle them with salt and pepper, and top with the remaining butter. Set aside.

4. Heat the remaining butter in a small skillet. Add the bread crumbs, parsley, and garlic and cook the mixture for 1 minute, stirring until it is well blended.

5. Preheat the broiler.

6. Set the scallop shells under the broiler, about 5 to 6 inches from the flame, and broil for 5 minutes. Sprinkle the scallops with a little of the bread crumb mixture, then return them to the oven for another 2 minutes, or until the bread crumbs are lightly browned.

7. Serve the scallops immediately, with French bread and a well chilled dry white wine.

Notes

Brochettes of scallops in green peppercorn sauce

Serves: 4 to 6
Preparation time: 25 minutes
Cooking time: 15 minutes

Green peppercorns have suddenly become the "in" spice on most French menus. They are often used indiscriminately on anything from ducks to fish. I was therefore somewhat skeptical when I first had this dish, but was pleasantly surprised. Neither the bacon nor the peppercorns should overpower the delicate flavor of the scallops.

Ingredients

3 large egg yolks
1 tablespoon cold butter
2 teaspoons tarragon vinegar
Salt and freshly ground white pepper
1¼ cups hot melted butter
1 to 1½ teaspoons crushed green
     peppercorns
16 to 24 one-inch cubes of bacon
20 to 30 large sea scallops
Freshly ground black pepper
Juice of 1 lemon

Garnish:
Lemon quarters
Parsley

Preparation

1. In the top part of a double boiler combine the egg yolks, cold butter, vinegar, salt, and white pepper. Place the pan over simmering water and beat with a whisk or electric hand beater until the mixture is thick and a faint steam rises from the pan. (Be careful not to overheat it, or the yolks will curdle.) Add 1 cup of the melted butter by droplets, beating constantly. When all the butter is absorbed and the

sauce is thick and smooth, remove the pan from the heat and add the crushed peppercorns. Taste and correct the seasoning, then place the saucepan in warm water until serving time.

2. Bring water to a boil in a small saucepan. Add the bacon cubes and blanch them for 5 minutes, then drain and dry well on paper towels.

3. Preheat the broiler.

4. Alternate the scallops and bacon on wooden skewers, starting with a scallop, then a piece of bacon, a scallop, and so forth. Season with salt and pepper. Put the skewers in a baking dish and sprinkle with the remaining ¼ cup melted butter and lemon juice, then place the baking dish under the broiler, about 6 to 8 inches from the source of heat. Broil the brochettes for 6 minutes on one side, then turn and broil for 5 minutes on the other side, basting them two or three times with the pan juices.

5. Place the brochettes on a round serving platter, with a bowl of the sauce arranged in the center. Garnish the platter with lemon quarters and sprigs of parsley and serve immediately.

Remarks

You may substitute mushroom caps for the bacon cubes or use both. The sauce can be made well in advance and kept warm. Whisk it from time to time if it seems to separate.

fish

Brochettes of shrimp in tarragon butter

Serves: 6
Preparation time: 20 minutes
Cooking time: 12 to 15 minutes

Since shrimp is by far the most popular shellfish in this country, I often wonder why most restaurants serve them so unimaginatively. Here is a pleasant change from the ever-present shrimp cocktail with its monotonous sauce . . .

Ingredients

1 cup softened butter
3 tablespoons finely minced fresh tarragon leaves
2 tablespoons finely minced fresh parsley
Juice of 1 lemon
1 teaspoon Dijon mustard
Salt and freshly ground black pepper
30 large raw shrimp, peeled
15 slices of bacon, each cut in half

Garnish:
Lemon quarters

Preparation

1. In a small saucepan combine the butter, tarragon, parsley, lemon juice, and mustard. Add salt and a heavy grinding of black pepper and simmer the mixture for 2 to 3 minutes. Set aside.

2. Preheat the broiler.

3. Season the shrimp with salt and pepper, then wrap each one in half a slice of bacon and thread on wooden skewers. Place the brochettes in a baking dish and dribble half the tarragon butter over them, keep the remaining butter warm. Place the pan under the broiler, 3 to 4 inches from the source of heat, and broil

the shrimp for 6 to 7 minutes on each side, basting them several times with the butter in the pan.

4. Place the brochettes on a serving platter, pour the remaining butter over them, and garnish with lemon quarters. Serve immediately.

Remarks

For a more substantial course, the shrimp brochettes can be served on a bed of curry-flavored rice.

Notes

Sautéed shrimp tasca

Serves: 6
Preparation time: 30 minutes
Cooking time: 2 to 3 minutes

The *tasca* is a way of life in Spain. It is a bar with a long counter displaying innumerable hors d'oeuvres, both hot and cold, a place where Spaniards nibble on *tapas* and drink a glass of wine or two before dinner. *Tapas* are Spain's contribution to the hors d'oeuvre world, some of which can easily be prepared at home. Here is an old-time favorite of mine.

Remarks

This is an appetizer that must be prepared at the last minute, and is therefore most suitable for serving in the living room or on a terrace with pre-dinner drinks. The shrimp must be quite spicy, so do not skimp on chili peppers. It is best to test the dish once before making it for guests.

Notes

Ingredients

1½ pounds small shrimp
Coarse salt
2 to 3 whole, dried hot chili peppers
6 large cloves garlic, peeled and halved
¾ cup fruity olive oil
1 tablespoon finely minced fresh parsley

Preparation

1. Peel and devein the shrimp. Dry them thoroughly in paper towels, then sprinkle with salt and set aside. Break the chili peppers in half; slice the garlic cloves in half. Set aside.

2. Heat the oil in 6 individual flameproof dishes until it is almost smoking. Add half a chili pepper, 2 pieces of garlic, and 6 to 8 shrimp to each dish. Sauté, uncovered, for 1 or 2 minutes, or until the shrimp turn pink, turning them once with a wooden spoon. Immediately remove from the heat, sprinkle with parsley, and serve piping hot directly from the dishes, accompanied by French bread and a glass of chilled white wine.

Baked red snapper in sauce russe

Serves: 4
Preparation time: 25 minutes
Cooking time: 40 minutes

Sorrel is widely used in Russian cooking, where the sauce used in this dish originated. Here is a French adaptation of a cold sorrel sauce that with the addition of fresh herbs becomes an elegant accompaniment to grilled or baked fish. It goes equally well with hard-boiled eggs, and I often serve it as a dip for raw vegetables.

Ingredients

1   red snapper (2½ to 3 pounds)
Salt and freshly ground black pepper
Juice of 1 lemon
1   teaspoon fennel seed
3   tablespoons olive oil
2   tablespoons butter
¼   cup white wine

Sauce russe:
2   cups fresh sorrel leaves, tightly packed
3   hard-boiled egg yolks
1   raw egg yolk
1½ tablespoons tarragon vinegar
½   tablespoon Dijon mustard
¾   cup olive oil
1   tablespoon finely minced fresh tarragon
2   tablespoons finely minced chives
1   tablespoon finely minced fresh parsley
Salt and freshly ground pepper

Garnish:
Sprigs of fresh parsley
Lemon quarters

Preparation

1. Start with the sauce. Wash the sorrel leaves thoroughly under cold water. Place in a saucepan and cook over low heat until the sorrel "melts" and is reduced to a soft puree. Pour the sorrel into a strainer and let cool.

2. In the container of a blender combine the egg yolks, raw egg, vinegar, and mustard. Blend the mixture at top speed for 30 seconds. Turn speed to low and add the olive oil by droplets until the sauce is thick and smooth. Add the sorrel and blend the mixture at top speed for 30 seconds.

3. Pour the sauce into a bowl. Add the herbs, salt, and pepper, taste and correct the seasoning. Set aside.

4. Season the fish with salt, pepper, and lemon juice. Sprinkle the cavity with fennel seed.

5. Preheat the oven to 350 degrees.

6. Heat the olive oil and butter in a large baking dish until it is foaming. Place the fish in the dish. Baste with the oil in the pan and bake for 25 minutes, adding 2 tablespoons of wine every 10 minutes and basting the fish several times with the pan juices.

7. Preheat the broiler.

8. Run the fish under the broiler for 3 to 4 minutes, or until the top is nicely browned. Do not overcook.

9. Carefully transfer the fish to a serving platter. Pour the pan juices over, garnish with parsley and lemon quarters, and serve with the sauce on the side.

(continued)

Fillets of sole à la basquaise

Serves: 4 to 6
Preparation time: 20 minutes
Cooking time: 20 minutes

Though Basque cooking is usually a robust and simple cuisine, it also offers dishes of great refinement. I was quite taken with this dish, which illustrates the flair of that region's cooking.

Ingredients

2   egg yolks
1   teaspoon cornstarch
½   cup plus ½ tablespoon water
4 to 6 medium-sized fillets of sole
Salt and freshly ground white pepper
2   tablespoons butter
2   tablespoons finely minced shallots
½   green pepper, cored, seeded and thinly
    sliced
2   ripe tomatoes, peeled, seeded and
    finely chopped
½   cup finely diced prosciutto
1   bay leaf
Pinch of dried thyme
½   cup white wine
¾   cup hot melted butter

Garnish:
2   tablespoons finely minced fresh parsley

Preparation

1. Combine the egg yolks and cornstarch in a small bowl. Add the ½ tablespoon water and whisk the mixture until it is smooth and well blended. Set aside.

2. Season the fillets with salt and pepper and set aside.

3. Heat the butter in a large, heavy, flame-proof baking dish. Add the shallots, green

Remarks

To vary the recipe and for easier serving, have the fish market fillet the fish. Bake for 12 minutes and serve with the sauce poured over the fish. Serve with French bread as an appetizer or as a main course with small new potatoes cooked until barely tender.

Notes

Stuffed squid al porto

Serves: 6
Preparation time: 25 minutes
Cooking time: 1 hour

pepper, tomatoes, prosciutto, bay leaf
and thyme. Cook for 2 minutes, then add
the wine and ½ cup water and bring to
a boil. Reduce the heat and add the fillets.
Cover the dish with buttered waxed paper
and simmer over very low heat for 8
minutes.

4. Carefully remove the fillets to a deep
serving platter. Place the platter over a
pan of hot water and keep the fillets warm.

5. Strain the poaching liquid into a small,
heavy saucepan, discarding the bay leaf
but reserving the vegetable mixture. Cook
the poaching liquid over high heat until
it is reduced to ¾ cup. Remove the saucepan from the heat and cool slightly, then
whisk in the egg yolk mixture. Return
the saucepan to the lowest possible heat
and slowly whisk in the hot melted butter,
being careful not to overheat the sauce
or the yolks will curdle. When all the butter
has been added and the sauce is thick
and smooth, add the reserved vegetable
mixture. Taste the sauce and correct the
seasoning. Set aside.

6. Wipe up any liquid that may have accumulated on the fish platter, and spoon
the sauce over the fish. Sprinkle with
parsley and serve immediately, accompanied by crusty French bread and a
chilled white wine.

Notes

Ingredients

6   medium squid or 12 small ones
¾   cup olive oil
1   onion, finely minced
¼   cup minced fresh parsley
2   ripe tomatoes, peeled, seeded and
    chopped
Salt and freshly ground black pepper
½   teaspoon dried oregano
½   to ¾ cup fresh, white bread crumbs
4   cloves garlic
1   large egg
½   cup dry white wine

Preparation

1. Have the fish market clean the squid,
leaving the sacs whole and reserving the
tentacles. Mince the tentacles fine.

2. Heat 2 tablespoons of the oil in a heavy
skillet. Add the tentacles and cook over
high heat until they turn white, then add the
onion and 2 tablespoons of the parsley
and cook until the onion is soft and lightly
browned. Add the tomatoes, salt, pepper,
and oregano and cook until all the tomato
juices have evaporated and the mixture is
thick. Remove the pan from the heat, then
add ½ cup bread crumbs, 2 cloves of
the garlic, mashed, and the egg. Combine
the mixture well with a fork. Taste and
correct the seasoning, then, if the stuffing
seems too soft, add another ¼ cup of
bread crumbs.

3. Stuff the squid loosely and sew up the
opening. Season with salt and pepper.

4. Preheat the oven to 350 degrees.

5. Oil a large baking dish. Arrange the squid in one layer, then add the remaining garlic cloves, whole but peeled, and dribble with the remaining oil and 2 tablespoons of the white wine. Bake for 45 minutes, basting with the juices in the pan and adding 2 more tablespoons of white wine every 15 minutes. Turn the squid once during the cooking.

6. When the squid are done, discard the garlic cloves. Transfer carefully to a serving platter, dribble the pan juices over them, and sprinkle with the remaining parsley. Serve immediately.

Remarks

The squid can be stuffed several hours ahead of time and prepared in the baking dish. Once cooked, however, they should be served as soon as possible.

Notes

Grilled swordfish steaks in herb butter

Serves: 4
Preparation time: 10 minutes
Cooking time: 15 minutes

Swordfish is one of the more popular fish in this country. It is a fish that demands little, and can be delicious when prepared quite simply. It is unfortunate, therefore, that it is almost impossible to get a properly cooked piece of swordfish in a restaurant, where it is so often featured on the menu. The secret of any well-prepared fish steak is simple: make sure it is fresh and never overcook it.

Ingredients

4   swordfish steaks, each cut ¾-inch thick
Juice of 2 lemons
Coarse salt and freshly ground black pepper
8   tablespoons (1 stick) butter
½   cup olive oil
4   large cloves garlic, finely minced
2   tablespoons finely minced fresh oregano
1   tablespoon finely minced fresh tarragon
3 to 4 tablespoons minced fresh parsley

Garnish:
8   new potatoes cooked in their jackets

Preparation

1. Sprinkle the swordfish steaks with the juice of 1 lemon, salt, and pepper and set aside for 30 minutes to 1 hour.

2. In a small saucepan heat the butter, olive oil, remaining lemon juice, salt, pepper, garlic, oregano, tarragon, and 2 tablespoons parsley. Simmer the mixture for 2 to 3 minutes, then set aside.

Marinated fish à la créole

Serves: 6
Preparation time: 25 to 30 minutes
Cooking time: 10 minutes

3. Preheat the broiler.

4. Pour half the butter and herb mixture into a shallow baking dish. Arrange the steaks in one layer and pour the remaining butter over them. Place the dish under the broiler, 3 to 5 inches from the source of heat, and broil for 6 to 8 minutes, basting the steaks several times with the pan juices. Carefully turn the steaks with two spatulas and broil for another 6 to 8 minutes, basting several times. Test the fish for doneness by piercing it with the tip of a sharp knife; it should flake easily.

5. Transfer the fish to a serving platter. Spoon the pan juices over it, then garnish with the cooked potatoes and sprinkle with parsley. Serve immediately.

Notes

Ingredients

2 pounds fillets of Boston mackerel or flounder
Juice of 1 lemon
¾ cup olive oil
Large pinch of dried thyme
Pinch of dried marjoram
All-purpose flour
Salt and freshly ground black pepper
1 cup water
1 small carrot, peeled and thinly sliced
1 large onion, thinly sliced
½ green pepper, thinly sliced
½ red pepper, cored and thinly sliced
½ cup white wine vinegar
2 bay leaves
6 peppercorns
1 tablespoon sugar
Large dash of Tabasco

Garnish:
Finely minced fresh parsley
2 tablespoons finely minced pimiento
Heavy grinding of coriander seeds
6 to 8 black Greek olives

Preparation

1. Arrange the fish fillets in a glass or enameled baking dish and sprinkle with the lemon juice, 2 tablespoons of the olive oil, the thyme, and marjoram. Let the fish fillets marinate for 30 minutes, turning them once or twice. Dry the fillets thoroughly on paper towels.

2. In a shallow dish combine flour, salt, and pepper. Dredge the fillets in the seasoned flour, shaking off the excess. Set aside on a double layer of paper towels.

3. Heat ¼ cup of the olive oil in a large, heavy skillet. Add the fillets, a few at a time (do not crowd the pan), and cook over medium heat until nicely browned on both sides, turning each fillet carefully with two spatulas so as not to break it.

4. Transfer the fish to a rectangular enameled baking dish and set aside.

5. Bring the 1 cup of water to a boil in a 2-quart saucepan. Add the carrot, then reduce the heat and simmer, covered, for 5 to 8 minutes, or until barely tender. Add the onion and simmer for 2 more minutes, then add the green and red peppers, and the remaining olive oil, vinegar, bay leaves, peppercorns, sugar, and Tabasco. Simmer the mixture for 2 to 3 minutes, then pour it over the fish. Cover the dish with foil and refrigerate for 24 hours.

6. Forty-five minutes before serving, bring the fish back to room temperature. Sprinkle with parsley, pimiento, and a heavy grinding of coriander seeds and garnish with black olives. Serve as an appetizer, accompanied by French bread, a bowl of sweet butter, and a slightly chilled white wine.

Remarks

Though I personally prefer mackerel for this kind of preparation, other fish, such as cod, Atlantic sea perch, and whiting, lend themselves equally well to this preparation. If you have cold leftover fish, such as bass, you can marinate it in the same cooked marinade for 4 to 6 hours and serve it slightly chilled (but not cold).

eggs, quiches, and crepes

The egg is one of the most marvelously basic and versatile of foods. Unfortunately, its preparation in this country is usually limited to two or three ways. Compared to the French, who have undoubtedly created more egg-based dishes than any other country in the world, our own imagination and repertory seems terribly meager. Masters of variety, the French use the ordinary egg as well in peasant or country cooking as in their *grande cuisine,* where many of the egg dishes are used to highlight expensive garnishes like truffles and fois gras. Quite often the French serve eggs with complicated sauces, such as Madeira or hollandaise.

Through the years, I have been fascinated by the ways in which different countries explore the potential of the simplest foods and ingredients. In Mediterranean countries eggs are mainly served as lunch and supper dishes. In northern Spain they are used to make thick, pie-shaped omelets, containing potatoes, artichokes, or onions, that are cut into wedges and eaten either hot or cold as part of an hors d'oeuvre table before a meal, or as light snacks. The *frittade,* or open-faced omelette, is also extremely popular in Mediterranean peasant cooking. Here the eggs are used to bind all sorts of ingredients, such as sausages and bacon, or vegetables like tomatoes, leeks, or potatoes. The classic Basque omelette, the *pipérade,* is a hearty mixture of green peppers, onions, and tomatoes. And in Spain eggs are even used with rice. *Arroz cubano* is a steamed rice dish topped with a fried egg and tomato sauce and fried bananas.

There is no good reason why the use of eggs should be so limited in this country, and it is a shame we have paid so little attention to them. Eggs are a basic food and shouldn't be confined to the breakfast table. They are easily adaptable, easily prepared, and can be turned quickly into filling meals with the addition of any number of simple and fresh foods. Recently, I was served sautéed scallops and scrambled eggs; it was one of the most unusual yet delicious combinations.

We must understand, however, that precisely because egg dishes are so basic and simple, they need to be perfectly prepared and require a cook's skill and mastery of the pan. Even in its humblest form— scrambled, fried, or boiled for example— an egg demands slow, even cooking. Scrambled eggs can be a great dish when moist and creamy, but miserable when dry and lumpy. To the knowledgeable cook, a rubbery fried egg is as noticeable as an overcooked vegetable. I'm afraid that many cooks have never mastered the art of properly boiling an egg, but take it for granted that we are born with that knowledge. Furthermore, few people seem to know how to hard-boil an egg the right way. It should not be overcooked at a fast boil, but should be simmered for 8 minutes and rolled back and forth a few times to center the yolk. Probably lots of Americans don't even know the taste of a good egg. We have become so used to eating in fast food restaurants, where eggs are often slaughtered on a grill.

Even the omelet, which has gained enormous popularity in recent years, is still considered somewhat special, and has not yet become part of the everyday cook's repertory. Once you have seen an omelet properly done and learned the technique, you will quickly take to it and use it frequently and creatively.

Poached eggs, too, have been sadly neglected in this country. Again, this is probably because many cooks think they are hard to prepare. However, the egg poacher makes cooking them as simple as any other egg dish. I use poached eggs as a topping for braised spinach and broccoli or with freshly cooked asparagus. The beauty of this egg is that it adapts itself to all seasons, and there are very few vegetables that do not have an affinity to it.

In combination with cream, eggs have produced some of the great classics, such as quiche Lorraine and the Onion and Bacon Tart in this book (see page 167). These are still considered first-course dishes in France, but I feel that they are really too filling for an appetizer, and can and should stand on their own as one-dish meals. They go very well served with a salad and warm, crusty bread.
Other egg-based classics such as soufflés and crêpes have been considered as part of *haute cuisine,* but I think they should also be thought of as inexpensive and versatile ways to use leftovers or as a use for expensive ingredients in small quantities, such as crabmeat and shrimp. To me, there is nothing simpler and more exciting than the crêpe. The variety of flavorings it can be eaten with is enormous, and they can be made in quantity and very

successfully frozen for later use. I am a firm believer in serving crêpes throughout the year, either as appetizers or as the main course in a simple but satisfying meal.

Every country offers us distinctive ways to work with the egg. The creative cook should select the best of them and use them with the proper understanding of the ingredients involved; he or she will naturally come up with some delicious and inexpensive dishes.

Russian eggs

Serves: 4 to 6
Preparation time: 10 minutes
Cooking time: 10 minutes

When people say they hardly know how to boil an egg, they are closer to the truth than they think, since there is very definitely a right and a wrong way to do it. The eggs should not be overcooked, or they will be rubbery and hard to peel. The yolks should be centered and not discolored in any way.

To ensure this, place room-temperature eggs in a saucepan with cold water to cover. Bring to a boil, then lower the heat and simmer for 8 to 10 minutes. Roll the eggs to and fro every few minutes to center the yolks, and finally run them under cold water to stop further cooking. All by itself, a bowl of hard-boiled eggs served with coarse salt is a simple, pleasing appetizer at all times. In this recipe, hard-boiled eggs are dressed in a slightly sharp mayonnaise and garnished with lumpfish caviar, chives, and cucumber.

Ingredients

4 to 6 hard-boiled eggs
1 large raw egg
½ teaspoon Dijon mustard
¼ teaspoon dry mustard
1 teaspoon white wine vinegar
½ to ¾ cup vegetable oil
2 tablespoons chopped scallion, white part only
2 tablespoons chili sauce
¼ cup Danish lumpfish caviar
Salt and freshly ground white pepper

Garnish:
Thinly sliced, unpeeled cucumber
Finely minced chives

Preparation

1. Peel the eggs, then cut them in half lengthwise and place them, cut side down, on a rectangular serving dish. Set aside.

2. In the container of a blender combine the raw egg, mustards, and vinegar. Blend the mixture at high speed for 30 seconds, and, continuing to blend, start adding the oil, by droplets, until the sauce gets very thick. Add the scallion and chili sauce and blend again, then pour the mixture into a mixing bowl. Add 3 tablespoons of the caviar and season with salt and pepper. Chill the sauce for 2 to 4 hours.

3. Just before serving, pour the sauce over the eggs. Arrange the cucumber slices in an overlapping pattern along the dish, sprinkle with chives and the remaining caviar, and serve, accompanied by thinly sliced, buttered pumpernickel.

Remarks

This sauce is even better when prepared the night before. It can also be served as a dip for the *crudité* basket with a side bowl of hard-boiled eggs.

Notes

Eggs tonnato

Serves: 6 to 8
Preparation time: 15 minutes
Cooking time: 10 minutes

Hard-boiled eggs are a natural for the hors d'oeuvre table. I serve them stuffed or in a well-flavored mayonnaise, such as this tuna and anchovy one that I adapted from the famous Italian dish of cold, finely sliced veal called *vitello tonnato*.

Ingredients

6 to 8 hard-boiled eggs
2 raw eggs
1 to 2 tablespoons lemon juice
Salt and freshly ground white pepper
¾ to 1 cup olive oil
3 to 4 minced anchovy fillets
2 tablespoons finely minced scallion,
    white part only
3 ounces tuna
⅛ teaspoon cayenne pepper

Optional:
2 tablespoons heavy cream

Garnish:
2 tablespoons well-drained capers
1 bunch fresh watercress leaves
Cherry tomatoes
Black Greek olives

Preparation

1. Cut a ¼-inch lengthwise slice off each egg and place the eggs on a round serving platter; discard the slices.

2. In the container of a blender, combine the raw eggs, 1 tablespoon of lemon juice, salt, and pepper. Blend the mixture at high speed for 30 seconds, then, continuing to blend, add the oil drop by drop, until the mixture is thick and smooth.

Add the anchovies, scallion, and tuna and blend again. Add a pinch of cayenne, then taste the mixture and correct the seasoning, adding a little more lemon juice if necessary. If the sauce seems too thick (it should be of pouring consistency), stir in the 2 tablespoons of heavy cream.

3. Pour the sauce over the eggs, covering them completely. Sprinkle the eggs with capers, and decorate the platter with a border of watercress leaves. Place small bunches of cherry tomatoes and black olives around the eggs and serve well chilled but not cold, accompanied by crusty French bread, or as part of an hors d'oeuvre table.

Remarks

The tuna and anchovy mayonnaise can also be served as a dip with a basket of raw vegetables. If served as a dip, add the capers and a few minced black olives to the sauce, and let the mixture marinate for 2 to 4 hours before serving.

Notes

Eggs en tapenade

Serves: 6
Preparation time: 25 minutes
Cooking time: 10 minutes

A *tapenade* is a Provençal "dip" made of olives, anchovies, and capers pounded in a mortar with a pestle and served with raw vegetables and crusty French bread. I have always found the classic *tapenade* a bit too salty and the taste somewhat overpowering. Here is my modified version: the proportions are purposely high, since the *tapenade* can be served either as a dip or, as here, as a topping for hard-boiled eggs.

Ingredients

8   hard-boiled eggs
2   tablespoons sweet butter
8 to 10 black Greek olives, finely minced
1   can (3½ ounces) of tuna in olive oil
2   tablespoons well-drained capers
2   tablespoons minced anchovies
2   large cloves garlic, mashed
1   tablespoon chili sauce
Juice of 1 lemon
2   tablespoons finely minced onion
3   tablespoons Mayonnaise (see page 208)
3   tablespoons heavy cream
Heavy grinding of black pepper
¼   cup finely minced fresh parsley

Garnish:
2   red peppers, thinly sliced

Preparation

1. Cut 6 of the eggs in half lengthwise. Remove the yolks carefully and mash them, together with the butter, into a fine paste in a small bowl. Refill the eggs with the butter and yolk mixture. Mince the remaining 2 eggs.

2. In the container of a blender combine the olives, tuna, capers, anchovies, garlic, chili sauce, lemon juice, onion, mayonnaise, and heavy cream. Blend the mixture at top speed until smooth. Taste for seasoning, adding a heavy grinding of black pepper. Pour the mixture into a bowl and chill.

3. An hour before serving time, place the eggs on a round serving platter. Top each with a spoonful of the *tapenade*, sprinkle with the parsley and minced eggs and garnish the platter with red pepper rings. Serve with crusty French bread and a dry white wine.

Remarks

Serve the remaining *tapenade* as a dip, accompanied by endives sliced in half lengthwise, raw zucchini sticks, celery, and radishes. It will keep in a covered jar, well refrigerated, for 2 weeks.

Notes

Baked eggs à la polonaise

Serves: 4
Preparation time: 15 minutes
Cooking time: 20 minutes

A good brunch or light supper dish, the essence of which lies in the quality of the mushrooms. Usually made with the marvelous wild mushrooms of Central Europe, it is nevertheless worth duplicating with our own cultivated variety.

Ingredients

4   tablespoons butter
2   tablespoons finely minced shallots
½   pound mushrooms finely minced
Salt and freshly ground white pepper
2   tablespoons all-purpose flour
1¼ cups hot milk
Pinch of freshly grated nutmeg
4   eggs
1   tablespoon freshly grated Parmesan cheese

Preparation

1. Preheat the oven to 350 degrees.

2. In a small heavy skillet melt 2 tablespoons of the butter. When the butter is very hot, add the shallots and cook them for 1 minute, or until they are soft. Add the mushrooms and cook until they are lightly browned and all their juice has evaporated, then season the mixture with salt and pepper and set aside.

3. Melt the remaining butter in a small, heavy saucepan. Add the flour and cook for 1 minute, without browning, stirring constantly. Add the hot milk all at once and whisk with a wire whip until the sauce is thick and smooth. Add salt, pepper, and nutmeg, then remove from the heat and set aside.

4. Place a heaping tablespoon of the mushroom mixture into each of 4 porcelain ramekins. Break an egg into each one, centering the yolk. Season the egg with a pinch of salt and a grinding of white pepper and top with a little of the sauce, covering the egg completely. Sprinkle each ramekin with a little cheese and set the dishes in the oven. Bake for 6 minutes, then put under the broiler and broil for 1 or 2 minutes, close to the flame, until the top is browned; watch carefully, as the cheese must not burn. Serve immediately.

Remarks

The mushroom mixture and the sauce can be made 1 or 2 days ahead of time. Both can be prepared an hour or two before serving and kept warm in a pan with hot water. The baking of the eggs, however, must be done at the last minute.

Notes

Scrambled eggs niçoise

Serves: 4 to 6
Preparation time: 10 minutes
Cooking time: 20 minutes

This light supper dish calls for leftover *ratatouille*, a marvelous and versatile summer casserole of eggplant, zucchini, tomatoes, and onions that can be served either hot or cold.

Ingredients

2   cups leftover Ratatouille (see page 108)
1   cup cubed slab bacon
5   tablespoons sweet butter
2   tablespoons finely minced fresh parsley
8 to 9 large eggs
Large pinch of salt
Freshly ground white pepper
Pinch of cayenne pepper

Preparation

1. Put the *ratatouille* in a small, heavy, flameproof casserole and heat over a low flame for 15 to 20 minutes, or until well heated through. Keep warm.

2. Cook the bacon in a small, heavy skillet, over medium heat, until almost crisp. Drain on a double layer of paper towels, then add to the *ratatouille* and set aside.

3. Combine 2 tablespoons of the soft butter and the parsley in a small bowl. Mash the mixture with a fork until it is well blended and set aside.

4. Break the eggs into a large bowl and beat with a wire whisk for 1 minute. Add salt, pepper, and cayenne and set aside.

5. Melt the remaining butter in a heavy 8- to 10-inch iron skillet (the skillet must be well seasoned or the eggs will stick). Pour the eggs into the skillet and cook them over medium heat, stirring gently until they start to set. As soon as they begin to set, stir rapidly until they form a fluffy custard. (Do not overcook, scrambled eggs should be creamy and just hold their shape.) Remove the pan from the heat, then stir in the parsley butter and a heavy grinding of pepper.

6. Pour the eggs into an oval serving dish, surround them with the *ratatouille*, and serve immediately.

Remarks

For a variation, omit the bacon and sauté 8 Italian link sausages in 2 tablespoons of olive oil and serve with the eggs. Other herbs, such as a mixture of chervil and chives, can be added to the eggs instead of parsley.

Notes

eggs, quiches, and crepes

Poached eggs on sorrel puree

Serves: 6
Preparation time: 10 minutes
Cooking time: 35 to 40 minutes

In Mediterranean cooking, poached, fried, and scrambled eggs are often served as appetizers or as simple main courses for a family dinner. Sorrel has a particular affinity for eggs, but other purees, such as broccoli or spinach, can be substituted for the sorrel.

Ingredients

4   tablespoons butter
2   large shallots, finely minced
2   tablespoons minced fresh parsley
3   pounds fresh sorrel, washed and stems removed
Salt and freshly ground white pepper
1   cup Crème Fraîche (see page 206)
Beurre Manié (see page 213)
6   large eggs
¼   cup melted butter

Garnish:
Bread triangles sautéed in Clarified Butter (see page 225)

Preparation

1. Melt the butter in a large, heavy, flame-proof casserole. Add the shallots and 1 tablespoon of the parsley and cook the mixture over low heat for 5 minutes, or until soft but not browned. Add the sorrel, cover the casserole, and simmer for 30 minutes, stirring frequently. The sorrel will "melt" down to a soft puree; season it with salt and pepper and add the *Crème Fraîche.* Raise the heat and cook the mixture, uncovered, until it is thick and most of the cream has evaporated. Add the *beurre manié* and stir until it is well

blended into the puree. (If the sorrel seems stringy, pass the puree through a fine sieve.) Pour into a deep, oval serving dish and keep warm.

2. Poach the eggs in an egg poacher. As soon as they are done, arrange them on the puree and sprinkle with salt, pepper, and the remaining parsley. Dribble the melted butter over the eggs, arrange the bread triangles around the puree and serve immediately.

Remarks

The puree can be made hours ahead of time and kept warm in a double boiler. The bread triangles can be made several hours ahead and reheated in the oven. If you do not have an egg poacher and find the skillet method of poaching eggs too difficult, make *oeufs mollets,* which are soft-boiled eggs prepared as follows:

Notes

Oeufs mollets

1. Bring the eggs to room temperature.

2. Bring water to a boil in a large saucepan. Lower the eggs carefully into the water, then reduce the heat and cook over medium heat for 6 minutes, turning them frequently.

3. Immediately run the eggs under cold water to stop further cooking. Peel them carefully and serve immediately.

Notes

Fried eggs à la provençale

Serves: 4 to 6
Preparation time: 15 minutes (plus 1 to 2 hours draining time)
Cooking time: 10 minutes

Eggs fried in olive oil and served accompanied by sautéed eggplants, tomatoes, or other fresh vegetables are a staple of the Mediterranean peasant kitchen. Serve them as a beginning to a meal or as a main course for a plain family supper, accompanied by saffron-flavored rice.

Ingredients

2   medium eggplants
Salt
½ to ¾ cup olive oil
1 to 1½ cups Provençal Tomato Fondue
    (see page 207)
2   tablespoons finely minced fresh parsley
1   clove garlic, finely mashed
4 to 6 large eggs
Freshly ground black pepper

Garnish:
Bread triangles fried in olive oil

Preparation

1. Cut the eggplants, unpeeled, crosswise into ½-inch slices. Sprinkle the slices with salt and let them drain on a double layer of paper towels for 1 to 2 hours.

2. Dry the eggplant thoroughly. Heat 3 tablespoons of the oil in a large, heavy skillet and add the slices, a few at a time, and cook over medium heat until nicely browned on both sides (you may need more oil). Arrange them as they are done on a round serving platter and set aside.

3. Heat 1 tablespoon of the oil in a small saucepan. Add the tomato fondue, parsley,

and garlic. Simmer the mixture for 5 minutes, or until well heated through, then set aside.

4. Heat 3 tablespoons of oil in a large, heavy skillet. Break the eggs carefully into the hot oil and cook over low heat until the whites are set, spooning the oil over. Season with salt and pepper, then carefully transfer to the serving platter. Spoon the tomato fondue around the eggs, encircling them without covering the yolks. Sprinkle with a heavy grinding of black pepper, garnish with fried bread triangles, and serve immediately.

Notes

Frittade de bayonne

Serves: 4
Preparation time: 10 minutes
Cooking time: 15 minutes

The *frittade*, an open-faced omelet, is a staple in Mediterranean peasant cooking, since it can be made with innumerable ingredients and is a good way of using leftovers.

Ingredients

¼ pound medium-sized mushrooms
4 tablespoons olive oil
½ onion, thinly sliced
1 large tomato, cubed
1 large clove garlic, finely minced
⅔ cup cubed, cooked ham
Salt and freshly ground white pepper
1 tablespoon finely minced fresh parsley
8 whole eggs
Dash of Tabasco
2 tablespoons butter

Preparation

1. Preheat the oven to 350 degrees.

2. Wipe the mushrooms with a wet paper towel. Remove and discard part of the stems and slice the mushrooms thin. Set aside.

3. Heat 2 tablespoons of oil in a heavy, 10-inch skillet. Add the onion and cook over low heat until it is very soft and lightly browned, then add the mushrooms. Raise the heat and cook until the mushrooms are lightly browned. Add the tomato and garlic and continue cooking until most of the tomato juices have evaporated, then add the ham, salt, pepper, and parsley and cook until the ham is heated through. Taste the mixture for seasoning. Set aside.

4. Beat the eggs in a mixing bowl until just blended, then season with salt and pepper and a dash of Tabasco. Add the mushroom mixture.

5. Wipe the pan out with paper towels. Heat the butter and remaining oil in the pan, and when the butter is very hot, add the egg and vegetable mixture. Cook until the bottom is set, then transfer the pan to the oven and bake for 3 to 5 minutes, or until the top is set and lightly browned. Do not overcook, as the *frittade* must not be dry. Serve immediately.

Remarks

The vegetable mixture can be made well ahead of time. It is equally good as a filling for lunch crêpes or as an accompaniment to grilled sausages.

Notes

Frittata catalana

Serves: 4
Preparation time: 15 minutes (plus 30 minutes draining time)
Cooking time: 15 minutes

There are so many exciting appetizers, both hot and cold, that can be made with eggs. Here is one I particularly like to serve as a start to a simple summer meal.

Ingredients

1 to 2 small potatoes
Salt
1   medium zucchini, finely cubed
2   tablespoons butter
2   tablespoons olive oil
½   red onion, thinly sliced
1   small green pepper, cubed
½   cup finely cubed sweet red pepper or canned Italian roasted red peppers
2   tablespoons finely minced fresh parsley
6 to 8 eggs
2 or 3 drops of Tabasco
Freshly ground white pepper
2   tablespoons freshly grated Parmesan cheese

Preparation

1. Preheat the oven to 350 degrees.

2. Cook the potato in salted water until it is barely tender, then peel and cut it into thin slices. Set aside.

3. Sprinkle the zucchini with salt and let drain in a colander for 30 minutes.

4. Heat the butter and oil in a heavy 8-inch, skillet. Add the sliced potato and cook until it is nicely browned on all sides. Remove to a side dish with a slotted spoon.

5. To the oil in the pan add the zucchini and cook until lightly browned, then add

the onion and peppers and cook for 2 to 3 minutes, or until the onion is soft but not browned. Return the potato slices to the pan, along with the parsley, and season the mixture with salt and pepper. Set the pan aside.

6. In a bowl combine the eggs, salt, pepper, Tabasco, and Parmesan. Beat the mixture until it is fluffy. Return the skillet to the heat, and as soon as the pan is very hot, pour the egg mixture over the vegetables. Cook the *frittata* until the bottom is set and lightly browned. Set the pan in the oven and cook until the top of the eggs are set and slightly puffed. Serve immediately, directly out of the pan, accompanied by French bread and a bowl of sweet butter.

Remarks

I often serve this dish along with a platter of prosciutto or assorted sausages, for a light summer supper.

Notes

Omelette soufflée au gruyère

Serves: 2
Preparation time: 10 minutes
Cooking time: 5 minutes

The souffléed omelet is usually eaten as a dessert, but I find that it lends itself equally well to the light appetizer category.

Ingredients

4   large eggs, separated
Salt
Freshly ground white pepper
3   tablespoons finely grated Gruyère cheese (or a mixture of Parmesan and Swiss)

Optional:
1   tablespoon finely minced chives
2   tablespoons sweet butter

Preparation

1. Preheat the oven to 325 degrees.

2. In a stainless steel bowl combine the egg whites with a pinch of salt and beat until they are stiff but not dry. Set aside.

3. In another bowl beat the yolks, adding a pinch of salt, pepper, 2 tablespoons of the cheese, and the optional chives. Fold the yolk mixture carefully into the beaten whites, and set aside.

4. Heat the butter in a heavy, 8-inch skillet until it just begins to brown. Add the egg mixture, flatten the top with a spatula, and cook over medium heat for 2 or 3 minutes, lifting up the edge of the omelet gently to let most of the uncooked mixture seep to the bottom. As soon as it is browned, remove the skillet from the heat and with a large spatula fold the omelet in half.

5. Sprinkle the omelet with the remaining cheese, then place the skillet in the oven for 3 minutes. Remove and slide the omelet onto a serving plate, and serve immediately.

Remarks

Such fillings as sautéed, minced mushrooms, cooked spinach, or sautéed chicken livers can be added to the omelet just before folding it in half. These omelets can never be made successfully in quantity. If serving 4 people, use 2 skillets.

Notes

Onion and bacon tart

Serves: 6 to 8
Preparation time: 20 minutes
Cooking time: 1 hour and 20 minutes

■●

Ingredients

3   tablespoons butter
1   tablespoon olive oil
4   medium onions, peeled and finely chopped
1   cup finely cubed slab bacon
3   eggs
1   cup heavy cream
Salt and freshly ground white pepper
1   eight-inch Basic Tart Shell (see page 211), partially baked
2   tablespoons freshly grated Parmesan cheese

Preparation

1. Heat 2 tablespoons of butter and the oil in a large, heavy skillet. Add the onions, then lower the heat and cook, covered, for 45 minutes, stirring several times and scraping the bottom of the pan to prevent the onions from sticking.

2. While the onions are cooking, bring water to boil in a small saucepan. Add the bacon cubes and cook for 3 to 4 minutes, then drain.

3. Heat the remaining butter in a small, heavy skillet. Add the cubes of bacon and sauté until almost crisp, then drain on paper towels.

4. In a mixing bowl combine the eggs and cream. Season with salt and pepper and set aside.

5. Preheat the oven to 350 degrees.

6. When the onions are done, season with salt and pepper and fold them, to-

eggs, quiches, and crepes

gether with the bacon, into the cream mixture.

7. Pour the mixture into the tart shell, sprinkle with Parmesan, and bake the tart for 30 minutes, or until the top is nicely browned. Serve warm or at room temperature.

Notes

Quiche grecque

Serves: 12 to 14
Preparation time: 40 minutes (plus 1 hour draining time)
Cooking time: 1 hour

■■●

More than a quiche, this is an inexpensive and hearty meat pie. It is too substantial to be served as an appetizer, but is excellent for buffet entertaining and as a main course for a simple supper accompanied by a green salad and a glass of wine. It is useful to make two at a time, as the finished quiche freezes successfully and is good to have on hand for last-minute entertaining.

Ingredients

2 eggplants (1 small and 1 medium-sized)
Salt
4 tablespoons butter
2 tablespoons finely minced shallots
1 teaspoon finely minced garlic
1¼ pounds finely ground lamb or beef
1 whole egg
Freshly ground white pepper
Pinch of ground allspice
Large pinch of freshly grated nutmeg
¾ pound mushrooms, sliced
6 to 8 tablespoons olive oil
2 Basic Tart Shells (see page 211)

The topping:
4 tablespoons butter
¼ cup all-purpose flour
2 cups hot milk
3 egg yolks
Salt and freshly ground white pepper
3 to 4 tablespoons finely grated fresh Parmesan cheese

Preparation

1. Peel and dice the small eggplant, then place it in a colander. Sprinkle with salt

and let drain for at least 1 hour. Cut the medium-sized eggplant, unpeeled, into ½-inch slices, then place on paper towels and sprinkle with salt and let drain as well.

2. Heat 2 tablespoons of the butter in a small skillet. Add the shallots and garlic and sauté until soft but not browned, then remove from the heat and set aside.

3. In a mixing bowl combine the lamb, whole egg, salt, pepper and spices. Add the shallot mixture and set aside.

4. In the same skillet heat 2 tablespoons of the butter and sauté the sliced mushrooms until nicely browned, season and set aside.

5. Heat 3 tablespoons of the olive oil in a large skillet. Add the eggplant cubes and cook until well browned (you may need more oil), then drain on paper towels and add to the meat mixture. Taste for seasoning.

6. Heat the remaining oil in the skillet and brown the eggplant slices. Drain them on paper towels and reserve.

7. Partially bake the tart shells for 10 minutes in a preheated 350-degree oven. While the shells are baking make the topping.

8. Heat 4 tablespoons of butter in a heavy saucepan. Add the flour and cook it for 2 minutes, without browning, stirring with a wire whisk. Add the hot milk all at once and whisk the mixture until it is smooth and thick; add salt, pepper, nutmeg, and the egg yolks and blend well.

9. Make a layer of eggplant slices in the baked tart shells. Top with a little of the meat mixture and then cover with the sliced mushrooms. Add another layer of meat and then the butter and milk topping and sprinkle with the cheese.

10. Place the quiches in the oven and bake for 1 hour. (If the tops begin to get too brown cover with foil.) Let the quiches stand for 20 minutes before serving.

Notes

eggs, quiches, and crepes

Quiche tropezienne

Serves: 6 to 8
Preparation time: 45 minutes
Cooking time: 1 hour

■■●

Though slow in gaining popularity in this
country, the classic cheese and bacon
quiche has now become a staple in the
repertory of many cooks. A good quiche
should have an excellent crust, and the
custard must be high and well flavored.
For best results use a French porcelain
quiche pan, rather than a metal one with
removable bottom, and bake the quiche
at the last possible minute. Those who
claim that prebaked and frozen quiches are
as good as those made fresh at the last
minute must never have tasted the "real
thing."

Ingredients

1   8- to 9-inch Basic Tart Shell (see
     page 211), unbaked
6 to 8 littleneck clams
2   tablespoons butter
3   tablespoons finely minced shallots
½   cup diced bacon
1½ cups heavy cream
3   eggs
Salt and freshly ground white pepper
Few drops of Tabasco

Preparation

1. Freeze the pastry shell in the pan for 2
to 4 hours or overnight.

2. Scrub the clams thoroughly under cold
running water, then place in a saucepan
and cook, partially covered, over medium
heat until they open, removing them as
they open to a side dish. As soon as the
clams are cool enough to handle, shell
them and cut each one into 3 or 4 pieces.
Reserve the clam juice.

3. Preheat the oven to 350 degrees.

4. Strain the clam juice through a double
layer of cheesecloth and reduce it in a
small, heavy saucepan to 2 tablespoons.
Reserve.

5. Heat the butter in a small, heavy skillet.
Add the shallots and bacon and cook for
3 or 4 minutes, or until the shallots are
soft but not browned. Remove all but 2
tablespoons of fat from the pan, then add
the clams and heat through. Set the pan
aside.

6. Prick the bottom of the frozen shell.
Line with foil and 2 cups of dried white
beans or rice and bake for 15 minutes
or until the dough is set. Remove the foil,
together with the beans or rice, and fill
with the clam mixture. Set aside.

7. In a mixing bowl combine the cream,
eggs, salt, pepper, Tabasco, and clam
juice. Whisk the mixture until it is well
blended and pour it into the shell.

8. Bake the quiche for 50 minutes, until
it is nicely browned, or until a knife in-
serted an inch from the pastry edge comes
out clean. Serve immediately.

Remarks

If you are making the quiche in a porcelain
dish you will need ½ cup more cream and
1 additional egg. A quiche made in a metal
dish should be unmolded and placed on
a cookie sheet before adding the cream
and egg mixture.

Quiche du midi

Serves: 6 to 8
Preparation time: 20 minutes
Cooking time: 50 minutes to an hour

A quiche is an inexpensive appetizer that lends itself to using leftovers creatively. Once you have mastered making the crust you can prepare several tart shells, freeze them, and when needed fill with either a vegetable, cream, or meat mixture.

Ingredients

1   frozen Basic Tart Shell (see page 211)
3   eggs
Salt and freshly ground white pepper
2   cups leftover Ratatouille (see page 108)
2   tablespoons freshly grated Parmesan cheese
6 to 8 black Greek olives

Preparation

1. Preheat the oven to 350 degrees.

2. Remove the shell from the freezer. Line with waxed paper and fill with dried beans or rice, then bake for 20 minutes. Remove the beans and paper, prick the bottom of the shell in several places and continue baking for 10 minutes, or until lightly browned. Remove the shell from the oven, and when cool enough to handle, unmold it onto a cookie sheet. Set aside.

3. In a large mixing bowl whisk the eggs for 1 or 2 minutes. Add salt, pepper, and the *ratatouille*. Stir the mixture until it is well blended, then pour it into the shell. Sprinkle with the Parmesan, then return the quiche to the oven and bake for 20 or 30 minutes, or until it is well heated through and lightly browned.

4. Carefully transfer the quiche to a serving platter, garnish with olives, and serve warm or at room temperature.

Quiche provençale

Serves: 6 to 8
Preparation time: 15 minutes
Cooking time: 1 hour 20 minutes

This Provençal quiche is often called "pizza" in the south of France, since its taste is somewhat similar. I have never been much of a pizza fan, yet this quiche is a staple of my kitchen as soon as good tomatoes are available. Vary the quiche by adding finely sliced, sautéed mushrooms or zucchini to the tomato mixture or by topping it with finely sliced garlic sausages instead of anchovies.

Ingredients

2   tablespoons butter
1   tablespoon olive oil
4   large onions, thinly sliced
Salt and freshly ground black pepper
Pinch of granulated sugar
1½ to 2 cups Provençal Tomato Fondue (see page 207)
½   teaspoon dried oregano
¼   teaspoon dried thyme
¼   teaspoon dried basil
1   8-inch Basic Tart Shell (see page 211) prebaked
6 to 8 anchovy fillets
6 to 8 black Greek olives

Preparation

1. Heat the butter and oil in a large, heavy skillet. Add the onions and season with salt, pepper, and a pinch of sugar. Cover and cook over low heat, stirring frequently, for 1 hour; the onions should be "melted" and lightly browned.

2. When the onions are done, add the tomato fondue, salt, pepper and herbs; taste and correct the seasoning. Pour the

tomato mixture into the tart shell, arrange the anchovies and olives in a decorative pattern.

3. Preheat the oven to 350 degrees.

4. Bake the quiche for 20 minutes, or until bubbly and well heated through. Carefully transfer the quiche to a serving platter, cool, and serve at room temperature.

Remarks

This quiche should be prepared in a metal quiche pan with a removable bottom. Taste the anchovies before placing them in the quiche; if too salty, marinate in a little cold milk for 15 minutes, then drain well on paper towels.

Notes

Crêpes farcies niçoise

Serves: 6 to 8
Preparation time: 35 minutes
Cooking time: 45 minutes

To many people, crêpes mean only crêpes Suzette. There are, however, innumerable ways of preparing these delicious pancakes for appetizers as well as desserts. Personally, I find entree crêpes more interesting than dessert crêpes, and have tried to create a variety of fillings for them.

Ingredients

1   large eggplant, unpeeled and cubed
2   small zucchini, cubed
Salt
¾   cup olive oil
2   medium onions, thinly sliced
1   green pepper, thinly sliced
1   red pepper, thinly sliced, or 1 cup thinly sliced pimiento
4   large, ripe tomatoes, seeded, peeled, and chopped
2   tablespoons minced fresh basil or 1 teaspoon dried
½   teaspoon dried oregano
2   tablespoons minced fresh parsley
2   large cloves garlic, minced
Freshly ground black pepper
12 to 16 Entrée Crêpes (see page 212)
12 to 16 thin slices of prosciutto or finely sliced baked ham
¾   cup melted butter
½   cup finely grated fresh Parmesan cheese

Preparation

1. Sprinkle the cubed eggplant and zucchini with salt and let drain, separately, on paper towels for 30 minutes to 1 hour, then dry the vegetables thoroughly with paper towels.

2. Heat ½ cup of the olive oil in a large, heavy skillet. Add the eggplant cubes and sauté over high heat until they are browned on all sides. Remove with a slotted spoon to a side dish.

3. Add the remaining oil to the pan. Add the zucchini and cook over high heat until they are nicely browned. Remove to a side dish.

4. Add the onions, peppers, and tomatoes to the skillet. Cook the mixture until the onions and peppers are soft and all the tomato juices have evaporated, then add the basil, oregano, parsley, garlic, salt, and pepper. Reduce the heat, return the zucchini and eggplant cubes to the pan, and cook the vegetable mixture for 5 to 6 minutes. Set aside.

5. Preheat the oven to 350 degrees.

6. Line each crêpe with a thin slice of prosciutto, then fill with a heaping table-spoonful of the vegetable mixture. Roll up the crêpes, tucking in the ends, and place in a well-buttered baking dish. Dribble the melted butter over them, and sprinkle with cheese, then cover the dish and bake for 15 to 20 minutes, or until the crêpes are well heated and the cheese is melted.

7. Serve immediately, right out of the baking dish.

Notes

Crêpes farcies à la monegasque

Serves: 6 to 8
Preparation time: 35 minutes
Cooking time: 35 minutes

Ingredients

1½ sticks unsalted butter
4   anchovy fillets, finely minced
3   tablespoons fruity olive oil
2   cups thinly sliced onion
2   cloves garlic, finely minced
4 to 6 ripe tomatoes, peeled, seeded, and chopped
1   teaspoon dried oregano
Salt and freshly ground white pepper
6   pimiento-stuffed green olives, thinly sliced
6   black Greek olives, pitted and cut in half
½ cup finely chopped pimiento
¾ pound shrimp, cooked, peeled, and cubed
12 to 16 Entrée Crêpes (see page 212)

Preparation

1. Combine the butter and anchovies in a small saucepan and heat until the butter is melted. Whisk the mixture until the anchovies are completely incorporated into the butter, then set aside and keep warm.

2. Heat the oil in a large, heavy skillet. Add the onion and garlic and cook, partially covered, until the onion is soft and lightly browned. Add the tomatoes, oregano, salt, and pepper, then bring to a boil and cook over high heat until all the tomato juices have evaporated and the mixture is thick. Add the olives, pimientos, and shrimp and cook for 2 minutes longer, until well heated through. Taste and correct the seasoning.

3. Preheat the oven to 325 degrees.

Crêpes farcies à la bernoise

Serves: 6
Preparation time: 20 minutes
Cooking time: 35 minutes

4. Place a heaping tablespoonful of the mixture on each crêpe. Roll them up and arrange in one layer in a well-buttered rectangular baking dish. Dribble the anchovy butter over the crêpes, then place the dish, covered with foil, in the center of the oven. Bake for 20 minutes, or until the crêpes are well heated through.

5. Serve immediately, right from the baking dish.

Notes

Ingredients

6 to 8 large leeks
Salt
2   cups cubed slab bacon (about 1½ pounds)
1½   sticks unsalted butter
Freshly ground white pepper
2   tablespoons finely minced fresh parsley
½   teaspoon dried thyme
3   hard-boiled eggs, finely minced
12 to 14 Entrée Crêpes (see page 212)
½   cup finely grated Parmesan cheese

Preparation

1. Wash the leeks thoroughly under cold running water. Trim the root ends and remove the greens (reserving them for stocks and soups). Slice the leeks, then set aside.

2. Bring salted water to a boil in a 2-quart saucepan. Add the bacon and cook for 3 to 4 minutes, then drain and dry thoroughly on paper towels.

3. Heat 2 tablespoons of the butter in a large, heavy skillet. Add the bacon and cook until it is almost crisp, then remove with a slotted spoon to a side dish.

4. Discard all but 3 tablespoons of fat from the pan. Add the leeks, cover, and cook over low heat for 10 minutes, or until very tender. Season with salt and pepper, then add the bacon, parsley, thyme, and hard-boiled eggs. Cook for 2 more minutes, or until well heated through, and set aside.

5. Preheat the oven to 325 degrees.

Dill crêpes tivoli
Serves: 4 to 6
Preparation time: 1 hour

6. Melt the remaining butter in a small saucepan, then set aside and keep warm.

7. Place a heaping tablespoonful of the leek and bacon mixture on each crêpe, then roll them up, and arrange in one layer in a well-buttered baking dish. Dribble with butter and sprinkle with the Parmesan, then cover the dish with foil and bake for 20 minutes, or until the crêpes are well heated through.

8. Serve immediately, right from the baking dish.

Notes

Crêpes, like soufflés, are both easy and inexpensive to make. There are many ways to serve and flavor them. It is useful to have a batch of crêpes in your freezer at any time. Reheat them and fill with either a hot filling or a cold one, such as this.

Ingredients
8 ounces cream cheese, softened
1 cup sour cream
Salt and freshly ground white pepper
2 tablespoons finely minced fresh dill
¼ pound smoked salmon, finely minced, or 1 jar (7½ ounces) of red caviar
12 to 16 Entrée Crêpes (see page 212), flavored with dill
1 cup melted butter

Preparation

1. In a mixing bowl combine the cream cheese and sour cream. Mash with a fork until the mixture is smooth and well blended, then add salt, pepper, the dill, and the smoked salmon or caviar. Blend again and taste for seasoning.

2. Fill each crêpe with a teaspoon of the mixture and fold into a triangle. Place the crêpes, in an overlapping pattern, in serving dish. Dribble with melted butter and serve immediately.

Remarks
Both the crêpes and the filling can be made well in advance. Once the crêpes are filled, however, they should be served immediately.

eggs, quiches, and crepes

Scandinavian spinach and dill crêpes

Serves: 4 to 6
Preparation time: 25 minutes
Cooking time: 45 minutes

Ingredients

2   pounds spinach
Salt
1½ sticks unsalted butter
½   cup finely minced scallion, green part included
Freshly ground white pepper
2   tablespoons finely minced fresh dill
1   large clove garlic, mashed
3   tablespoons Crème Fraîche (see page 206) or sour cream
12 to 14 Entrée Crêpes (see page 212), flavored with dill
3   tablespoons finely grated Gruyère or Parmesan cheese

Preparation

1. Remove the stems from the spinach, then wash the leaves thoroughly under cold running water.

2. Bring salted water to a boil in a large casserole. Add the spinach and cook for 5 minutes. Drain in a colander, and as soon as the spinach is cool enough to handle, squeeze out the moisture with your hands. Chop fine and reserve.

3. Melt 4 tablespoons of the butter in a large, heavy skillet. Add the scallion and cook over low heat until soft but not browned, then add the spinach. Season with salt and pepper, cover, and cook over low heat for 5 minutes. Add the dill, garlic, *crème fraîche* or sour cream. Raise the heat and cook the mixture for another 2 or 3 minutes, or until all the moisture has evaporated. Taste and correct the seasoning.

4. Melt the remaining butter in a small saucepan. Set aside and keep warm.

5. Preheat the oven to 325 degrees.

6. Fill the crêpes with the spinach mixture and roll them up, tucking in the ends. Arrange in one layer in a well-buttered baking dish. Spoon the melted butter over the crêpes and sprinkle with the cheese, then cover the dish loosely with foil and bake for 25 minutes, or until the crêpes are heated through and the cheese is melted.

7. Serve immediately, right from the baking dish.

Remarks

The crêpes can be kept hot for an hour in a turned-off oven.
For a variation, add 1 finely minced hard-boiled egg to the spinach mixture and/or 6 finely minced, cooked and shelled shrimp. In Scandinavia a flat anchovy fillet or a piece of smoked fish is often added to each crêpe; it is an interesting change.

Notes

pasta, rice, and breads

Though the world of pasta includes innumerable varieties, by far the best known and most popular outside Italy is spaghetti. This should not be surprising, because it is one of the easiest foods to cook, and is also extremely inexpensive. For as little as two or three dollars, a family of four to six can eat a filling meal once or twice a week. Spaghetti goes very well with inexpensive ingredients like tomatoes, oil, garlic, and parsley or canned tuna, pimientos, and black olives, or even simply with a little fresh butter and grated cheese. Aside from its wonderful quality of providing the cook with an easy, good one-dish meal, pasta is marvelously versatile and combines well with all sorts of vegetables, making it possible to take advantage of every season's fresh offerings. Tomatoes, mushrooms, eggplants, peppers, and herbs, as well as seafood and ground meats, all combine wonderfully with spaghetti and other varieties of pasta.

In recent years, pasta has become increasingly popular all over Europe, but is still nowhere near as popular as in this country. In fact, spaghetti has virtually become an American food. This is all the more amazing since the majority of Italian restaurants overcook it or sauce it too heavily, sometimes with canned concoctions. It is unfortunate that the majority of American spaghetti lovers have never had properly cooked spaghetti, let alone other types of pasta. Italians, aside from always slightly undercooking their pasta, also sauce it sparingly, so as to let the quality of the pasta speak for itself.

Making homemade pasta has recently become more popular here. Though extremely rewarding and not difficult to do if you own a pasta machine, it is time consuming and requires a good deal of space. Fresh pasta is sold in most Italian specialty stores in large metropolitan areas, and I find it well worth looking for. Freshly made fettucini or ravioli, store bought or homemade, is far superior to the commercial varieties available on the supermarket shelf. Most cooks, however, have to make do with store-bought varieties, and though our commercial pasta does not have the quality of the Italian brands, it is nevertheless excellent when properly cooked and sauced.

Most pasta is based on the same dough and simply cut in different shapes. In Italy, to add to the confusion, different names are given to almost identical kinds of pasta, depending on the region. When choosing spaghetti or other pasta, however, you should have in mind the kind of sauce you will be serving with it. Thin spaghetti (also called "spaghettini") is best with seafood sauces and other sauces based on olive oil. The regular spaghetti is more suitable to butter and cream sauces, and some prefer it also for tomato sauces. Thick tubular pasta such as macaroni and rigatoni lend themselves best to meat sauces. Although pasta can be considered a basic and simple food, it requires as much care as any other dish. Like other "basics," pasta can also be as outstanding and memorable as any dish from the *grande cuisine*.

Rice is by far the most popular grain in the world. It has always played a major role in Middle and Far Eastern cooking, but surprisingly enough in France, where food is probably better understood than anywhere else in the world, the cooking of rice has been practically ignored. Of all the European countries, Italy has mastered the art of cooking rice best.

The special rice grown throughout the rich Po Valley has inspired some of the great, by now classic, dishes that were originally part of the peasant cuisines of the area. Soil and climate once more are seen to place an indelible stamp on the basic foods of each nation. As an example, the rice grown in the Piedmont province of Italy is especially suited to the unique method of slow braising that makes a perfect *risotto*, such as the simple Lemon Risotto on page 119. Another specialty of the Piedmont is *risotto alla piemontese*, which combines rice with the rare and aromatic white truffle found in the same province. From Lombardy comes *risotto alla milanese*, a creamy, saffron-flavored rice dish with kernels that look like little grains of gold. But the creativity and imagination of Italian rice cooking does not stop with these dishes. *Risotti* can be as varied and as differently sauced as pasta. Seafood, seasonal vegetables such as peas, asparagus, and zucchini, as well as tomatoes and mushrooms, have all lent their delicious flavors to the riches of Italy.

Although rice is to northern Italy what pasta is to southern Italy, *risotto*, unlike pasta, has never gained widespread popularity either in Europe or in the United States. This is probably because making a *risotto* is somewhat more difficult than cooking pasta. Few Italian restaurants, even in Italy, excel in the art of *risotto* making—a great shame, since it can be one of the world's great dishes when properly done.

Traditionally, the *risotto* is served separately at the beginning of the meal, not as an accompaniment to the main course. There are exceptions, such as the *risotto alla milanese*, which is served along with the classic braised veal knuckles—the *osso buco*. But in Italy today, where diets are as important as they are here, *risotto* is usually served alone as a lunch dish, followed by a simple green salad and a light dessert like fruit and cheese. *Risotti* make perfect one-dish meals; they are as inexpensive as pasta and provide a wonderful way to make use of leftovers of meats or stews, or of chicken livers or fresh tomato sauce.

Though Italian rice is naturally best suited for *risotto*, it is not always available in this country. I have found that long-grain Carolina rice is an excellent substitute. Do not make the dish with parboiled rice, for it cannot properly absorb the liquid, and you won't achieve the creamy texture characteristic of the best *risotti*. But just as with pasta and other foods, once you come to a basic understanding of the nature of rice, you will recognize that it is a superb carrier of sauces, meats, and vegetables.

Bread is the most basic food of the Western world. In one way or another, it is used extensively in both elegant and peasant cooking, either with the meal or as a basis for the meal itself.

Many countries, especially in Central and Northern Europe, have produced innumerable varieties of bread. Scandinavians, for example, use ryes, pumpernickels, and brown breads as the basis for their smorgasbord, a beautiful array of elegant open sandwiches. The dark, crusty breads of Central Europe are quite different, and are particularly good as accompaniments to hearty soups, such as split-pea and cabbage, as well as the one-dish meals in this book. Indeed, it is important to understand how certain breads relate to certain dishes.

The long, thin, crusty loaf of French bread is by far the most popular and versatile member of the bread family. Italy, Spain, and Greece all have produced their own version of this classic, a fact that is understandable because the bread has an affinity to any part of the meal.

The French love their bread at the beginning and end of nearly every repast. It goes wonderfully with an appetizer salad and equally well with a good piece of cheese. French bread is also widely used in cooking. Fried in olive oil, it is added to many peasant soups or served on the side.

I have chosen some of the lesser-known peasant bread dishes for this book, including Pan Basquaise (see page 195) and Pan Catalan (see page 196). I like their heartiness and gutsy flavor, and they are a sampling of how bread can be used creatively as the center of the meal.

The simple white loaf of bread is, in my opinion, the most suitable for sandwiches using cold chicken, leftover turkey, or almost any other cold meats. White bread is also the basis for some classics, like the *French croque monsieur,* a cheese and ham sandwich fried in butter, as well as for the Toast Genevoise in this book (see page 199). These make good openers to simple meals.

Sautéed white bread is a wonderful base for poached or scrambled eggs, and for sautéed vegetables such as spinach and mushrooms. It can also be used imaginatively, as in Crostini alla Romana (see page 194) and Brochettes of Chicken Livers (see page 117).

In recent years there has been a fantastic revival in home bread making. We have become keenly aware that a good bread is not easy to find, and what we do find on the supermarket shelf is more often than not dull and tasteless. If a good bakery is not nearby, learning to make your own can be well worth your time, as well as great fun. It should be remembered that every dish gains importance with the right bread, and there is really no end to the possibilities it gives the creative cook.

Gnocchi in anchovy butter

Serves: 4
Preparation time: 15 minutes
Cooking time: 25 minutes

Ingredients

2 cups milk
½ cup semolina
2 egg yolks
4 tablespoons butter
½ cup plus 2 tablespoons freshly grated
   Parmesan cheese
Salt and freshly ground white pepper
Pinch of freshly grated nutmeg

Anchovy butter:

6 tablespoons butter, softened
1 teaspoon lemon juice
2 shallots, finely minced
1 tablespoon finely minced fresh parsley
4 anchovies, finely minced
Salt and freshly ground white pepper

Preparation

1. Begin by making the anchovy butter.
In a mixing bowl combine the butter, lemon
juice, shallots, parsley, and anchovies.
Mash with a fork until the mixture is well
blended, then season with salt and pepper
to taste and chill until ready to use.

2. Bring the milk to a boil in a large, heavy
saucepan. Add the semolina in a light,
steady stream, stirring constantly until the
mixture gets very thick. Cook for 3 to 4
minutes, stirring constantly, then remove
the saucepan from the heat. Beat in the
egg yolks, butter, and the ½ cup of
Parmesan and blend thoroughly. Season
with salt, pepper, and a pinch of nutmeg
and set aside.

3. Rinse a rectangular baking dish with
cold water. Spoon the semolina mixture

into the dish and flatten it evenly with your
hands to a thickness of ½ inch. Chill
for 1 hour.

4. Preheat the oven to 325 degrees.

5. With a cookie cutter or a small glass,
cut the chilled semolina into small disks.
Arrange them, slightly overlapping, in one
layer in a well-buttered baking dish. Dot
with bits of anchovy butter and sprinkle
with the remaining cheese. Bake for 15
minutes, then run the *gnocchi* under the
broiler for 2 to 3 minutes, or until lightly
browned. Serve immediately right from
the baking dish.

Remarks

When making the *gnocchi* in the summer
or early fall, add 1 tablespoon of finely
minced fresh oregano, basil or mint to
the anchovy butter.

Notes

Spaghettini and clams primavera

Serves: 4 to 6
Preparation time: 45 minutes
Cooking time: 25 minutes

Spaghettini in clam sauce is an old time favorite, but is, unfortunately, often a disappointment. The secret is simple: the clams must be fresh and the spaghetti not overcooked.

Ingredients

3   dozen small clams
¼ cup water
⅓ cup olive oil
1   tablespoon finely minced shallots
6   peppercorns
2   tablespoons finely minced fresh oregano or 1 teaspoon dried
1   bay leaf
1   teaspoon all-purpose flour mashed together with 1 tablespoon butter
½ cup finely minced fresh parsley
2   teaspoons finely minced garlic
1   tablespoon minced fresh oregano or marjoram
Salt
1   pound thin spaghetti
Freshly ground black pepper

Preparation

1. Scrub the clams thoroughly under cold running water, removing as much sand as possible, then soak in a large bowl of cold water for 2 or 3 hours.

2. In a large, heavy, flameproof casserole combine the water, oil, shallots, peppercorns, oregano, and bay leaf. Add the clams, cover the casserole and steam the clams until they open. As soon as some open, remove them with a slotted spoon to a side dish and continue steaming the others. When the clams are cool enough to handle, remove them from their shells and cut each into three to four pieces. Set aside.

3. Strain the clam juice through a fine sieve and return it to the casserole. Reduce the broth to 1 cup and whisk in the butter and flour paste, just enough to thicken the broth lightly. Add the parsley, garlic, oregano, and clams and set aside. Keep warm.

4. Bring 5 quarts of salted water to a boil in a large flameproof casserole. Add the spaghetti and cook over high heat for 8 to 9 minutes, or until barely done; the spaghetti should still be slightly chewy. Add 1 to 2 cups cold water to the pot to stop the spaghetti from further cooking. Drain.

5. Return the spaghetti to the pot or put into a deep serving bowl. Pour the sauce over the spaghetti and toss lightly with 2 forks, then add a heavy grinding of black pepper and serve immediately.

Notes

Spaghettini and mussels alfio

Serves: 4
Preparation time: 35 minutes
Cooking time: 30 minutes

■●

Aside from a spectacular antipasto table, Alfio's in Milan offers some of the best seafood dishes in the city. The spaghettini with mussels, served in individual earthenware dishes, are marvelously fresh and an old-time favorite of mine.

Ingredients

1   onion, finely minced
½ cup white wine
1   Bouquet Garni (see page 214)
24 to 32 fresh mussels, well scrubbed
6   Tablespoons olive oil
½ cup finely minced fresh parsley
4   large cloves garlic, finely minced
2   cups Fresh Tomato Sauce (see page 207)
2   teaspoons dried oregano
Salt and freshly ground black pepper
1   pound thin spaghetti

Optional:
1   Beurre Manié (see page 213)

Preparation

1. Place the onion, white wine, *bouquet garni*, and mussels in a large, flameproof casserole. Bring to a boil, then reduce the heat, cover, and simmer the mussels until they open. Set aside to cool, then remove the mussels to a side dish with a slotted spoon.

2. Raise the heat and reduce the poaching liquid to ½ cup. Strain and reserve.

3. Heat the oil in a large, heavy saucepan. Add half the parsley and 2 cloves of the garlic. Cook the mixture over low heat for 2 or 3 minutes without browning, then add the tomato sauce, the reserved poaching liquid, the oregano, salt, and pepper. Simmer the sauce for 5 minutes, then, if the sauce seems thin, whisk in the *beurre manié*. Add the mussels, in their shells, heat through and set aside. Keep warm.

4. Bring salted water to a boil in a large, flameproof casserole. Add the spaghetti and cook over high heat for 9 to 12 minutes, or until barely tender. As soon as the spaghetti is done, add 4 cups of cold water to the pot to stop further cooking, then drain the spaghetti and pour into a deep serving bowl or into individual earthenware dishes.

5. Pour the mussels and sauce over the spaghetti, toss with 2 serving spoons, and sprinkle with the remaining parsley and garlic. Add a heavy grinding of black pepper and serve.

Remarks

You may cook the mussels ahead of time and reheat them in the sauce just before cooking the spaghetti. The mussels in the tomato sauce, without the spaghetti, make an excellent appetizer by themselves.

Notes

pasta, rice, and breads

Spaghettini alla rustica

Serves: 4
Preparation time: 10 minutes
Cooking time: 10 to 12 minutes

Here is a dish I discovered in a small Basque restaurant. Since it is rare to find spicy dishes in Italian cooking, I have a feeling that the dish got spicier as it traveled across France to the Basque country.

Ingredients

Salt
1 pound thin spaghetti
¾ cup fruity olive oil
4 cloves garlic, cut in half
1 to 2 dried hot chili pepper, cut in half
2 tablespoons minced fresh parsley
15 shrimp, peeled and cubed
Freshly ground black pepper

Garnish:
2 tablespoons minced fresh parsley
2 cloves garlic, finely minced

Preparation

1. Bring plenty of salted water to a boil in a large casserole. Add the spaghettini and cook for 8 to 9 minutes, or until barely tender.

2. While the spaghetti is cooking, heat the olive oil, together with 2 cloves of the garlic, peeled but left whole, and the chili pepper, in a large, heavy skillet. As soon as the garlic is browned, remove and discard. Add 2 tablespoons of the parsley and the shrimp and cook for 1 or 2 minutes, or until the shrimp turn bright pink. Season with salt and pepper, then remove the pan from the heat, discard the chili pepper, and set aside.

3. Drain the spaghetti, add to the skillet, and toss lightly in the oil and shrimp mixture. Add a heavy grinding of black pepper and garnish with garlic and parsley. Serve immediately.

Remarks

This dish should be quite spicy. Test it the first time with one chili pepper; you may increase it to two for a heartier spicy flavor.

Notes

Spaghettini in tuna and anchovy sauce

Serves: 4
Preparation time: 10 minutes
Cooking time: 20 minutes

Ingredients

½ cup olive oil
½ cup finely minced parsley
4 large cloves garlic, finely minced
½ cup finely minced fresh basil
2 tablespoons finely minced fresh oregano or 1 teaspoon dried
2½ cups Fresh Tomato Sauce (see page 207)
1 can (7½ ounces) tuna in olive oil
6 anchovy fillets, finely minced
10 oil-cured black olives, pitted and cut in half
Salt and freshly ground black pepper
1 pound thin spaghetti
1 cup finely cubed mozzarella cheese

Preparation

1. Heat the oil in a large, heavy skillet. Add 2 tablespoons of the parsley, half the minced garlic, the basil, and oregano and cook for 2 minutes. Add the tomato sauce and simmer, partially covered, for 10 minutes. Add the tuna, anchovies, and black olives and heat through. Season with salt and pepper and set aside. Keep warm.

2. Bring salted water to a boil in a large, flameproof casserole. Add the spaghetti and cook over high heat for 8 to 9 minutes, or until barely tender. As soon as the spaghetti is done, add 4 cups of cold water to the pot to stop further cooking. Drain and pour into a large serving bowl.

3. Add the sauce and toss the spaghetti with 2 forks. Sprinkle with the remaining parsley, garlic, and the cheese, add a generous grinding of black pepper, and serve immediately.

Cold rice ring andalouse

Serves: 6 to 8
Preparation time: 35 minutes
Cooking time: 20 minutes (for the rice)

Ingredients

2½ cups Mayonnaise (see page 208)
1 can (3½ ounces) tuna in oil
3 large cloves garlic, mashed
Juice of 1 lemon
2 tablespoons chili sauce
1 tablespoon tiny, well-drained capers
Salt and freshly ground black pepper
1½ cups long-grain Carolina rice, cooked until tender
1 small cucumber, peeled, seeded, and cubed
1 ripe tomato, finely cubed
1 green pepper, cored, seeded, and cubed
4 to 6 radishes, cubed
2 tablespoons finely minced scallion
2 tablespoons finely minced fresh parsley
½ cup black olives, pitted and cut in half
2 tablespoons olive oil

Garnish:
8 cooked, shelled, and deveined shrimp
Sprigs of fresh watercress

Preparation

1. In the container of a blender combine half the mayonnaise, the tuna, 2 cloves of the garlic and half the lemon juice. Blend the mixture at high speed until smooth. Taste and correct the seasoning. Set aside.

2. In a bowl combine the remaining mayonnaise with the chili sauce, remaining garlic, and capers. Blend thoroughly, season with salt and pepper, and set aside.

3. In a large bowl combine the cooked rice with the tuna mayonnaise. Fold thoroughly and pour the rice into a well-oiled ring mold. Chill until serving.

4. In a mixing bowl combine the cucumber, tomato, green pepper, radishes, scallion, parsley and olives. Season with salt and pepper, sprinkle with the remaining lemon juice and olive oil, and toss lightly. Chill.

5. Thirty minutes before serving, unmold the rice onto a round platter. Fill the center with the vegetable salad, spoon the chili-flavored mayonnaise over the rice, garnish with shrimp, and surround with sprigs of watercress.

Notes

Baked rice à la catalane

Serves: 4 to 6
Preparation time: 35 minutes
Cooking time: 50 minutes

There is no doubt that the *paella* is synonymous with Spanish cooking. It is, however, an intricate dish to prepare, one that demands many ingredients, several of which are quite expensive. There are innumerable simple and inexpensive versions of the *paella* that the everyday Spanish cook serves her family. This is one I grew up with.

Ingredients

Salt
½ cup fresh peas
½ cup diced fresh green beans
1 cup cubed, lean salt pork
2 tablespoons chicken fat or vegetable oil
4 to 5 chicken wings, cut in half and tips removed
Freshly ground black pepper
3 to 4 chicken livers, trimmed and cut in half
1 large onion, finely minced
3 cloves garlic, minced
3 large tomatoes, peeled, seeded and chopped
1 teaspoon saffron
1½ cups raw long-grain Carolina rice
½ cup cooked chick-peas (see page 30)
2 cups Chicken Stock (see page 203) or water

Garnish:

Finely sliced *chorizo* or garlic-flavored sausage
Strips of pimiento
Finely minced fresh parsley
Lemon quarters

Preparation

1. Bring salted water to a boil in a sauce-pan. Add the peas and cook until they are barely tender, or for about 5 to 6 minutes. Remove with a slotted spoon to a bowl and reserve. Add the beans to the sauce-pan and cook for 5 or 6 minutes, or until barely tender. Drain and add to the bowl with the peas.

2. Bring water to a boil in a saucepan. Add the salt pork and cook for 5 minutes, then drain and dry thoroughly with paper towels.

3. Heat the chicken fat in a large, heavy skillet. Add the salt pork and cook until very crisp, then remove the cubes to a side dish with a slotted spoon.

4. Add the chicken wings to the skillet and cook over moderate heat until nicely browned on all sides. Season with salt and pepper and remove to the side dish.

5. Discard all but 3 tablespoons of fat from the pan. Add the chicken livers and cook them quickly over high heat until well browned, then season with salt and pepper and remove with a slotted spoon to the side dish.

6. To the fat remaining in the pan add the onion and garlic. Cook over medium heat until the onion is soft and lightly browned. Add the tomatoes, saffron, salt, and pepper and cook the mixture until it is thick and all the tomato juices have evaporated. Preheat oven to 350 degrees.

7. Add the rice and stir until it is well blended with the tomato mixture. Return the chicken wings to the pan, together with the salt pork, chicken livers, beans, peas, and chick-peas. Add 2 cups of chicken stock or water. Season with salt and pepper, bring to a boil, cover, and set in the middle part of the oven. Bake for 25 to 30 minutes, or until the rice is tender and all the stock has been absorbed. Remove the pan from the oven, garnish with sliced sausage and strips of pimiento, sprinkle with parsley, and place lemon quarters around.

8. Serve immediately, directly from the skillet.

Remarks

The entire dish can be made ahead of time up to the step of adding the rice. Once the dish is baked, however, it should be served as soon as possible. Since chick-peas take a long time to cook, you may use a good canned variety for this dish. You can also substitute cooked white beans for the chick-peas. Other vegetables, such as zucchini and artichoke hearts, can be added to the rice as well.

Notes

pasta, rice, and breads

Arroz cubano

Serves: 4
Preparation time: 20 minutes
Cooking time: 40 to 45 minutes

Although *arroz cubano* means "Cuban rice," this dish is actually Spanish. In northern Spain it is the usual fare in every simple home at least once a week. Fried bananas served together with tomato sauce may sound like a strange combination, but I think it is delicious.

Ingredients

6   tablespoons butter
1   small onion, peeled and finely minced
1½ cups raw long-grain Carolina rice
3   cups hot water
Salt
4   slightly green bananas
All-purpose flour
½   cup olive or peanut oil
4   whole eggs
Freshly ground white pepper
1½ to 2 cups hot Provençal Tomato
     Fondue (see page 207)

Preparation

1. In a heavy, 2-quart saucepan melt 3 tablespoons of the butter. Add the onion and cook until soft but not browned, or for about 3 minutes. Add the rice and cook, stirring, until it turns an opaque white, then add the hot water all at once. Bring to a boil, add a large pinch of salt, and reduce the heat. Cover the saucepan with a sheet of buttered waxed paper and the lid and simmer the rice for 25 to 30 minutes.

2. While the rice is cooking, dredge the bananas lightly in flour, shaking off the excess. If the bananas are large, cut them in half crosswise.

3. Heat ¼ cup of the oil in a large skillet. Add the bananas and cook for 2 or 3 minutes on each side, or until nicely browned. Remove the bananas to a large, oval serving platter.

4. When the rice is done, whisk in the remaining butter. Spoon the rice into the center of the platter, flatten it out slightly with a spatula, and form into an oval. Cover the dish and keep warm.

5. Heat the remaining oil in a large skillet. Break the eggs into it, one by one, and cook over low heat until the whites are set, spooning a little oil over the yolks. Season the eggs with salt and pepper and transfer them carefully to the serving dish, topping the rice.

6. Spoon the tomato fondue around the platter, between each banana, and serve immediately.

Remarks

In the summer I often substitute warm leftover Ratatouille (see page 112) for the bananas and flavor the rice with a few finely minced basil or mint leaves.

Notes

Risotto con calamari

Serves: 4 to 6
Preparation time: 20 minutes
Cooking time: 45 minutes

Most European countries as well as the United States have always ignored the tremendous versatility of rice, generally serving it only as an accompaniment to main courses. Italy is the only European country to have concocted marvelous creations with rice, and this *risotto* is proof of Italian cooks' ingenuity.

Ingredients

2 to 3 small very fresh squid
¼ cup olive oil
3 large cloves garlic, minced
1 small dried hot chili pepper
1 cup peeled, seeded, and chopped tomatoes
1 teaspoon tomato paste
½ teaspoon dried oregano
¼ cup finely minced fresh parsley
¼ cup white wine
1 bay leaf
Salt and freshly ground black pepper
1½ cups raw Italian (Arborio) or long-grain Carolina rice
4 to 5 cups Light Chicken or White Stock (see pages 201 or 204)
½ teaspoon finely grated lemon rind

Preparation

1. Have the fish market clean the squid for you. Cut them into small cubes.

2. Heat the oil in a heavy, 3-quart sauce-pan. Add 2 cloves of the garlic, the chili pepper, tomatoes and paste, oregano, 2 tablespoons of the parsley, and the wine. Cook over high heat until all the wine has evaporated. Add the squid, bay leaf, salt and pepper, then reduce the heat and cook the mixture, partially covered, for 20 minutes, stirring it from time to time.

3. Mix in the rice and stir to cover it well with the tomato mixture. Add ½ cup of stock, bring it to a boil, stirring constantly with a wooden spoon until all the stock has been absorbed. Continue adding the stock, about ¾ cup at a time, stirring constantly until it is absorbed. (The rice should be finished in 25 minutes; it should be creamy and slightly chewy.) Taste for seasoning, adding salt and a heavy grinding of black pepper if necessary. Remove the rice from the heat, stir in the remaining parsley and garlic and the lemon rind.

4. Pour the rice into a warm serving bowl and serve immediately.

Remarks

A *risotto* is one of those easy yet tricky dishes. The rice must be stirred constantly, and each cup of stock should evaporate completely before the next one is added. A good *risotto* is creamy, not dry, and the kernels must still retain some chewiness. A good *risotto* is only learned by experience, but once mastered it is well worth the effort.

Risotto genovese

Serves: 4
Preparation time: 10 minutes
Cooking time: 25 to 30 minutes

Because I have a passion for fresh herbs, especially basil, I try to incorporate them into as many dishes as I can during the summer season. This variation of the classic Italian *pesto* is particularly interesting, and for a change is not used with spaghetti.

Ingredients

2   tablespoons butter
2   tablespoons finely minced scallion
1   cup raw Italian (Arborio) rice or long-grain Carolina rice
3 to 4 cups Light Chicken Stock (see page 204)
½   cup heavy cream
½   cup finely cubed prosciutto or Westphalian ham
Salt and freshly ground black pepper
1   clove garlic, mashed
2   heaping tablespoons Basil Paste (see page 210)
1   tablespoon finely grated fresh Parmesan cheese
Garnish:
1   bowl of freshly grated Parmesan

Preparation

1. In a heavy 2-quart saucepan melt the butter. Add the scallion and cook for 2 minutes, or until soft but not browned. Add the rice and stir for a minute or two to coat it well with the butter. Add 1 cup of stock and bring it to a boil, then reduce the heat and simmer the rice, stirring constantly, until all the stock has been absorbed. Continue adding the stock, 1 cup at a time, cooking the rice, uncovered, until all the stock has been absorbed and the rice is tender but still slightly chewy. The rice should be done in 25 minutes.

2. Add the cream and prosciutto, salt, and pepper. Cook for 2 or 3 minutes, or until the prosciutto is heated through and the cream has been absorbed.

3. Add the garlic and the basil paste and incorporate it gently into the rice. Taste and correct the seasoning, then pour into a warm serving dish. Sprinkle with Parmesan and serve immediately, accompanied by a bowl of freshly grated Parmesan.

Remarks

Though most *risotti* are served as first courses in Italy, this dish is an excellent accompaniment to roast leg of lamb, shish kebab, or a ragoût of beef.

Notes

Risotto à l'indienne

Serves: 4 to 6
Preparation time: 25 minutes
Cooking time: 30 to 35 minutes

Though the use of curry is rare in Italian cooking, I find that it gives great character to this lovely *risotto* created at the Al Porto restaurant in Milan.

Ingredients

7   tablespoons butter
1   tablespoon vegetable oil
1   onion, finely minced
2   cloves garlic, finely minced
1   large, ripe tomato, peeled, seeded, and chopped
1   teaspoon tomato paste
10 to 12 shrimp, peeled, deveined, and diced
1½ teaspoons curry powder
Salt and freshly ground black pepper
1½ cups raw Italian (Arborio) rice or long-grain Carolina rice
⅓   cup white wine
4 to 5 cups Light Chicken (see page 204) or White Stock (see page 201)
⅓   cup heavy cream
½   cup freshly grated Parmesan cheese

Garnish:
2   tablespoons finely minced fresh parsley

Preparation

1. Heat 2 tablespoons of butter and the oil in a small, heavy skillet. Add the onion and garlic and cook until the onion is soft but not browned, then add the tomatoes and tomato paste and cook the mixture for 2 to 3 minutes, until most of the tomato juices have evaporated. Add the shrimp, curry powder, salt, and pepper and continue cooking for 3 to 4 minutes, or until the shrimp turn pink. Set the pan aside.

2. Heat 3 tablespoons of butter in a heavy-bottomed, 2-quart saucepan. Add the rice and stir until it is well coated with the butter. Add the wine and continue cooking over high heat until the wine has evaporated, then add 1 cup of warm stock and cook, stirring constantly with a wooden spoon, until all the stock has been absorbed before adding more stock. Continue adding the stock, 1 cup at a time, until the rice is almost tender.

3. Add the cream and shrimp mixture to the rice, as well as salt and a heavy grinding of black pepper, and continue stirring the rice until it is done, or for about 25 minutes; it should be creamy and still somewhat chewy. Remove the rice from the heat and beat in the remaining butter and Parmesan.

4. Garnish the rice with the parsley and serve immediately.

Remarks

Risotto should be made at the last minute. However, it can be kept warm for 30 to 40 minutes in the top part of a double boiler. The shrimp mixture can be made well in advance.

Lemon risotto

Serves: 6
Preparation time: 10 minutes
Cooking time: 25 to 30 minutes

Here is a specialty from the Piedmont area of Italy. It is a good, simple dish that can be served as an appetizer, a light supper dish, or as an accompaniment to roast chicken or duck.

Ingredients

3   egg yolks
½ cup finely grated fresh Parmesan cheese
1½ to 2 tablespoons lemon juice
5   tablespoons unsalted butter
1   medium onion, finely minced
1½ cups Italian (Arborio) rice or long-grain Carolina rice
4 to 5 cups hot Chicken Stock (see page 203)
Salt and freshly ground white pepper

Garnish:
Bowl of freshly grated Parmesan

Preparation

1. In a small mixing bowl combine the egg yolks, Parmesan, and lemon juice. Whisk the mixture until well blended and set aside.

2. Heat 3 tablespoons of the butter in a heavy, two-quart saucepan. Add the onion and cook until soft but not browned. Add the rice and cook until it is well coated with the butter and turns an opaque white. Add ½ cup of the chicken stock and cook over medium heat, stirring constantly, until all the liquid has been absorbed. Continue adding the stock, ½ cup at a time, stirring constantly and waiting till all the stock is absorbed before adding more.

3. After 20 minutes taste the rice, it should be slightly soft yet still somewhat chewy. Add the remaining stock, ¼ cup at a time, still stirring constantly. (Do not drown the rice; it should be creamy but not runny.) Season with salt and pepper.

4. Remove the saucepan from the heat. Add the yolk mixture and fold it into the rice, then taste and correct the seasoning, adding more lemon juice if you like. Add the remaining butter and stir gently until the butter is melted.

5. Serve immediately, with additional freshly grated Parmesan on the side.

Notes

Risotto verde

Serves: 4 to 6
Preparation time: 20 minutes
Cooking time: 45 minutes

The ingenuity of Italian cooks who successfully combine rice with the best of the season's produce in one simple dish is remarkable. Here is a sample of northern Italian cuisine at its absolute freshest.

Ingredients

3 to 4 stalks of asparagus
Salt
½ cup shelled fresh peas
Pinch of sugar
6 tablespoons butter
1½ cups diced zucchini
Freshly ground white pepper
1 onion, finely minced
1½ cups Italian (Arborio) rice or long-grain Carolina rice
4 to 5 cups Light Chicken Stock (see page 204)
2 tablespoons freshly grated Parmesan cheese

Garnish:
Finely minced fresh parsley

Preparation

1. Remove the tough ends of the asparagus. Scrape them with a vegetable peeler and set aside.

2. Bring salted water to a boil in a large saucepan. Add the asparagus and cook until tender, or for about 7 to 9 minutes. Remove them with kitchen tongs and place on a double layer of paper towels to drain. Cut into small rounds and set aside.

3. Add the peas, together with a good pinch of sugar, to the boiling water. Cook for 10 minutes, or until tender. Drain and set aside.

4. Heat 2 tablespoons of the butter in a heavy 3-quart saucepan. Add the zucchini and cook over medium heat until soft and lightly browned. Season with salt and pepper and remove to a side dish with a slotted spoon.

5. Add 2 more tablespoons of butter to the saucepan. Add the onion and cook until it is soft but not browned, then add the rice and cook for 1 minute, stirring to coat the rice well with the butter. Add 2 cups of stock and bring to a boil. Reduce the heat and simmer, partially covered, for 5 to 6 minutes, stirring several times until all the stock has been absorbed. Add more stock and continue simmering the rice, stirring frequently, until it is tender but still slightly chewy. The rice should be done in 25 to 30 minutes, and by the time it is done it should have absorbed 4 to 5 cups of stock.

6. When the rice is almost done, stir in the peas, asparagus, and zucchini. Stir carefully. Cover the saucepan and finish cooking.

7. When the rice is done, fold in the remaining butter and Parmesan cheese. Taste and correct the seasoning, adding a good grinding of pepper. Put the risotto in individual soup plates, sprinkle with parsley, and serve with additional freshly grated Parmesan on the side.

Crostini alla romana

Serves: 6 to 8
Preparation time: 15 to 20 minutes
Cooking time: 5 minutes

Most Mediterranean countries uses bread ingeniously in their everyday meals. The Basques have the Pan Basquaise (see page 195), and the Spaniards make wonderful use of ripe tomatoes in the Pan Catalan (see page 196). Here is a Roman dish made with anchovies and garlic that I consider one of Italy's best dishes.

Ingredients

1½ sticks unsalted butter
6 to 7 anchovy fillets, finely mashed
2   cloves garlic, mashed
6 to 8 slices of mozzarella or fontina
        cheese, cut ⅛-inch thick
12 to 16 slices of French bread, cut
        ¼-inch thick
Vegetable oil for frying
1   cup milk
3   eggs, beaten lightly

Preparation

1. Heat the butter in a small saucepan over low heat. Add 4 of the anchovies and the garlic and simmer, stirring, for 3 to 5 minutes, or until the anchovies are reduced to a paste. Set aside and keep warm.

2. Place a slice of mozzarella and a bit of mashed anchovy between 2 slices of bread, making 6 to 8 sandwiches.

3. Heat the oil in a deep, heavy skillet to the depth of one inch until hot but not smoking.

4. Dip the sandwiches in the milk and then in the beaten egg. Fry the sandwiches in the hot oil on both sides until they are golden brown, carefully regulating the heat; the bread must not burn and the cheese must have time to melt.

5. Drain the *crostini* on paper towels and place on a serving platter. Serve immediately with the anchovy and garlic butter on the side.

Notes

Pan basquaise

Serves: 4 to 6
Preparation time: 15 minutes
Cooking time: 10 minutes

Here is a robust appetizer typical of the Basque country. I find it especially suitable for outdoor entertaining, lunches and barbecues. Serve with a full-bodied red wine or *sangria* and plenty of napkins.

Ingredients

2 ⸱ loaves of French bread
4 tablespoons olive oil
4 large red peppers, roasted, peeled and finely sliced (see page 31)
⅔ cup flaked tuna in olive oil
Salt and freshly ground black pepper
2 tablespoons wine vinegar
4 tablespoons finely minced fresh parsley
3 cloves garlic, finely minced

Garnish:
4 hard-boiled eggs, sliced
8 black Greek olives
Finely minced parsley
Olive oil

Preparation

1. Preheat the oven to 350 degrees.

2. Cut the loaves of bread in half lengthwise and then crosswise into 4-inch pieces.

3. Heat 3 tablespoons of the oil in a heavy, 10-inch skillet. Add the peppers and cook them over high heat for 2 or 3 minutes, then add the tuna, salt, and pepper, continuing to cook until the tuna is heated through. Add the vinegar, 2 tablespoons of the parsley, and garlic and cook the mixture until the vinegar has evaporated, or for about 2 more minutes. Remove the pan from the heat, taste the mixture for seasoning, and set aside.

4. Place the bread on a baking sheet and toast it in the oven until it is warm and crisp, but not brown.

5. Place the bread on a serving platter and top with the pepper and tuna mixture. Garnish with sliced eggs and top each slice with an olive, pitted and cut in half lengthwise. Dribble a little oil over each piece of bread and sprinkle with the remaining parsley. Serve warm or at room temperature.

Notes

pasta, rice, and breads

Pan catalan

Serves: 4 to 6
Preparation time: 10 minutes
Cooking time: 2 to 3 minutes

Here is a dish that is as true to Catalan cooking as apple pie is to the American kitchen. *Pan catalan* is a peasant dish, simple and delicious. When you first serve it your guests may regard it skeptically, but never mind—they will soon appreciate the wholesome flavor of this sandwich.

Ingredients

1   loaf of French bread, cut in half lengthwise
2   cloves garlic, cut
3 to 4 ripe tomatoes
Fruity olive oil
Salt

Garnish:
8 to 12 slices of finely sliced prosciutto
Finely sliced garlic sausage
Finely sliced Bermuda onion
A bowl of black Greek olives

Preparation

1. Preheat the broiler.

2. Rub the bread with the cut side of a garlic clove, then cut each half crosswise into 3 pieces. Place the bread under the broiler and toast until it is lightly browned, but do not let it burn.

3. Cut the tomatoes in half crosswise; rub the toasted bread with the cut side of the tomato, soaking the bread with the tomato pulp. Discard the peel. Dribble the "tomato bread" with olive oil and sprinkle lightly with salt.

4. Top each piece of bread with a ring of Bermuda onion and an olive. Serve immediately, with a side platter of prosciutto and sliced sausages.

Remarks

Pan catalan is often served in northern Spain as an accompaniment to a potato omelet (see Frittata Catalana, page 165), with a side platter of *chorizo* (Spanish sausage) or other garlicky, spicy sausage.

Notes

Toast à l'anglaise

Serves: 4 to 6
Preparation time: 15 minutes
Cooking time: 40 minutes

Leftover roast beef is mostly reserved for that ever-so-dull roast beef sandwich often heavily soused with Russian dressing. Here is a delicious way to use leftover roast beef. Serve it as a light appetizer or luncheon dish.

Ingredients

4   tablespoons butter
2   teaspoons Dijon mustard
Worcestershire sauce
Salt and freshly ground black pepper
1   tablespoon vegetable oil
3   onions, thinly sliced
8 to 12 slices of white bread, crust
    removed
4 to 6 slices rare roast beef
½   cup Clarified Butter (see page 213)

Garnish:
4 to 6 dill gherkins
Sprigs of parsley

Preparation

1. Combine 2 tablespoons of the butter and the mustard in a small bowl. Add a few drops of Worcestershire sauce and a pinch each of salt and pepper. Mash the mixture with a fork until smooth and well blended, then set aside.

2. Heat the remaining butter and the oil in a heavy skillet. Add the onions and cook, covered, over low heat for 30 minutes, or until very soft and lightly browned. Drain the onions and set aside.

3. Spread the bread slices with the mustard butter. Place a slice of roast beef on half the bread slices, top with a little of the onion mixture, and cover with the remaining bread.

4. Heat the clarified butter in a large skillet, add the sandwiches, and sauté them on both sides until nicely browned. Transfer to a serving platter and top each one with a dill gherkin, finely sliced lengthwise, and a sprig of parsley.

5. Serve immediately.

Notes

Avocado toast à la mexicaine

Serves: 4
Preparation time: 10 minutes
Cooking time: 5 minutes

Ingredients

4   slices of white bread, cut ½ inch thick
½   cup Clarified Butter (see page 213) or
    4 tablespoons butter and 2 tablespoons
    vegetable oil
4   slices Canadian bacon
2   tablespoons olive oil
¼   cup fresh, white bread crumbs
2   tablespoons finely minced fresh parsley
1   large clove garlic, finely minced
1   ripe avocado
Salt and freshly ground black pepper
1   ripe tomato, sliced

Preparation

1. Preheat the broiler. Remove the crusts
from the bread. Heat the clarified butter
in a large, heavy skillet and sauté the bread
slices until they are nicely browned on
both sides. Remove to a baking sheet.

2. To the fat remaining in the pan add the
Canadian bacon. Cook for 1 minute on
each side, then remove to a side dish.
Add the olive oil to the pan and heat. Add
the bread crumbs, parsley, and garlic and
cook the mixture for 2 minutes, or until
the bread crumbs are browned. Set aside.

3. Peel the avocado and cut it in half
lengthwise. Remove the pit, then slice it
thin crosswise. Arrange the avocado slices
on the bread, season with salt and pepper,
and top with a slice each of bacon and
tomato. Spoon a little of the bread crumb
mixture over each piece of toast.

4. Run the toast under the broiler for 2 to 4
minutes or until heated through.

5. Transfer to individual plates and serve
immediately.

Notes

pasta, rice, and breads

Toast genevoise

Serves: 4 to 6
Preparation time: 10 minutes
Cooking time: 10 minutes

Open toasted sandwiches are common appetizers for family dining in many Central European countries. Some countries, such as Sweden and Denmark, have actually created masterpieces in decorating open sandwiches. This variation is quickly prepared, and therefore especially useful for weekend and brunch entertaining.

Ingredients

½ cup Clarified Butter (see page 213) or
   4 tablespoons butter and 2 tablespoons vegetable oil
4 to 6 slices of white bread, cut ½-inch thick
Dijon mustard
4 to 6 slices baked or boiled ham
1 to 1½ cups grated Gruyère cheese

Garnish:
4 to 6 dill gherkins, thinly sliced lengthwise
Bermuda onion rings
Sprigs of fresh parsley

Preparation

1. Preheat the oven to 375 degrees.
Heat the clarified butter or mixture of butter and oil in a large skillet. Add the bread slices, two at a time, and sauté until they are nicely browned on both sides. Remove to a baking sheet, and when all the slices are done (if not using clarified butter you may need more butter), spread each slice with a thin layer of mustard and top with a slice of ham and 2 tablespoons of cheese.

2. Place in the oven and bake until the cheese is melted and lightly browned.

3. Arrange the sandwiches on individual plates, garnish each one with dill gherkins, an onion ring, and a sprig of parsley, and serve immediately.

Notes

Sliced tomatoes à la jardinière

Serves: 4 to 6
Preparation time: 10 minutes

Open sandwiches are a popular snack in both Scandinavia and Central Europe. Using the staples of your kitchen they can be prepared with a great deal of imagination, and make excellent last-minute appetizers or lunch dishes.

Ingredients

3   tablespoons unsalted butter, softened
1   can imported sardines (preferably
    skinless and boneless), well drained
Lemon juice
Salt and freshly ground black pepper
1   cup Mayonnaise (see page 208)
⅓   cup minced fresh parsley
2   tablespoons minced scallion, green
    part only
4 to 6 slices of white bread, cut ¼-inch
    thick
2   large beefsteak tomatoes
2 to 3 hard-boiled eggs, sliced
1   small red onion, thinly sliced

Optional:
2   tablespoons dill or chervil

Garnish:
Boston lettuce leaves
Black Greek olives

Preparation

1. Combine the sardines and butter in a bowl and mash with a fork until the mixture is smooth and well blended. Add a few drops of lemon juice, salt, and pepper and chill for 10 minutes.

2. In the container of a blender combine the mayonnaise, parsley, and scallions.

Puree the mixture at top speed for 30 seconds, or until smooth, then add the optional dill or chervil. Taste and correct the seasoning and set aside.

3. Remove the crust from the bread. Toast lightly and spread with a thick mixture of the sardine butter, then place the slices on individual plates and set aside.

4. Cut the tomatoes lengthwise into 4 to 6 thick slices (reserving the end pieces for salads or soups) and arrange them on the bread, top with egg slices and an onion ring. Spoon the mayonnaise over the entire sandwich, then garnish with another onion ring and an olive. Arrange tiny leaves of Boston lettuce around each sandwich and serve.

Remarks

The sardine butter and the mayonnaise can be prepared several days ahead of time. Once the sandwich is assembled, however, it should be served as soon as possible, for there is nothing less attractive than soggy bread.

Notes

basics

White or beef stock

Makes: About 3 quarts
Preparation time: 10 minutes
Cooking time: 3 hours

Ingredients

2 to 3 pounds veal knuckle bones
2 to 3 pounds beef soup bones, including
  some beef shank
2 carrots, peeled and cut in half
2 stalks celery, trimmed and cut in half
2 leeks, some of the green included,
  well rinsed
1 parsley root or parsnip, trimmed and
  cleaned
3 to 4 sprigs fresh parsley
1 teaspoon dried thyme
1 tablespoon salt
3½ quarts water, more if necessary

Preparation

1. Combine all the ingredients in a flameproof 9-quart casserole or stock pot, making sure there is enough water to cover
the bones by 1 inch. Bring to a boil, skim
carefully, then reduce the heat and simmer
the stock, partially covered, for 3 hours,
skimming several times.

2. When the stock is done, let it cool,
uncovered, then strain into a large bowl
and chill overnight. The next day degrease
the stock carefully and refrigerate in
covered jars or freeze.

Remarks

Refrigerated stock should be brought back
to a boil every 3 to 4 days. Frozen stock
will keep for 2 to 3 months.

Light white stock

Makes: About 2½ quarts
Preparation time: 10 minutes
Cooking time: 2 hours

Ingredients

3 quarts cold water
4 to 6 chicken wings and giblets
2 pounds meaty soup bones
Salt
1 carrot, peeled and cut in half
1 stalk celery, trimmed
1 whole onion, unpeeled
½ head garlic, unpeeled
3 large sprigs fresh parsley
5 peppercorns
1 bay leaf

Optional:
1 pig's knuckle or 1 pound lean salt pork

Preparation

1. Combine all the ingredients in a large,
flameproof casserole. Bring to a boil, then
reduce the heat and simmer for 2 hours,
skimming frequently.

2. When done, strain the broth, degrease
it thoroughly, and cool, uncovered. When
completely cool, refrigerate in a covered
jar or freeze.

Notes

Brown stock

Makes: About 3 quarts
Preparation time: 20 minutes
Cooking time: 5 to 6 hours

Brown stock is by far the most important stock in French cooking. All great sauces are based on it, and I have never seen a good restaurant without a large stock pot simmering away at the corner of the stove. Once you realize the incredible potential a good stock can give to the simplest food, you will never want to be without it.

Ingredients

4 to 5 pounds veal knuckle bones, cracked
2 to 3 pounds meaty beef bones, including some beef shank
2 cups coarsely chopped onion
2 cups carrots, peeled and cubed
1 large stalk, celery trimmed and cubed
1 head garlic, unpeeled
1 teaspoon dried thyme
4 large sprigs parsley
1 bay leaf
1 to 2 ripe tomatoes
Salt

Optional:
2 leeks, well rinsed and coarsely chopped
Mushroom stems
1 peeled parsnip or parsley root

Preparation

1. Preheat the oven to 500 degrees.

2. Arrange the meat bones in one layer in a large, shallow baking dish. Place the dish in the center of the oven and cook for 30 to 40 minutes, or until the bones are well browned. Reduce the heat to 375

degrees, then scatter the onions, carrots, and celery over the bones and continue cooking until the vegetables are well browned.

3. Transfer the bones and vegetables to a flameproof 9-quart casserole or stock pot. Add the garlic, thyme, parsley, bay leaf, whole tomatoes, salt, and optional leeks, mushroom stems, and parsnip. Add enough water to cover and bring to a boil, then reduce the heat and simmer the stock, partially covered, for 5 to 6 hours, stirring frequently.

4. Remove the stock from the heat, strain into a large bowl, and cool completely. Degrease the stock carefully and refrigerate in covered jars or freeze.

Notes

Concentrated brown stock

Makes: About 2½ cups
Preparation time: 5 minutes
Cooking time: 30 to 40 minutes

Here is a simple version of the classic brown sauce. After you make this, using a well-flavored brown stock, it will take only 5 minutes to reheat, and will give you an instant sauce. Use it on anything from poached eggs, braised celery hearts, chicken livers, pan-fried steaks, or roast duck.

Ingredients

6   cups Brown Stock (see page 202)
2   tablespoons potato starch or arrowroot
1   tablespoon tomato paste
½   cup white wine
Salt and freshly ground white pepper

Preparation

1. Bring the stock to a boil in a heavy-bottomed, 2-quart saucepan, then reduce it over medium heat by one-third.

2. While the stock is simmering, combine the potato starch or arrowroot, tomato paste, and wine in a small bowl. Whisk the mixture until it is well blended, then stir the mixture into the hot stock and continue cooking for 2 or 3 minutes, or until the stock has thickened. Season lightly with salt and pepper, then cool the stock and refrigerate in covered jars or freeze.

Remarks

Instead of white wine you may use Madeira or port to flavor the stock. Do not season it too highly; as it is usually used to deglaze a pan, it will reduce more during its final cooking and can easily become too salty.

Chicken stock

Makes: About 2½ quarts
Preparation time: 10 minutes
Cooking time: 2 hours

Chicken stock is by far the simplest and most versatile of stocks. It is used as a base for most soups and in all sauces calling for chicken wings, chicken livers, and many vegetables. It is both easy to make and inexpensive.

Ingredients

3 to 4 pounds chicken necks, wings, and gizzards
2   carrots, peeled and cut in half
2   stalks celery, trimmed and cut in half
2   large leeks some of the green included, well rinsed
1   parsnip, scraped
1   parsley root or several large sprigs of parsley
5   peppercorns
1   tablespoon salt
3 to 3½ quarts water

Preparation

1. Combine all the ingredients in a large stock pot or flameproof casserole. Bring to a boil, skim carefully, then partially cover and cook over low heat for 2 hours.

2. When done, strain the stock into a large bowl. Chill overnight. The next day carefully degrease and refrigerate in covered jars or freeze.

Remarks

Refrigerated stock must be brought back to a boil every 3 or 4 days and cooled completely before returning it to the jars. It can be frozen for about 2 months.

Light chicken stock

Makes: About 2 quarts
Preparation time: 10 minutes
Cooking time: 50 minutes

A quick light chicken stock can be made with little effort by using a few wings and some chicken trimmings (necks and gizzards) and "doctoring" up the taste with 2 chicken bouillon cubes. This kind of stock is suitable for vegetable soups, particularly those made with vegetables of strong individual flavor such as broccoli, cauliflower and sorrel.

Ingredients

1 to 1½ pounds chicken trimmings
1   carrot, scraped and cut in half
2   celery stalks, well rinsed and cut in half
3 to 4 stalks parsley
1   large onion, peeled
2   chicken bouillon cubes or 2 packages of powdered chicken broth
Pinch of salt

Preparation

In a 3-quart saucepan combine the chicken trimmings with the carrot, celery, parsley, onion and bouillon cubes. Add 6 to 8 cups of water; bring to a boil, reduce the heat and simmer for 45 to 50 minutes. Season with a pinch of salt and strain the stock into a large bowl. Chill for 2 to 4 hours, remove the fat and pour the stock into a covered jar. Refrigerate or freeze.

Fish stock

Makes: About 1 quart
Preparation time: 10 minutes
Cooking time: 50 minutes

Ingredients

3   tablespoons butter
1   large onion, finely minced
2   leeks well rinsed and finely sliced
1   large carrot, peeled and thinly sliced
1   stalk celery, sliced
3   pounds fish trimmings (preferably cod necks)
1   cup dry white wine
1   Bouquet Garni (see page 214)
4   peppercorns
Pinch of salt
4 to 5 cups water

Preparation

1. Melt the butter in a large, heavy casserole. Add the onion, leeks, carrot, and celery and cook over low heat for 5 minutes, or until the vegetables are soft and lightly browned. Add the fish trimmings, wine, *bouquet garni*, peppercorns, salt, and enough water to cover. Bring to a boil, then reduce the heat and simmer, partially covered, for 45 minutes, skimming frequently.

2. When the stock is done, strain it through a fine sieve, pressing down with a wooden spoon to extract all the juices out of the vegetables. Cool and refrigerate in a covered jar or freeze.

Remarks

Refrigerated stock must be brought back to a boil every 2 or 3 days. This stock is good for making light fish *velouté* sauces, or for poaching fish and in soups. For a stronger, more full-bodied sauce as called for in several recipes in this book, the stock must be reduced by half.

Sauce béchamel à l'ancienne

Makes: About 3 cups
Preparation time: 10 minutes
Cooking time: 2 hours

Béchamel sauce is the most basic of French sauces. It is extremely versatile, and appears over and over again in many different dishes of the French cuisine. Other countries such as Greece, Italy, and Spain have adopted the sauce, but unfortunately it usually loses something in the translation, and invariably tastes pasty and uninteresting. For a while I stopped using this sauce, but recently I rediscovered it by adapting the old-fashioned method of making it. The result is a smooth and delicate sauce that lends itself to a great many uses.

Ingredients

4   tablespoons unsalted butter
½   cup all-purpose flour
4½   cups warm milk
1   onion stuck with 1 whole clove
1   small Bouquet Garni (see page 214)
Salt and freshly ground white pepper
3   egg yolks
¼ to ½ cup heavy cream

Optional:
Pinch of freshly grated nutmeg

Preparation

1. Preheat the oven to 300 degrees.

2. Heat the butter in a heavy, enameled 2-quart saucepan over low heat. As soon as it is melted, add the flour and cook for 1 or 2 minutes, without letting it brown, stirring constantly with a wire whisk. Add the warm milk all at once and whisk constantly until the mixture is thick and smooth. Remove the pan from the heat and add the onion and *bouquet garni*, then season with salt and pepper, cover, and place the pan in the center of the oven. Cook the sauce for 2 hours, whisking it from time to time.

3. While the sauce is cooking, combine the egg yolks with ¼ cup heavy cream. Whisk the mixture thoroughly and set aside.

4. When the sauce is done, remove the saucepan from the oven, discard the onion and *bouquet garni*, and whisk the yolk mixture into the sauce. If it seems too thick, add the remaining cream. Correct the seasoning, adding a grinding of fresh nutmeg if you wish.

Remarks

The sauce will thicken as it cools, and will thin out when it is reheated. It can be frozen and used as needed.

Notes

Crème fraîche

Makes: 2 cups
Preparation time: 5 minutes

The French use *crème fraîche* the way we use heavy cream. It is actually soured cream that is far superior to our commercial sour cream. Whereas sour cream will curdle in a hot sauce, *crème fraîche* will not, and a spoonful or two of this delicious cream will enrich the simplest of dishes.

Ingredients

2 cups very fresh heavy cream
6 teaspoons buttermilk

Preparation

Combine the heavy cream and buttermilk in a jar and whisk the mixture until well blended. Cover the jar and let it stand in a warm place for 24 hours, checking the cream once or twice and whisking again. It is done when it has the consistency of sour cream. Refrigerate.

Remarks

Crème fraîche keeps well for 1 to 2 weeks. It can also be sugared and served with berries or poached fruit.

Notes

Hollandaise

Makes: 1½ cups
Preparation time: 5 minutes
Cooking time: 10 minutes

Ingredients

4 egg yolks
1 teaspoon white wine vinegar
2 tablespoons Crème Fraîche (see opposite) or heavy cream
1 cup hot Clarified Butter (see page 213)
Salt and freshly ground white pepper

Optional:
1 teaspoon lemon juice
2 tablespoons cold water

Preparation

1. Combine the egg yolks, vinegar and *crème fraîche* in the container of a blender. Blend the mixture at high speed for 30 seconds, then turn the blender to medium speed and add half the butter by droplets. The mixture will become very thick.

2. Pour the mixture into a saucepan and set over the lowest possible heat. Whisk in the remaining butter in a slow stream until it is all incorporated in the sauce, then season with salt and pepper. If the sauce is too thick, beat in the cold water. Taste, and if the sauce is not tangy enough, add the lemon juice. Keep the sauce warm in a pan of warm, not hot, water.

Remarks

The sauce can be made well in advance and kept warm in a pan of warm water, but it must be whisked every 30 minutes. If the hollandaise shows signs of curdling, whisk in a tablespoon of iced water and beat vigorously until it is smooth again.

Fresh tomato sauce

Makes: About 4 cups
Preparation time: 25 minutes
Cooking time: 2 hours

Ingredients

3   tablespoons fruity olive oil
1   cup finely minced onion
1   stalk celery, finely minced
1   small carrot, peeled and finely minced
3   tablespoons finely minced fresh parsley
3   cloves garlic, finely minced
2   tablespoons chopped fresh basil or 1 teaspoon dried
1   large sprig fresh oregano or ½ teaspoon dried
1   bay leaf
4 to 5 pounds ripe tomatoes, peeled and coarsely chopped
2   tablespoons tomato paste
Salt and freshly ground black pepper

Preparation

1. Heat the oil in a large, flameproof casserole. Add the onion, celery, carrot, parsley, garlic and herbs, then cook over low heat until the onion is soft but not browned. Add the tomatoes, tomato paste, salt, and pepper. Partially cover and cook until all the tomato juices have evaporated and the sauce is thick (about 1½ hours), stirring several times during cooking to prevent the sauce from scorching. Taste and correct the seasoning.

2. Strain the sauce through a food mill and refrigerate in covered jars or freeze.

Remarks

Frozen, the sauce will keep for 2 to 3 months. Otherwise, 2 to 3 weeks. The sauce can also be left unstrained if you like a heartier, chunky sauce.

Provençal tomato fondue

Makes: About 4 cups
Preparation time: 20 minutes (plus 24 hours draining time)
Cooking time: 25 to 35 minutes

Since discovering this marvelous tomato puree in the south of France, I have never been without it. When I run out of my fresh garden tomato supply, I make it successfully with a good brand of canned tomatoes. It can be used as a topping for omelets, for quiches, fried eggs, or as an accompaniment to grilled or sautéed fish.

Ingredients

4 to 5 pounds fresh tomatoes, peeled
Salt and freshly ground black pepper
½   cup olive oil
¾   cup finely minced shallots
2   cloves garlic, minced
½   bay leaf
1   sprig fresh thyme or ¼ teaspoon dried
1   tablespoon tomato paste
½   cup melted butter
½   cup chopped fresh basil or marjoram

Optional:
1   teaspoon meat glaze

Preparation

1. Quarter the tomatoes, then sprinkle them with salt and place them in a colander. Let drain for 24 hours.

2. Heat the oil in a large, heavy-bottomed saucepan. Add the tomatoes, shallots, garlic, bay leaf, and thyme and cook over high heat for 20 to 30 minutes, stirring every few minutes to prevent the mixture from scorching. When the puree is very thick and all the tomato water has evaporated, add the tomato paste and meat glaze. Season with salt and pepper and set aside.

3. Combine the melted butter with the basil or marjoram in the container of a blender. Blend the mixture at high speed for 30 seconds, then pour it into the tomato puree. Blend together well, then correct the seasoning and store in a covered jar in the refrigerator, for up to 2 weeks, or freeze.

Remarks

Other herbs, such as oregano or summer savory, can be used to flavor the puree. All, however, should be fresh.
I rarely make any concessions to canned vegetables, but I have successfully made the puree with a good brand of canned tomatoes, as I mentioned above. These must also drain for 24 hours.

Notes

Mayonnaise

Makes: About 1½ cups
Preparation time: 5 minutes

There is absolutely no comparison between homemade mayonnaise and the commercial variety. Many people still think that making mayonnaise is a difficult task, but thanks to the blender it is now both quick and failproof. Aside from binding a salad, a good mayonnaise can be flavored with finely minced fresh herbs or spices, such as curry or cumin, and served as a dip and an accompaniment to a raw vegetable basket.

Ingredients

2   eggs
1   teaspoon white wine vinegar
1   teaspoon Dijon mustard
Pinch of salt
¾ to 1 cup vegetable oil
Small pinch of granulated sugar (optional)

Preparation

1. In the container of a blender combine the eggs, vinegar, mustard and salt. Blend the mixture at high speed for 30 seconds, then reduce the speed slightly and start adding the oil, by droplets. As the mayonnaise begins to thicken, add the remaining oil in a slow stream. Taste and correct the seasoning, add the optional sugar if you like your mayonnaise on the sweet side.

2. Scrape the mayonnaise into a jar, cover, and refrigerate.

Remarks

Homemade mayonnaise can be kept for 2 weeks. If you prefer the flavor of lemon rather than vinegar, substitute 1 tablespoon of lemon juice for the vinegar.

Vinaigrette provençale

Makes: About ½ cup
Preparation time: 5 minutes

No commercial salad dressing can match the flavor and freshness of homemade dressing. A good dressing gives the right tone to every meal, and is plain proof of the cook's attention to details.

Ingredients

1   teaspoon Dijon mustard
1   clove garlic, mashed
2   tablespoons finely minced scallion
1½ tablespoons excellent wine vinegar
6   tablespoons good-quality olive oil
    (such as Berio or Bertolli)
Salt and freshly ground black pepper

Preparation

In a screwtop jar combine the mustard, garlic, scallion, vinegar, olive oil, a good pinch of salt, and a heavy grinding of black pepper. Close the jar tightly and shake vigorously until the dressing is smooth and well blended. Taste and correct the seasoning. If refrigerated, bring back to room temperature before using and shake again until well blended.

Remarks

Vinaigrette can be made in large quantities, and will keep for several days. When making vinaigrette ahead of time, do not mash the garlic, but add the whole peeled clove to the jar and remove before serving. You may flavor the vinaigrette with a teaspoon of anchovy paste, 1 tablespoon of tiny, well-drained capers, or with other herbs, such as chervil, dill, or finely minced fennel tops.

Lemon vinaigrette

Makes: About ½ cup
Preparation time: 5 minutes

This slightly sweet lemon vinaigrette lends itself particularly well to mild and tender greens such as Boston, Bibb, and field lettuce. For an interesting variation, add a few thinly sliced raw mushrooms to the vinaigrette and marinate for 30 minutes before adding to the greens.

Ingredients

Juice of 1 lemon
1   teaspoon Dijon mustard
1   teaspoon granulated sugar
6   tablespoons mild olive oil or walnut
    oil (see remarks)
2   tablespoons finely minced scallion or
    dill
Salt and freshly ground white pepper

Preparation

In a screw-top jar combine the lemon juice, mustard, sugar, oil, and scallion or dill. Add a pinch of salt and a good pinch of freshly ground pepper, close the jar tightly and shake until the vinaigrette is smooth and well blended. Taste and correct the seasoning. If refrigerated, bring the vinaigrette back to room temperature before using and shake once more until the dressing is well blended.

Remarks

For variety, add 1 to 2 tablespoons heavy cream or Crème Fraîche (see page 206) to the dressing.
In recent years I have used walnut oil imported from France in place of olive oil. It is available here in specialty stores, and gives a salad an interesting, nutty flavor.

Basil paste (or other herb paste)

An herb paste is the best way to preserve the essence of fresh herbs for fall and winter months. Use for flavoring soups and sauces. The herbs that lend themselves best are basil, tarragon, marjoram, sage and oregano.

Ingredients

3 to 4 cups tightly packed basil leaves (or other herb leaves)
Fruity olive oil (preferably Plagniol)

Preparation

Rinse the basil leaves carefully under cold running water and dry them thoroughly on paper towels. Put the leaves in the container of a blender or in an electric food mill. Add just enough oil to get a smooth purée. Spoon the purée into freezer containers, refrigerate or freeze.

Remarks

The herb pastes can be made in large quantities but should only be frozen in small containers. A mixture of your favorite herbs can be puréed together and lightly seasoned with salt. Do not add garlic to an herb paste as it tends to give it a bitter taste after a while.

Notes

Cooked white beans

Preparation time: 10 minutes (plus 1 hour soaking time)
Cooking time: 2 to 3 hours

Ingredients

2 cups dried white beans (preferably Great Northern)
Salt
5 peppercorns
1 onion, peeled and stuck with 1 whole clove
1 carrot, peeled and cut in half
1 stalk celery, trimmed
1 large sprig fresh parsley
1 sprig fresh thyme or ½ teaspoon dried

Preparation

1. Preheat the oven to 325 degrees.

2. Put the beans in a large, flameproof casserole with plenty of water to cover. Bring to a boil, then immediately remove from the heat. Cover and set aside for 1 hour.

3. Add salt and the peppercorns, onion, carrot, celery, parsley, and thyme. Place the casserole in the oven and cook the beans for 2 to 3 hours, or until they are very tender. Drain and use for salads and soups.

Remarks

If the beans are not to be used immediately let them remain in their poaching liquid.

Basic tart shell

Makes: 1 eight- to ten-inch tart shell
Preparation time: 20 minutes (plus 1 hour
  resting time)
Cooking time: 25 to 30 minutes

Ingredients

2 cups sifted all-purpose flour
Large pinch of salt
12 tablespoons cold unsalted butter
5 tablespoons ice-cold water, more if
  necessary

Preparation

1. Place the flour and salt in a large mixing bowl. Add the cold butter in tiny bits and work the flour and butter mixture with fingers until it resembles corn flakes. Add the cold water and knead the dough just until it forms a smooth mass. (You may need another tablespoon of water.) Flour the dough lightly, wrap in waxed paper and chill for an hour before rolling out.

2. When ready to roll out the dough, place it on a lightly floured marble or Formica surface. Lightly flour the rolling pin and roll out the dough, always working away from you, into an even circle of ⅛ inch thickness. Carefully roll up the dough onto the rolling pin and unroll over either porcelain or metal quiche pan. Press the dough gently into the bottom and sides of the pan. Trim off the excess dough by rolling the pin over the top of the pan.

3. Preheat the oven to 350 degrees.

4. Prick the dough in several places with the tip of a sharp knife. Line the shell with waxed paper and fill with dried beans to keep the crust from puffing during baking. Place the tart shell on a cookie sheet and bake for 25 minutes. Remove the shell from the oven. Carefully lift out the paper and

beans and fill the tart shell with desired filling.

Remarks

The dough can be refrigerated for several days or frozen. I find it best to make 2 or 3 shells at a time, then line them with a sheet of foil and wrap in another sheet of foil and freeze. The frozen shell is then lined with waxed paper and beans and baked for 40 minutes instead of 25.

Notes

Entrée crêpes

Makes: 12 to 14 crêpes
Preparation time: 5 minutes (plus 1 to 2
    hours resting time for the batter)
Cooking time: 30 minutes

Ingredients

1   cup all-purpose flour
1½ cups milk
3   whole eggs
Salt and freshly ground white pepper
3   tablespoons cool melted butter

Preparation

1. In the container of a blender combine
the flour, milk, eggs, salt, and pepper.
Blend the mixture at top speed for 30
seconds, then scrape down the sides of
the jar with a rubber scraper and blend
again for 30 seconds. Whisk in the melted
butter, pour the batter into a mixing bowl,
and let stand at room temperature for
1 to 2 hours.

2. Heat a 6-inch crêpe pan and brush it
lightly with butter. When the pan is very
hot, remove it from the heat and add 2
tablespoons of the batter. Quickly turn
the pan in all directions to coat its entire
surface; pour out excess batter. Place the
pan over medium heat and cook the crêpe
until it is lightly browned, then loosen it
with the tip of a sharp knife. Lift the edge
and quickly turn it with your fingers. Brown
the crêpe lightly on the other side and
slide it onto a plate. Brush the pan again
lightly with butter before making the next
crêpe.

Remarks

Crêpes can be frozen very successfully.
Place a sheet of waxed paper between
each one, then wrap the entire batch in
foil and freeze. When ready to use, defrost
the crêpes at room temperature, then place
the wrapped package in a 300-degree
oven until the crêpes are thoroughly
heated through (about 1½ hours to 2
hours). Open the package and test a crêpe
to ensure that all are done.
For variety, crêpes can be flavored with
spinach or herbs. For spinach crêpes, add
½ cup cooked, thoroughly drained and
chopped spinach to the batter and puree
for 30 seconds at top blender speed. For
fines herbes crêpes, add 2 tablespoons
finely minced chives and parsley to the
batter and puree. To make dill crêpes, add
2 tablespoons of minced fresh dill to the
batter and puree at top speed.

Notes

Beurre manié

Clarified butter

A *beurre manié* is used in both classic and peasant cooking to thicken sauces. It is a flour and butter paste that can be formed into a ball and refrigerated successfully in a covered jar. It is useful to make several of these balls at a time and keep for later use.

Ingredients

1   tablespoon unsalted butter
1   tablespoon all-purpose flour

Preparation

Combine the butter and flour on a plate. Blend the mixture with a fork until it is smooth and all the flour has been incorporated into the butter. Form the mixture into a small ball with your hands and chill.

Remarks

Quite often you will need to add only a little *beurre manié* to a sauce to give it the right consistency. Add it in small amounts and keep the rest in the refrigerator.

Notes

Throughout this book you will find several recipes calling for bread or fish sautéed in butter. It is best to use clarified butter for this purpose, as it burns less easily and browns evenly. Clarified butter is excellent for making a brown butter and lemon sauce that can be served with a poached vegetable, such as cauliflower and broccoli, or as a light sauce for simply grilled fish steaks, such as salmon and swordfish.

Preparation

Melt unsalted butter in a small, heavy-bottomed saucepan over low heat. As soon as the foam starts to subside, remove the pan from the heat and carefully skim off the foam with a spoon. Pour the liquid yellow butter into a bowl or jar, being careful not to include the milky white residue in the bottom of the pan.

Remarks

Clarified butter can be made in quantities and refrigerated for 2 weeks in covered jars or frozen.

Bouquet garni

A *bouquet garni* is a classic combination
of three herbs used to flavor soups,
sauces, and stocks.

Ingredients

3 to 4 large sprigs fresh parsley
1   bay leaf
1   large sprig fresh thyme or 1 teaspoon
    dried

Optional:
1   small celery stalk with leaves

Preparation

Combine all the ingredients as follows:
when using fresh thyme, tie the herbs
together with a small piece of kitchen
string; if using dried thyme, wrap the
bouquet in a small piece of cheesecloth
and tie it with kitchen string.

Remarks

Parsley should never be used in dried
form; it has no taste whatsoever.

Notes

index

index

About the Author

Perla Meyers, a resident of New York City, studied at the École Hotelière in Lausanne, the Cordon Bleu in Paris and the Hotel Sacher in Vienna. She spends three months each year in Europe, working in the kitchens of such well-known restaurants as Grand Vefour in Paris, Troigros and Paul Bocuse in Lyon. She has also worked in many small country restaurants in Spain, Italy and Portugal, and she teaches creative cooking in The Perla Meyers Cooking School in New York City.